A COMPASS FOR DEEP HEAVEN: NAVIGATING THE C·S·LEWIS RANSOM TRILOGY

"This unique and necessary exploration of Lewis's science fiction Trilogy is both instructive and enjoyable. The collaborative tapestry of scholarship, with renowned Inklings scholar Diana Pavlac Glyer as its guiding editor, is an essential work of critical examination. This book is a pure gem, inviting readers to revisit the trilogy with fresh eyes and deepen an appreciation for Lewis's long-neglected science fiction texts."
—CRYSTAL HURD Reviews Editor for *Sehnsucht: The C. S. Lewis Journal* and recipient of the 2020 Clyde S. Kilby Research Grant

"A dynamic and engaging fieldbook for interstellar travel, *A Compass for Deep Heaven* is an accessible resource for reading Lewis in his personal, religious, literary, vocational, and historical contexts. Beyond its utility as a resource for readers—a 'Compass' for navigating Lewis's cosmic fiction—this volume is a superb example of learning as scholarship. C. S. Lewis was a writer and thinker carefully formed by mentors, and he spent most of his life shaping the writing and thinking of others, so it is only fitting that a Lewis studies resource will emerge out of collaborative discovery. Well-written and carefully edited, *A Compass for Deep Heaven* succeeds in equipping curious readers for the adventure of reading these challenging books."
—BRENTON DICKIESON, curator of *A Pilgrim in Narnia*

"*A Compass for Deep Heaven* is an especially useful tool for providing direction to readers of the Ransom Trilogy. It does not pretend to be a multifunctional device that exhaustively explores the series, but instead, it offers a bird's eye view of a variety of topics that are essential to understanding these books. I especially appreciate the way that the authors of each essay deliberately engage with one another."
—WILLIAM O'FLAHERTY, author of *The Misquotable C. S. Lewis* and the host of the podcast "All About Jack."

"*A Compass for Deep Heaven* is a carefully-crafted and beautifully-edited volume of ten fine essays that explore a common theme: the mythological, philosophical, scientific, theological, ethical, and literary influences behind Lewis's science fiction. Each chapter references and builds on the others, offering multiple layers of critical and popular analysis. Detailed references and a good glossary provide added value. This useful *Compass* has already found its way onto the recommended reading list in the Romantic Theology program at Northwind Seminary."
—MICHAEL J. CHRISTENSEN, author of *C. S. Lewis on Scripture* and Professor of Theology and Academic Dean at Northwind Seminary

"I can say without reservation that Julianne Johnson's work is the best 'short study' on myth I have ever read. For that essay alone, I recommend that you take a look at the whole book and carefully consider it."
—CHARLIE W. STARR, author of *The Faun's Bookshelf: C. S. Lewis on Why Myth Matters*

"Much like Lewis's Ransom when he traveled into the Deep Heavens, readers will find this significant collection of essays full of possibilities and life. And as with any attempt to grapple with Lewis's books about the cosmos, these essays helpfully map out critical corners of Lewis's thinking, tackling such key subjects as science and the self, myth, the medieval and the modern—issues almost everywhere present in Lewis's writing. Best of all, these authors remind us to turn to Lewis again, crafting our own Compass on the way to Deep Heaven."
—ANDREW LAZO, scholar and speaker currently pursuing his doctorate on C. S. Lewis and the Inklings

"I was completely blown away with the quality of this project—the seriousness with which the authors approached the project, the high level of scholarship they displayed in it, and the quality of their writing."
—GAYNE JOHN ANACKER, co-editor of *Contemporary Perspectives on C. S. Lewis' 'The Abolition of Man'*

Most of the students in my C. S. Lewis seminar over the last three decades came to the class having read at least some of the Narnia books. Few had read any of the Space Trilogy, and many had never even heard of it. They needed much more help to get their heads around what Lewis was doing there than they did for Narnia or the popular apologetics. But now we have a book that collects under one cover a lot of the kind of help they needed. *A Compass for Deep Heaven* would make a great supplemental text for a course on Lewis or a great read for the fan who wants to go deeper into those books."
—DONALD T. WILLIAMS, Professor Emeritus of Toccoa Falls College and author of *Deeper Magic: The Theology behind the Writings of C. S. Lewis*

"I take very seriously the research, the careful collaboration, and the critical thinking that are displayed in each of the essays in this impressive volume. This collection should be read and studied. It marks an important step toward greater understanding of a neglected area of Lewis scholarship."
—SCOTT B. KEY, editor of *In Pursuit of Truth,* an online Journal of the C. S. Lewis Foundation

A COMPASS FOR DEEP HEAVEN: NAVIGATING THE C·S·LEWIS RANSOM TRILOGY

S. L. JENSEN • JULIANNE JOHNSON
JACOB E. MEYER • RACHEL M. ROLLER
J. D. WUNDERLY • MAYA MALEY
NOLAN ANDREW • DANIEL Z. HSIEH
DANIEL J. FRIEND • EVANGELINE M. PRIOR

EDITED BY DIANA PAVLAC GLYER
AND JULIANNE JOHNSON

FOREWORD LOUIS MARKOS
ILLUSTRATIONS WILL KELLY

SQUARE HALO BOOKS

In Christian art, the square halo identified a living person presumed to be a saint. Square Halo Books is devoted to publishing works that present contextually sensitive biblical studies, and practical instruction consistent with the Doctrines of the Reformation. The goal of Square Halo Books is to provide materials useful for encouraging and equipping the saints.

An earlier version of this essay collection was prepared under the title *Warnings from Outer Space: Backdrops and Building Blocks of C. S. Lewis's Science Fiction Trilogy* and published in 2019 by the Azusa Pacific University Honors College.

©2021 Square Halo Books, Inc.
P.O. Box 18954
Baltimore, MD 21206
www.SquareHaloBooks.com

All Scripture quotations, unless otherwise indicated, are taken from the Holy Bible, New International Version®, NIV®. Copyright ©1973, 1978, 1984, 2011 by Biblica, Inc.™ Used by permission of Zondervan. All rights reserved worldwide. www.zondervan.com The "NIV" and "New International Version" are trademarks registered in the United States Patent and Trademark Office by Biblica, Inc.™

ISBN 978-1-941106-2-11
Library of Congress Control Number: 2021910213

All rights reserved. No part of this book may be reproduced without permission from the publisher, except by a reviewer who may quote brief passages in a review; nor may any part of this book be reproduced, stored in a retrieval system or transmitted in any form by any means (electronic, mechanical, photocopying, recorded or other), without permission from the publisher.

Printed in the United States of America

TO THOSE
WHO LOVE
THE SILENT
PLANET

I am going to give advice.
I am going to issue warnings.
Advice and warnings about things
which are so perennial that
no one calls them "current affairs."
—C.S. Lewis "The Inner Ring"

CONTENTS

All references to the books of the Ransom Trilogy
are taken from the following collection:
Lewis, C. S. *The Space Trilogy*. Reissue edition.
New York: Simon & Schuster, 2011.
Parenthetical citations in the text refer to the
page numbers from this collection
and use the following title abbreviations:

OSP: Out of the Silent Planet

PER: Perelandra

THS: That Hideous Strength

FOREWORD

Although the space race of the last half century has taught us many things about stars and planets, moons and meteors, I would argue that science fiction has had a more profound and lasting impact on our vision of ourselves, our creator, and the cosmos in which we live than all the scientific discoveries of NASA.

Putting a man on the moon was certainly an amazing accomplishment and the pictures from the Hubble telescope are often breathtakingly beautiful, but have they really helped us come any closer to answering the big questions: *Who am I? Why am I here? What is my purpose?* Have they inspired us to seek out and define the nature of the good man, the good state, or the good life? Have they engaged us on a deep moral-ethical level, forcing us to wrestle with our beliefs and our actions?

I do not believe they have. But I do believe quite strongly that the best science fiction stories, novels, films, and television shows have opened our minds hearts, and imaginations to wider vistas and greater possibilities.

Though C. S. Lewis may not be as famous in the world of science fiction as Jules Verne or H. G. Wells, Arthur C. Clarke or Robert Heinlein, Isaac Asimov or Frank Herbert, Orson Scott Card or Philip K. Dick, Ursula K. Le Guin or Madeleine L'Engle, his Cosmic (or Ransom or Science Fiction) Trilogy deserves a place in any pantheon of influential novels in the genre. Lewis understood instinctively that the impulse behind much science fiction is not so different from that of Dante or Spenser, Swift or Coleridge.

As he explains it in "On Science Fiction," the writers of old could set their fantastical tales in a distant country or a faraway forest or the mountains of Tibet or the frozen antipodes because those exotic locales had not yet been fully explored. There were still many places on the earth where one might take seriously that most magical of warnings: "Here there be dragons." Even during the great Victorian age of exploration, H. Rider Haggard could set his adventure novels (*King Solomon's Mines*; *She*) in the as yet undiscovered regions of Africa.

By the turn of the twentieth century, however, the globe had been sufficiently charted to make it necessary for writers to look to the distant stars as a setting for their fantastical tales. "It is not difficult," writes Lewis, "to see why those who wish to visit strange regions in search of such beauty, awe, or terror as the actual world does not supply have increasingly been driven to other planets or other stars" ("On Science Fiction").[1]

The best science fiction, including and especially Lewis's Cosmic Trilogy, does not take us to the Moon or Mars, Venus or Jupiter as an end in itself. To the contrary, it takes us there for the same reason that Dante takes us to Purgatory or Spenser to the realm of faerie or Swift to Lilliput and Laputa or Coleridge to the pole and the equator: to enact, in an unfamiliar setting, a definingly human moral-emotional-spiritual struggle.

In that sense, science fiction is rather like the tragedies of ancient Greece. We do not have to believe in the Greek pantheon or in the veracity of their ancient myths and legends to be fully engaged in the ethical crises experienced by Oedipus or Antigone, Orestes or Electra, Jason or Medea. Just so, we do not have to believe that there are rational beings on Pluto or Alpha Centauri or the Orion Nebula to recognize and participate in the moral dilemmas faced by our astronaut protagonist.

Indeed, in a modern age that is often leery of taking on spiritual and metaphysical issues, moving the setting from the Christian Middle Ages (*Divine Comedy*) to a planet that possesses the same kind of temporal and religious hierarchy (*Out of the Silent Planet*) or from the prelapsarian Garden of Eden (*Paradise Lost*) to an unfallen Venus (*Perelandra*) might allow a Christian writer to steal past some watchful dragons. Better yet, if such an author can draw his readers in by taking them to Mars and Venus, then he just might be able to bring them back to Earth and allow them to see it again as if for the first time (*That Hideous Strength*). Better yet, such an author might be able to convince them that many of the struggles we experience on Earth are part of a greater, more cosmic struggle to which we are too often blind.

I will never forget the icy chill I felt the first time I reached the end of *Out of the Silent Planet* and was confronted with the narrator's dire and urgent warning that a kind of spiritual warfare was heading to earth, one that we moderns were not ready for. Given our materialism, our skepticism, and our ignorance of old books, the only way the narrator could convey his warning to us was through the medium of science fiction.

I am happy to say that the authors of this volume have cultivated the eyes to see and the ears to hear the many warnings contained in Lewis's Cosmic Trilogy—which we should really (as my friend and colleague Michael Ward has wisely insisted) stop calling the Space Trilogy, since part of Lewis's wake-up call consists of teaching moderns the difference between space and the heavens!

"There are two ways of getting home," writes G. K. Chesterton in the opening sentence of *The Everlasting Man*, "and one of them is to stay there. The other is to walk round the whole world till we come back to the same place."[2] I would add, and I believe Dante would agree, that the best way to understand our planet and its place in the cosmic drama is to leave our atmosphere (or solar system or galaxy) behind and then turn around and look back. When we do that, as the writers of this volume have done, we may just discover truths and falsehoods, blessings and dangers that we had previously stood too close to see.

The heavens tell the glory of God (Psalm 19), but they also display the signs and symbols of a terrifying but finally hopeful cosmic conflict (Revelation 12). Let us, along with Lewis, pay heed to the praise . . . and the warning.

Louis Markos
Houston Baptist University
January 2019

INTRODUCTION

S. L. JENSEN

Before the success of Chronicles of Narnia and *The Lord of the Rings* C. S. Lewis and J. R. R. Tolkien had a problem. After a few pints in a pub in Oxford, Lewis turned to his good friend and said, "Tollers, there is too little of what we really like in stories. I am afraid we shall have to try and write some ourselves."[3]

The suggestion must have seemed absurd at the time—neither of these men had completed a full-length novel, at least not of the kind Lewis proposed, and they did not expect to have much success.[4] Faced with a problem, the two made a wager to see who could solve it. But before they put pen to paper, a few more rules needed to be established.

First, they decided on two topics that they both found interesting: one would write about a journey through space, and the other about a journey through time. To determine which adventure each author would write about, they tossed up—flipped a coin—and with that, the decision was made. Lewis would go on to write about space and Tolkien, time.[5] Next, they agreed that "Each adventure would lead to the discovery of the literal truth behind a well-known myth."[6]

With the rules set and the wager in place, the two authors began their work. Tolkien encountered difficulty in completing the task. The version of the Atlantis-themed story he began, entitled *The Lost Road*, never made it past the first few chapters. Even so, Tolkien's work was not fruitless. Years later, in letters written to friends, he mentions that his work on *The Lost Road* inspired elements of *The Lord of the Rings.*[7] Lewis, on the other hand, was able to complete his space-travel story. For him, the wager resulted in *Out of the Silent Planet,* which became the base from which he would write the entire Ransom Trilogy.[8]

The road to publication was long, but once *Out of the Silent Planet* was published, the book became quite popular amongst most of its readers. However, there was some debate and confusion as to what Lewis was really trying to say. Many thought that the book was merely an interesting take on science fiction—a writer for *The Times Literary Supplement* described the book as "inferior to Wells" and declared that while as a story it was enjoyable, it could not compare with the godfather of science fiction.[9] However, another critic writing for *Theology* saw something deeper and said that the themes were "so skilfully blended that the non-Christian will not realize that he is being instructed until it is too late."[10]

Today, readers are often left just as perplexed by Lewis's science fiction. In *Out of the Silent Planet*, readers find a new take on a trip to Mars, which is filled with new creatures like *sorns* and *pfifltriggi* and a divine ruler over it all. But in *Perelandra*, although the space-travel element remains, readers also travel back to a land before the Fall in what appears to be a retelling of Genesis. Just when it seems like another Aslan/Christ-figure narrative set in space, *That Hideous Strength* brings readers back to Earth (now called Thulcandra) with a brand new cast of characters, a still-alive severed head, and the introduction of Merlin. And, to make things even more complex, the books allude to everything from H. G. Wells and the World Wars to medieval cosmology and Arthurian Legend along the way.

To begin to answer the question of what Lewis is doing within the Ransom Trilogy, it is important to acknowledge that Lewis's broad and eclectic interests heavily influenced his writing even beyond the Trilogy. Many of the themes that Lewis communicated in his writing were done through allusions to the ideas and works of others and explorations of his own experiences. As we seek to navigate the at times chaotic mingling of these influences, it is helpful to have context on Lewis's life and mind to serve as a compass.

Lewis as a Christian

While the wager may have been the catalyst to the creation of the Trilogy, when it comes to the content, Lewis's faith played a key role. Since Lewis is known for the many theological themes that appear in his books, it may come as a surprise that Lewis himself was not a Christian for a significant portion of his life. Although Lewis grew up attending church, "the Sunday services to which he went held little meaning for him. He had come away with no knowledge or understanding of Christianity"[11] and when he was in his early teens, he walked away from the faith. A self-proclaimed atheist, he devoted much of his time to studying philosophy, reading myths, and wholly immersing himself in whatever book he was working through.[12] Sometime in 1930, Lewis again became a theist, but his conversion from theism to Christianity was a gradual process that would not take place for some time.[13] However, there are a few moments in his life that he saw as milestones toward regaining his faith.

One such milestone occurred after a conversation with his atheist professor, T. D. Wendelton. It was due to their discussion that Lewis's interest in theism changed to an interest in Christianity. Wendelton stated over dinner one night that the Gospels contain substantial amounts of historical fact. Upon hearing this, Lewis was prompted to do a little digging of his own. Lewis realized that if the Gospels were non-historical, mythical accounts, they were very poor ones—they lacked the artistry and imagination that mark an enduring myth. Yet in realizing that they had stood the test of time, he concluded that they must contain some element of truth. At that point, Lewis felt a strong conviction to become a Christian, but he still was not fully convinced.[14]

Lewis believed that God existed and that the Gospels were historical books rather than works of fiction.[15] But it was only after a conversation with Tolkien and another friend, Hugo Dyson, that Lewis understood the place of elements in Christianity like sacrifice and communion that seemed to belong to pagan mythology rather than a historical account.[16] His conversion finally took place a few days later, sitting in the sidecar of his brother's motorcycle on their way to the zoo.[17] Later, on October 1, 1931, he described the experience in a letter to his friend Arthur Greeves by saying he had decided to cross the divide into Christianity.[18] This decision changed everything. Because of his faith, his "life had a new center."[19] He would discover that "There was no nook or cranny of his being that [his faith] did not eventually reach and transform."[20] The presence of Christian themes within his stories are the expression of a thoroughly and authentically converted man, not a self-righteous person who wanted to push his beliefs on others. So how then did Christian elements make their way into the Ransom Trilogy? The best way to answer this is to look at who Lewis was as a writer.

Lewis as a Writer

In his essay "Sometimes Fairy Stories May Say Best What's to Be Said," Lewis addresses the inferences many had made about faith and his works. He recounts how, when he wrote the Chronicles of Narnia, many thought he was trying specifically to "say something about Christianity to children."[21] Lewis's writing process was much more nuanced than this. He explains in his essay that, for him, a tale began as a series of mental pictures, and it was from these pictures that he was able to formulate a plot. He writes that the whimsical images of what would become Mr. Tumnus, the White Witch, and Aslan each created in him an itch that could only be satisfied through their manifestation into story.[22] To give another example, when writing *Out of the Silent Planet,* his study of *De Mundi Universitate* by Bernardus Silvestris likely inspired the way Lewis portrays Mars. When writing *Perelandra,* Lewis's mental picture of the floating islands was one of his main inspirations. Lewis did not start a story with a motive or something specific he wanted to say, but instead, focused on the image that was unfolding in the theater of his mind. Once the picture was complete, he put it onto paper. Typically, the pictures came first, and then everything else followed.[23]

Lewis also was known for doing most of his drafting in his head, meaning that many of the manuscripts for his books were written down in a single draft.[24] He was also quite opinionated on *how* one should tell a story. He wanted the characters to exist for the sake of the plot. Too often, he saw stories that only existed for the characters or for excitement, and while he did not entirely discount this type of writing, he was definitely critical of it. He thought that making a distinction between danger in a broad sense and perils that exist due to, say, one's location, forces the reader to experience the story in a totally different way.[25] The stakes must be high, but more importantly, the stakes must be affected by a character's environment. They must affect more than the character; they must affect us. This is what transforms a book from one that is read for the rush of pure excitement into one that is most fully enjoyed when it is read and reread.[26]

Navigating the Ransom Trilogy

Lewis's Christian faith, his approach to writing, and his beliefs about story underlie almost all of his writing, including the Ransom Trilogy. But in order to see the full picture of what Lewis is communicating in this often perplexing work, more exploration is required. The authors of this book have carefully selected ten topics that serve to orient readers of the Ransom Trilogy to the wide range of influences that Lewis draws from for this work.

In Chapter 1, "More than Myth," Julianne Johnson discusses how truth can be revealed through story, not just through reason or science. This concept was a key part of Lewis's personal philosophy and his motivation as a writer. This chapter unpacks Lewis's ideas about the nature and workings of myth. Then, it explores how the Trilogy uses myth to reveal Christian themes, specifically through the incorporation of supernatural beings, a trinitarian god, and concepts of human fallenness and redemption.

In Chapter 2 of this book, "The Monsters Are Due on Malacandra," Jacob E. Meyer focuses on science fiction as a literary genre and its influences on Lewis's writing and storytelling. The chapter discusses several authors who influenced Lewis's writing of the Trilogy, Lewis's relationship with previous works of science fiction, and the Trilogy's relation to some of Lewis's other works.

In Chapter 3, "Science on the Silent Planet," Rachel M. Roller investigates whether Lewis in fact hated science as some have claimed. She unpacks Lewis's definition of scientism, showing how, for Lewis, scientism is a skewed sense of morality that views the species' survival as the highest moral end and, when taken to an extreme, dehumanizes us by stripping us of pity, happiness, and freedom. After highlighting Lewis's warnings against scientism, this chapter presents Lewis's proposed solution: a vision for a "new Natural Philosophy."

Chapter 4, "The Wars of Our World," focuses on the historical context of World War II and how it relates to themes in the Trilogy. Author J. D. Wunderly addresses how the context of Lewis as a war survivor can uncover new perspectives on the Trilogy. The parallels between the dangerous philosophies of Nazi Germany and the N.I.C.E. as well as other historical connections are also addressed. The goal of this analysis is to understand the necessity of violence as a potential course of action and the importance of acting against the evils of our world.

Continuing on to Chapter 5, "Traversing the Medieval Cosmos," Maya Maley discusses how Lewis superimposed medieval cosmology's understanding of "the heavens" onto 20th-century outer space. She explores Lewis's relationship with the ancient and medieval models of the universe alongside the popular cosmology and anxieties of Lewis's society. This chapter illuminates the key areas where medieval images are presented in the Trilogy: Ransom's recognition of "the heavens," the reality of cosmic order and hierarchy, and the influence of the planetary spirits.

Writing from a theological perspective, Nolan Andrew uses Chapter 6, "The Perilous Problem of Pride," to discuss Lewis's pressing belief on the dangers of pride to a Christian's spiritual journey and its profound connection to the Trilogy. The chapter provides an in-depth exploration of what constitutes pride and narrows in on Lewis's personal connection with the most dangerous sin.

Daniel Z. Hsieh discusses Lewis's interaction with Arthurian Legend in Chapter 7, "Arthurian Legend in Deep Heaven." This chapter explores four main Arthurian elements that inform *That Hideous Strength.* Through the examination of these four elements, many literary and mythological layers that otherwise go unnoticed begin to emerge.

In a continuation of his discussion of Arthurian Legend, Daniel Z. Hsieh in Chapter 8, "Ransoming Logres," looks at how the four Arthurian elements discussed in the previous chapter work together to restore our understanding of human flourishing. As a result of sin and the Fall in Genesis, human relationships have been broken in several ways. But viewing the Trilogy through the lens of the influence of Arthurian Legend points to how these relationships can be restored.

Daniel J. Friend, in Chapter 9, "The Cosmic Tao," explores the importance of recognizing the difference between subjectivity and objectivity. He shows how natural law can restore order. He traces the themes of "bentness" in *Out of the Silent Planet*, divine law in *Perelandra*, and the transformation of the view of law in *That Hideous Strength*, while shedding light on Lewis's warnings about law and what is good.

Chapter 10 by Evangeline M. Prior, entitled "Voices in His Head," looks at the Trilogy through the lens of literary criticism and character development. It takes a more in-depth look into who is speaking with the narrative voice within each book and explains the significance of the variance. Finally, it calls for the awakening of the Cosmos, and all that results from its stirring.

With these ten explorations into the Ransom Trilogy's backdrops and building blocks, many elements in the Trilogy that seem out of place or confusing at first glance prove to be signs that Lewis uses to point readers toward truth about themselves, the world around them, and the divine.

Endnotes

1 C. S. Lewis, "On Science Fiction," in *Of Other Worlds: Essays and Stories*, ed. Walter Hooper (New York: HarperCollins, 2017), 107.
2 G. K. Chesterton, *The Everlasting Man* (New York: Dodd, Mead, & Company, 1925), xi.
3 J. R. R. Tolkien to Charlotte and Denis Plimmer, February 8, 1967, in *The Letters of J. R. R. Tolkien*, ed. Humphrey Carpenter (New York: Houghton Mifflin, 2000), 29.
4 J. R. R. Tolkien to Charlotte and Denis Plimmer, February 8, 1967, in *The Letters of J. R. R. Tolkien*, ed. Humphrey Carpenter, 29.
5 Diana Pavlac Glyer, *The Company They Keep: C. S. Lewis and J .R. R. Tolkien as Writers in Community* (Kent, OH: The Kent State University Press, 2007), 58.
6 John Garth, "When J. R. R. Tolkien Bet C. S. Lewis: The Wager that Gave Birth to *The Lord of the Rings*," *The Telegraph*, December 8, 2016, https://www.telegraph.co.uk/books/what-to-read/jrr-tolkien-bet-cs-lewis-wager-gave-birth-lord-rings/.
7 Glyer, *Company They Keep*, 59.
8 Glyer, *Company They Keep*, 58.
9 Walter Hooper, *C. S. Lewis: A Companion and Guide* (New York: HarperCollins, 1996), 214.
10 Hooper, *C. S. Lewis: A Companion and Guide*, 214.
11 George Sayer, *Jack: A Life of C. S. Lewis* (Wheaton, IL: Crossway, 1988), 61.
12 Jeffery D. Schultz and John G. West Jr., *The C. S. Lewis Readers' Encyclopedia* (Grand Rapids, MI: Zondervan, 1998), 22.
13 Alister McGrath, *C. S. Lewis—A Life: Eccentric Genius, Reluctant Prophet* (Carol Stream, IL: Tyndale House, 2013), 141.
14 Sayer, 222–23.
15 Sayer, 225.
16 This conversation will be discussed further by Julianne Johnson in Chapter 1.
17 McGrath, 141.
18 McGrath, 141.
19 Sayer, 227.
20 Walter Hooper, preface to *On Stories: And Other Essays on Literature*, by C. S. Lewis, ed. Walter Hooper (San Diego: Harcourt Brace & Company, 1982), ix–xxi.
21 C. S. Lewis, "Sometimes Fairy Stories May Say Best What's to Be Said," in *Of Other Worlds: Essays and Stories*, ed. Walter Hooper (New York: HarperCollins, 2017), 57.
22 Lewis, "Sometimes Fairy Stories," 57.
23 Hooper, preface to *On Stories*, xv.
24 Hooper, preface to *On Stories*, xvii.
25 C. S. Lewis, "On Stories," in *Of Other Worlds: Essays and Stories*, ed. Walter Hooper (New York: HarperCollins, 2017), 10–14.
26 Lewis, "On Stories," 17–18.

MORE THAN MYTH

JULIANNE JOHNSON

To call a work 'fiction means that the story isn't true.

Or, at least that is how the librarians explained it to me when I was young. But this definition didn't satisfy me. The more I read, the more I found that fictional stories were communicating something that was true, even if the events in the story didn't really happen. At first, this seemed like some kind of inexplicable and powerful magic. According to C. S. Lewis, it was not magic at work: it is myth.

Myth was a necessary component to the Ransom Trilogy before a single word was put to paper. When outlining the terms of the wager that inspired *Out of the Silent Planet*, Lewis and Tolkien agreed that the stories would each discover myth.[1] They didn't mean myth in the sense of Greek gods and heroes, creation narratives, and other such stories.[2] While the stories Lewis called 'myths' certainly communicate a similar sort of supernatural quality, myths are more than outdated tales and folk stories. They communicate truth about a reality that reaches beyond our usual experience.[3]

Myth, according to Lewis, describes a particular kind of story, one that offers a taste of divine reality and truth.[4] He calls says that "these stories may well be a *preparatio evangelica*, a divine hinting in poetic and ritual form at the same central truth which was later focussed and (so to speak) historicised in the Incarnation."[5] Myth reveals truth, and since God is truth and therefore the source of truth and reality, myth reveals a glimpse of the divine. As Lewis's faith matured and he continued to write, his ideas about myth strengthened and became a powerful tool in his storytelling, giving his readers access to the ideas that profoundly changed his life.

Enchanted by Myth

Myth had enchanted Lewis's imagination long before he began *Out of the Silent Planet.* From a young age, Lewis recognized that story could awaken images, desires, and feelings that other experiences did not. In *Surprised by Joy,* he shares that Norse mythology and the feelings of "northernness" that accompanied its stories inspired some of his early experiences of Joy, a feeling he described as a longing for the transcendent.[6] These stories were mythic in both senses of the word: the stories were myths because they were part of Norse mythology, and they were myths because they served as a gateway to an experience of the transcendent. He loved the effect that myth had on him, but he did not yet realize the extent of myth's power.[7]

Some of the challenges that enriched his understanding of myth also led him closer to faith in Christ. One of the major obstacles to Lewis's conversion was his perception of the divide between imagination and reason. While he treasured his early experiences of imaginative awakening that came from his experiences of Joy and reading mythical stories such as George MacDonald's *Phantastes,* he could not reconcile the understanding of reality given by his imagination with the understanding of reality given by reason. His imagination led him to consider a world beyond the material, but his reason remained unconvinced. Myth had baptized his imagination, but there was still a long way to go before he would realize how it could unify these seemingly opposing sides of himself.[8]

The reconciliation of reason and imagination was one of the major events that led to Lewis's conversion. In September of 1931, Lewis had a conversation with J. R. R. Tolkien and Hugo Dyson that connected his imaginative experiences of myth with his rational explorations into the reality of the Christian narrative.[9] Lewis saw that the events of the Christian narrative could be historically accurate, but he struggled to see how his experiences of transcendence and Joy could be explained and satisfied by a narrative that did not appear mythic to him. If Christianity was the only source of divine truth, why did its story lack the sense of Joy and wonder that he found in other stories? What would that sense of longing be directing him toward if Christianity was the final end?

Tolkien explained that all stories that we perceive as mythic echo divine truth—the source of which he recognized as the Christian God. The imaginative explorations of truth through story (myths) are related to the rational explorations of truth (facts) because they are two ways of approaching the same source of divine truth and reality. The Christian narrative uniquely brought both myth and fact together in the Incarnation—the true myth.

Lewis later processed this idea in a letter to his good friend Arthur Greeves. He writes that the expression of God through myth takes two forms: human myth and God's myth (true myth). Human myths are expressions of God through "the minds of poets, using such images as He found there," such as the pagan stories that enchanted Lewis during his childhood. On the other hand, God's myth is an expression of God through real historical events, specifically, the incarnation of Christ and the Christian narrative. In Christ's life, death, and resurrection was both the historical confirmation that the events really happened and the sense of myth to draw the mind upward to apprehend the events' greater meaning. Lewis explains it in this way:

> Now the story of Christ is simply a true myth: a myth working on us in the same way as the others, but with this tremendous difference that *it really happened* . . . .it is God's myth where the others are men's myths: i.e. the Pagan stories are God expressing Himself through what we call 'real things'.[10]

Human myths can point us in the right direction to discover reality, but God's myth actually affects reality. Human myths are limited because they can carry meaning, but they lack actuality. God's myth is a truthful, concrete expression of Himself that has actuality and meaning beyond the words of a story. Other myths could present fragments of divine truth, but only the story of Christ's incarnation shapes reality itself by changing the outcome of human life because in Christ was both myth and divine reality. His redemptive actions on Earth gave insight into a larger reality of God's presence and work but also manifested that presence and carried out that work. Lewis reflects on this revelation in *Surprised by Joy*, saying, "If ever a myth had become fact, had been incarnated, it would be just like this."[11]

Although Lewis had been open to the experience of myth in his encounters with stories of Norse mythology or in Wagner's opera, he had not approached the Gospels as myth. When he studied the Gospels previously, he had sought truth using reason rather than imagination. Once he approached Scripture as true myth as Tolkien and Dyson described, he was able to experience a meeting of his "demand for mythic wonder on the one side and rational reality on the other."[12] This led him to the realization that Christianity "is not 'a religion', nor 'a philosophy'. It is the summing up and actuality of them all."[13] The development of Lewis's understanding of myth was not the only factor in Lewis's conversion, but understanding the role of myth helps illuminate Lewis's emphasis on the connection between myth and faith.[14]

Discovering Myth in the Ransom Trilogy

For Lewis, the reconciliation of imagination and reason that came from his new understanding of the true myth of Christ was so significant that he wrote about how the divine interacts with the created world in many of his works, both fiction and nonfiction. Perhaps one of the most memorable statements of this occurs in *The Voyage of the Dawn Treader.* At the end of the story, Aslan comforts Lucy and Edmund about their final moments in Narnia and says, "'But there I have another name. You must learn to know me by that name. This was the very reason why you were brought to Narnia, that by knowing me here for a little, you may know me better there.'"[15] The Pevensie children travelled to a fantastic world where they got to know the divine through an experience that their lives in England could not offer. They watched Aslan love Narnia and then returned to England with a longing for the divine, which perhaps was only fully satisfied at the end of *The Last Battle.* The purpose of their experiences was not to leave them enchanted in Narnia, but to familiarize them with the divine so that they could return to England and know the divine even better.

In the same way, Ransom is plucked from his home world and brought to Malacandra and later Perelandra to experience a reality more in touch with the divine so that later he can return to his Silent Planet with an enhanced ability to know the divine there. But unlike the Pevensies, before Ransom returns to England, he must discover myth.

Myth and Reality

An early step in Ransom's journey toward myth brings him to realize that mythic stories present an image of reality, not just fantasy. While on Perelandra, Ransom encounters creatures similar to what people on Earth would call merfolk. The creatures' intense similarity to mermaids in human mythologies causes Ransom to wonder if "what was myth in one world might always be fact in some other" (*PER*, 88). Merfolk are not the only figures from Earth's mythologies that appear as reality on Perelandra. When Ransom first wakes up on Perelandra, the narrator says that "he saw reality, and thought it was a dream" and "recognised the garden of the Hesperides at once" at the sight of a tree with silver leaves (*PER*, 40). Ransom also recalls in this moment how the *sorns* on Malacandra are reminiscent of the cyclops from Greek myth.[16] The appearance of these creatures that Ransom recognized from Earth's mythologies shifts his understanding of reality. Somehow, stories on Earth have provided a glimpse of what is real in another place, suggesting that the separation between reality and fantasy may not be as clear as it seems.

At the end of *Perelandra*, after pondering this connection further, Ransom pictures the universe as connected like a spider's web, and he imagines that memories and images flow within this web. Ransom hypothesizes that the figures that appear in Earth's mythologies may bear the image of a deeper reality. These characters, stories, and themes are, in a sense, echoes of the unseen world. They serve as signposts, directing us to a greater understanding of what lies behind the world we know.

When gazing upon the figures of the Oyarsa of Malacandra and the Oyarsa of Perelandra, Ransom identifies them as Ares and Aphrodite from Greek mythology (*PER*, 172–73).[17] But his reason for this similarity is not that the gods of the Greeks are actually real; the reason is that there is a more fundamental truth about gender that is *embodied* by each Oyarsa, which is merely *communicated* by the Greek's stories.[18] The qualities of strength or beauty gathered from stories about Ares and Aphrodite were not arbitrary. Ransom's image of the web is his way of expressing that mythic stories can present us with images and ideas that are meaningful and representative of reality, even if that reality is currently beyond our reach.

Ransom's thoughts then lead him to suggest this definition of myth: "gleams of celestial strength and beauty" that have made their way to earthly minds through the web of the universe (*PER*, 172–73). The celestial or divine reality that is usually beyond the reach of human faculties could be understood in part through myth, but only as a gleam—a reflection, a shadow.

Myth Is Restricted

The full definition of myth that Ransom provides after gazing upon the Oyarsa of Malacandra and the Oyarsa of Perelandra is "gleams of celestial strength and beauty falling on a jungle of filth and imbecility" (*PER*, 173). A similar definition is found in *Miracles*, where Lewis defines myth as: "a real though unfocused gleam of divine truth falling on human imagination"[19] In essence, myth is a communication of divine truth or an image of divine reality that has been obscured by the fallen nature of the world. Although the truth that myth communicates is representative of reality, parts of the truth are lost in its translation into a form that humans can use and understand.

The incompleteness of our reception of myth is an idea that Ransom explores earlier in the Trilogy. In *Out of the Silent Planet*, he reflects upon his time on Malacandra's surface and comments that "the distinction between history and mythology might be itself meaningless outside the Earth" (*OSP*, 144). Ransom realizes that his experiences on Malacandra may eventually seem like a mythological tale to him as the experience itself gets further away in time from the present and the truth of his memory begins to fade. This realization leads him to an important observation: Although history is often associated with reality and myth with fantasy, this may not be the case outside of fallen Earth, since the fallen nature of the world affects humans' relationship to divine truth.

If history and mythology are not distinct, then stories would align exactly with reality. To understand what this looks like, we can recall that Genesis describes God speaking creation into existence, and the Bible later describes Christ's incarnation by saying, "The Word became flesh."[20] In these instances, God's Word, His *Story*, becomes *history*. The mythology of the Old Testament reveals itself as fact in the New Testament. There is no separation between the myth and the fact.

However, on Earth, story does not always match our understanding of history. Human mythologies present a variety of perspectives on what happened in the past, and the presence of multiple conflicting accounts means that some of them are simply untrue. These mythological stories may present some aspects of truth that lines up with divine reality, as Ransom explored in his contemplation of the Oyarsa of Malacandra and the Oyarsa of Perelandra appearing to him like Ares and Aphrodite, but they are flawed somehow. Myth cannot embody truth to us in the same way that it can in a heavenly context because there is a limitation, a separation.

Charles Moorman suggests an explanation for why truth and myth appear to be separate: "On the planets he visits, Ransom sees the substantive realities of what Earth men are used to [thinking] of as myths, presumably... because man is cut off from the truths which the heavens hold."[21] In essence, Ransom encounters myth as reality on other unfallen worlds because myth and reality are not distinct from one another outside of fallen Earth. With the introduction of sin comes the corruption of truth and therefore the separation between myth and fact. It is the "jungle of filth and imbecility" that corrupts the "gleams of celestial strength and beauty" that myth offers.

Closing the Gap

Presently, humans may not be able to experience or understand the divine in its fullness, but through myth, we can close some of the distance. Lewis explains that "In the enjoyment of a great myth we come nearest to experiencing as concrete what can otherwise be understood only as an abstraction" because "What flows into you from myth is not truth but reality (truth is always *about* something, but reality is that *about which* truth is), and, therefore, every myth becomes the father of innumerable truths on the abstract level."[22] According to Lewis, one of the ways myth allows us to experience the divine is it allows the imagination to encounter both the abstract and the concrete at the same time.

Lewis writes in his essay "Myth Became Fact" that the abstract and the concrete cannot be perceived together. We are forced to choose between thinking of the abstract or experiencing the concrete because we are unable to do both at the same time. For example, we can concretely experience the feeling of love, pain, or pleasure, but once we try to intellectually and abstractly grasp what Love, Pain, or Pleasure is in the complete, transcendent sense, the experiences become mere examples. In his words, "This is our dilemma … to lack one kind of knowledge because we are in an experience or to lack another kind because we are outside it."[23]

From a divine perspective, abstract truth and concrete experience are not separate; they are the same reality. What is apprehended by God is the entirety of what Is, without obscurity, hiddenness, or alteration. However, what is experienced by humans can be obscured, hidden, or altered by sin and our created nature.

The working of myth is different from pure abstraction or pure experience, and this is the key to its unique ability to relate glimpses of divine truth. Myth is not confined to the abstract or the concrete because it communicates both. In myth, truth and experience are received together as an experience of reality. Charlie W. Starr, an expert on Lewis's writings on myth, explains that myth presents a "vision of higher reality spoken to our imagination through story;" it is the imagination apprehending higher reality to the degree that is possible in light of human fallenness.[24]

Through myth, we may be able to access some degree of truth about the divine, but it is not a complete image of who God is in His entirety. However, God chooses to express Himself to us through obscured glimpses of divine truth so that we may know Him to the fullest extent possible in spite of our limitations. Lewis writes that myth is not true "in the sense of being a 'description' of God … but in the sense of being the way in which God chooses to (or can) appear to our faculties."[25] Although the glimpses we receive through myth form an incomplete image of God, it is out of His grace and love for us that He has chosen to reveal Himself at all in a way that we can comprehend. In this grace, Lewis saw opportunity, and so does Ransom.

The Work of Myth

For those who are skeptical of scripture and the true myth it carries (as Lewis was before his conversion), human myths provide another expression of the divine. Story brings a suspension of disbelief, or a setting aside of our criticisms and expectations for reality, which allows the imagination to interact more freely with the ideas presented. In an essay about the importance of fairy tales, Lewis says it this way:

> I thought I saw how stories of this kind could steal past a certain inhibition which had paralysed much of my own religion in childhood.... Supposing that by casting all these things into an imaginary world, stripping them of their stained-glass and Sunday school associations, one could make them for the first time appear in their real potency?[26]

Lewis recognized that many people have had negative experiences with religion that may prevent them from freely interacting with the myth presented by scripture. Representing divine truth within story puts it into a form that is accessible to readers who may not be open to experiencing the more effective true myth in scripture. After encountering these mythic retellings, readers not only encounter some form of divine truth, but they may also approach scripture differently since the ideas have already been smuggled into their minds and now feel familiar.

This belief is echoed in the last paragraphs of *Out of the Silent Planet* when Ransom says, "what we need for the moment is not so much a body of belief as a body of people familiarized with certain ideas" (*OSP*, 152). Lewis is not expecting his readers to immediately recognize and believe all of the ideas being communicated to them, but his work does present them for consideration.

We see later in the Trilogy that Ransom's theory works. Jane, one of the prominent characters in *That Hideous Strength,* wrestles with understanding her relationship with the cultural expectations she feels have been forced upon her as well as her relationship with the divine. The book begins with her bitter criticism of marriage, and throughout the story, she questions the religious notions of those around her. However, as she spends more time with Ransom and the company at St. Anne's, these perspectives begin to shift. As she passes through the garden on her way to see Grace Ironwood, Jane connects her image of the garden with the gardens in *Peter Rabbit, Romance of the Rose,* and other gardens she has read about (*THS*, 60). Her contemplation of these connections leads her to consider the deeper meaning of love, beauty, and the feminine. These works of literature have presented her with a mythic image of gardens that point her imagination toward higher things. Later, she even considers that "Maleldil might be, quite simply and crudely, God" as she reflects on the way Ransom inspires obedience and is ultimately obedient to Maleldil, and as she recalls the various experiences that have inspired her growing sense of the divine (*THS*, 231). In the end, it was not a well-reasoned argument, a convicting sermon, or a supernatural vision that led to Jane's submission to Maleldil: it was her gradual familiarization with the ideas the company at St. Anne's embodied, partly through story, that led her to believe.

From the circumstances that led up to his own conversion, Lewis saw that even if a person was not open to myth in its fullest expression (true myth through scripture), they may still be drawn toward God through the experience of myth from other sources. By familiarizing readers with Christian themes through the form of story, Lewis could present a reality to the reader that "the narrow and desperately practical perspectives of real life exclude," and "[set] before us an image of what reality may well be like at some central region."[27] If readers encounter myth in Lewis's stories, then it is possible that they will encounter a number of divine truths that books of doctrine and theology may not reveal with the same degree of approachability. Myth communicated through story is Lewis's way of smuggling Christian themes past the previous associations and narrow perspectives of real life present in the minds of his readers. Myth shows that there is an underlying, fundamental reality that we often ignore, and it turns us toward the divine in order to correct our view.

Divine Truth within the Ransom Trilogy

In the present age, readers may immediately place Lewis and his work within a Christian context. However, at the time of the wager, Lewis had been a Christian for less than a decade, and his early audience struggled to pick up on the Christian themes that appeared in his works, particularly with *Out of the Silent Planet, Perelandra,* and *That Hideous Strength.* Lewis writes in a letter to Sister Penelope that "out of about sixty reviews [of *Out of the Silent Planet*] only two showed any knowledge that my idea of the fall of the Bent One was anything but a private invention of my own!"[28] Readers and reviewers of the Trilogy did not recognize that the images presented in *Out of the Silent Planet* had their origin in the biblical truths; they did not recognize the myth present within the story that pointed back to God.

The audience's lack of recognition may suggest a failure on Lewis's part to clearly present this aspect of the Christian narrative, but Lewis saw it another way. He writes later in the same letter that "this great ignorance might be a help to the evangelization of England: any amount of theology can now be smuggled into people's minds under the cover of romance without their knowing it."[29] Author Colin Duriez suggests that one of the purposes of Lewis's fiction was to "undeceive his contemporaries" and reacquaint them with the basic Christian teachings that he thought they had lost touch with.[30] Lewis understood that myths reveal how the divine interacts with creation, and that the only true myth is the Christian narrative. So, in order to reacquaint his contemporaries with Christ despite their aversion to Christianity, he writes a myth of his own: a story of how the divine (Maleldil) interacts with creation. Even if the readers did not immediately pick up on the way myth linked images like the Bent One in the Trilogy and Satan in the Bible, Lewis believed that his stories could familiarize readers with Christian themes, ideas, and images that they may not normally be willing to consider.

However, for the reader who is aware of the myths working in the Trilogy, these themes, ideas, and images become clearer and richer. Since Lewis understood that myth was a way to see God, it is fitting that a few of the most prominent and potent ideas in the Trilogy that are revealed through myth are the existence of the supernatural and the nature of God.

Supernatural

For Lewis, the supernatural was not simply an element of fantasy within his works but an element of divine reality that cannot be ignored. He strongly advocated that Christianity could not be explained to someone without addressing the supernatural element that was inextricably bound to it.[31] The supernatural involves both good and evil forces including (but not limited to) the angels and demons that are at work in the everyday world.[32] Lewis's writing portrays both good and evil forces, providing a glimpse of a larger reality in which supernatural forces exist and affect the real world. In the words of Duriez, "In the style of Charles Williams, the supernatural world impinges on the everyday world of ordinary people . . . in both [the Ransom Trilogy and *The Screwtape Letters*], ordinary living is the theater of damnation and salvation."[33] The inclusion of the supernatural in Lewis's fiction provides a new vision of how the supernatural operates, challenging what is normally thought about the supernatural, stirring the imagination, and awakening a sense of myth.[34] The *eldila*, Oyéresu, and dark *eldila* are all types of supernatural beings that are present within the Trilogy and help give readers a glimpse of an expanded reality.

The first supernatural being that Ransom encounters during his planetary journeys are the *eldila*. *That Hideous Strength* describes the *eldila* as "those high creatures whose activity builds what we call Nature," indicating their general involvement in creating and maintaining the universe (*THS*, 199). They bring to mind angels because they are messengers and workers who carry out the will of Maleldil, the being who reminds the reader of the biblical God. In *Out of the Silent Planet* and *Perelandra*, we also see the ruling *eldila*, or Oyéresu, of the worlds teaching the *hnau* and beasts what is good, presiding over life and death, shaping the terrain, governing the *hnau*, administering justice, naming the animals and lands, and more.[35] Thus, it would seem that the role of the supernatural within the Trilogy is to build, maintain, and order reality itself. Although this is a fictional representation, it is consistent with what Lewis argues in his book, *Miracles*. This work emphasizes that supernatural beings exist and that their presence points to the fact that God created Nature and maintains Nature's existence.[36] The presence and role of the supernatural *eldila* and Oyéresu lead readers to consider that our reality is not self-sustaining or self-existent but that there is a greater power that controls and creates life as we know it.

One common argument against the suggestion that supernatural beings exist in our reality is that humans are generally unable to perceive or detect supernatural beings. The mythic portrayal of the supernatural within the Trilogy presents an explanation: the supernatural has a different relationship to matter and light than material beings do. This sense of otherness appears in several ways. Ransom describes the *eldila* as being like "tiny variations of light and shade" and "silvery noises . . . footsteps of light" that disappear the moment he tries to focus on them (*OSP*, 108–09). His eyes cannot easily distinguish them from their surroundings because they do not relate to light as matter does. Likewise, the *eldila* experience matter as permeable rather than solid and are able to pass through solid objects (*OSP*, 95).

Finally, their placement in and relationship to space is different. To a being with a planetary context, the world seems stationary, but because the supernatural beings have a heavenly context that is connected to a higher degree of reality, they perceive the world as in motion as it orbits the Sun. Although the residents of the planets perceive that they are not in motion, the Oyéresu and *eldila* must constantly be in motion in order to appear in one place on the planet's surface, as seen in *That Hideous Strength* during the meeting with Ransom and Merlin (*THS*, 317–18). Another example is found in *Perelandra*. Ransom describes the *eldila* as seeming aslant in relation to the horizon of the planet, but really, it was the heavenly sense of the vertical being impressed upon him, leading him to realize that it was his perspective that was skewed, not the *eldila* (*PER*, 170).

All these examples point to the idea that in the presence of the supernatural, Ransom gets a taste of a truer and more expansive sense of reality than his limited human experience can offer him. His reference point shifts from planetary to heavenly when he encounters the supernatural, showing that his sense of reality is not full and complete as he had believed. This description of how the supernatural interacts with the material highlights the otherness of the supernatural. Because of the effects of myth, the supernatural beings within the story prompt the reader to consider that supernatural beings might exist even outside of the Trilogy.

In addition to the angelic forces of good represented by the *eldila*, there is also an evil spiritual force at work. The dark *eldila* and the Bent One rule over Earth in an attempt to spread bentness and obscure the reality of Maleldil's ultimate power. There is a clear image of this dark spiritual warfare at the beginning of *Perelandra* when Lewis the character is travelling to Ransom's house. Along the way, he is plagued with inexplicable fear and strong oppression that tries to make him turn around and go back home. Lewis the character initially questions his sanity, but upon Ransom's arrival, it is revealed that the barrage was spiritual in nature (*PER*, 19–20). The dark *eldila* were trying to prevent Lewis the character from assisting Ransom and partaking in Maleldil's plan. The dark supernatural forces are at work within Weston and the National Institute of Coordinated Experiments (N.I.C.E.) as well, changing and manipulating them to cause them to lose their sensitivity to the divine and to twist their humanity until it is unrecognizable.

The inclusion of these dark supernatural forces emphasize the fact that not all spiritual forces are necessarily good. For the reader who may already be alert to the presence of the supernatural in reality, the idea of the dark *eldila* gives another, more sinister, aspect of supernatural reality to consider. This is just one example of the fact that myth is not limited to a single message but can convey multiple messages from the same vision of divine reality that it presents. The idea that any supernatural beings exist in reality may be an expansion of some readers' understandings of the world. But even with readers who have already accepted this aspect of divine reality, myth can continue to inform them by presenting another message.

Trinity

The Trilogy presents a variety of supernatural beings that affect the real world, expanding the image of reality, but it does not end there. Through the inclusion of Maleldil, the Trilogy also speaks to how reality is created and defined. In *Out of the Silent Planet,* Ransom hears about Maleldil through the *hrossa,* one of the native species on Malacandra. The *hrossa* tell Ransom that Maleldil is the being who created and now rules the world and that Maleldil does not exist in a specific physical location (*OSP*, 69). At this point in the story, Ransom is not fluent in Old Solar, so this description of Maleldil is likely a simplified version of what the *hrossa* were trying to convey. But, despite the limitation of the language barrier, this description identifies Maleldil as a creative, authoritative, and omnipresent god.

These qualities allude to the attributes of the biblical God, but it is Maleldil's trinitarian nature that solidifies the connection. *Out of the Silent Planet* introduces Maleldil the Old (similar to God the Father) and Maleldil the Young (similar to Christ), but the third member of the trinity that would bring to mind the Holy Spirit is not immediately clear in the first book of the Trilogy.[37] Some authors suggest that this third aspect of the trinity is represented by the work of the *eldila*.[38] However, the only definitive reference to the third aspect is found in *Perelandra* where the King of Perelandra shares that "For many hours I learned new things about Maleldil and about His Father and the Third One" (*PER*, 180). The exact role or description of the Third One is not given in this quote, but it is reasonable to connect the passages where Ransom speaks of the Holy Ghost or Holy Spirit with the Third One because of the way he overlaps his language of his Christian faith and his language of his belief in Maleldil. For example, Ransom speaks of the Holy Spirit during his initial debates with Weston. He distinguishes Weston's "blind, inarticulate purposiveness" from the Holy Spirit and clarifies that while God (Maleldil) is spirit, there are also other spirits that can deceive (*PER*, 79–80). Ransom is advised and comforted by a Voice in the darkness just before his physical fight with the Un-man (Weston, who is taken over by an evil spirit), and he calls upon the Holy Ghost when he defeats the Un-man and again in *That Hideous Strength* when he speaks to Merlin (*PER*, 122–27; *PER*, 155; *THS*, 268). A spirit that is purposeful and good and can be called upon for power and support matches a basic description of the Holy Spirit, which suggests that Ransom's references to the Holy Spirit are at the same time references to the Third One that the King mentions. From these examples, it is clear that Maleldil is a trinitarian being who echoes the trinitarian God of the Christian faith.[39]

However, it is important to note that the trinity that appears in Lewis's science fiction trilogy is not an exact representation of what scripture describes. Although the three parts of the trinity are presented, several inconsistencies appear when taking Lewis's presentation of the trinity in comparison to the presentation given by scripture, especially in the roles and interconnectedness of the trinity.[40] The trinity presented in the Trilogy is not meant to be an exact allegorical interpretation. Instead, it is an image that inspires a sense of the reality of the divine through myth. The purpose of the mythical image is not to be perfectly accurate but to familiarize people with the images and ideas found in scripture in order to point back to the true myth found in the life of Christ.

The myth-evoking image of the trinity found in Lewis's science fiction trilogy recalls a sense of God's otherness in comparison to humans, His immanent presence, and His undeserved, gracious love. Maleldil is described as a spiritual being who is above all else, and the *hrossa* conclude that "He is not *hnau*" which sets him apart from the other intelligent beings (*OSP*, 69). Maleldil's role as creator, ruler, and sustainer of life also gives him a sense of vast power and grandeur that places him as transcendent above the *hnau*. These factors show

Maleldil's otherness in the sense of his glory, yet in *Perelandra*, Tinidril is shown communicating with Maleldil freely and receiving knowledge from him. On the unfallen planet, Tinidril's relationship with Maleldil shows a supposal of what humankind's relationship with God could have been if sin had not separated us. Although God is transcendent and powerful, He is also immanent, and He is only apart from us because of our choice to sin. And thus, in order to remove the bentness that keeps Earth silent and separates its inhabitants from intimate relationship with Maleldil, Maleldil the Young "has taken strange counsel and dared terrible things, wrestling with the Bent One in Thulcandra" in order to restore and redeem fallen Earth (*OSP*, 120). Maleldil is powerful, yet near, and the actions of Maleldil the Young on Earth show the extent of his love for his creation.

This image is not new. It is the same sense of creation, fall, and redemption that the story of Christ shows clearly. Karen Mounts, who wrote a thesis on allegory in the Ransom Trilogy, explains that it would be out of place to directly reference the Bible within the context of worlds that did not have scripture, so instead, Lewis discusses "not what God has done on Earth, but explore[s] the very nature of God. This story not only explains God's role in Man's life, but also examines who God really is, His characteristics, and His temperament."[41] The mythical images and allusions to the trinity are one way that the Trilogy shows the nature of God without directly introducing scripture or lessons in theology. Instead, the reader encounters images of divine reality through the myth, and these images provide the reader with a glimpse of God's nature.

Eden and Sin

The Trilogy familiarizes readers with a sense of who God is and how He has ordered reality, and then builds upon this general understanding of God by alluding to the grand story of creation, fall, and redemption. Allusions to the biblical stories of the Garden of Eden and the sacrifice of Christ familiarize readers with God's myth through the vehicle of human myth. Lewis's retelling of life in the Garden of Eden is found in *Perelandra*, though the story's ending is different. Ransom is taken to the paradise-like planet and is able to prevent the Fall and the introduction of bentness. Ransom's experiences eating fruit parallel the unforbidden fruit of the Garden of Eden, and Tinidril's ability to hear directly from Maleldil parallels Adam and Eve's closeness with God before the Fall. These images evoke a sense of the goodness and perfection that existed before the Fall. When eating the fruit, Ransom comments, "It was like the discovery of a totally new *genus* of pleasures" (*PER*, 37). Even an action as ordinary as eating is new and better on Perelandra because creation has not been affected by bentness or sin. Tinidril is able to hear directly from Maleldil rather than relying on revelation through scripture or other means, as is necessary on Earth. *Perelandra* exposes readers to a supposed version of what Paradise was like before the Fall, which enchants the imagination to understand the great goodness of God's creation free from sin. This mythic image of reality stirs a sense of wonder and a desire for perfection that come with life as God intended.

The inclusion of the story of the Fall within *Perelandra* also provides a sense of the devastating nature of disobedience. Alongside the image of exquisite perfection and goodness looms the impending danger of bentness. Tinidril has been given a commandment that prevents her from sleeping on the Fixed Land, but the Un-man tries to convince her to disobey. With Ransom's guidance, Tinidril realizes that the nature of the commandment is not to restrict but to allow her to express love for Maleldil: "We cannot walk out of Maleldil's will: but He has given us a way to walk out of *our* will" (*PER*, 102). Tinidril's choice to obey gives her an opportunity to surrender her own will and thus express respect for Maleldil's plan. The nature of sin is that we refuse to let go of our own will instead of surrendering to God's. From Tinidril's growing understanding of sin, the reader also sees why sin is so devastating: our stubborn decision to stay in our own will leads to destruction where there could have been goodness.

This threat of disobedience still exists as long as the Un-man remains on Perelandra, so Ransom realizes he must kill the Un-man in order to make sure that Perelandra remains unfallen (*PER*, 120–27). As a result of his struggle to kill the Un-man, his heel is injured, which is another allusion.[42] In Genesis God gives a promise: "And I will put enmity between you [the serpent] and the woman, and between your offspring and hers; he will crush your head, and you will strike his heel."[43] Ransom's bleeding heel alludes to this scriptural promise and is a reminder that even though Perelandra has been saved, Earth and humanity remain fallen and separated from the goodness expressed on Perelandra.[44] Although the outcome of Lewis's work is different from scripture, the effect of the inclusion of this narrative is that readers encounter the mythic story in a new way. This portrait of an Eden-like world presents the goodness of remaining in God's plan, contrasting it with the gravity of choosing sin and revealing a glimpse of what was lost as a result of the Fall.

Redemption

God's myth communicated in the Bible presents both fall and redemption; the Trilogy also includes a sense of both.[45] The retelling of Christ's redemptive actions on Earth is found in the story of Maleldil the Young preventing the Bent One from overtaking Earth. This story is mentioned when Ransom speaks to

Oyarsa on Malacandra and again when Ransom is debating with the Un-man on Perelandra (*OSP*, 120; *PER*, 102–04). In both instances, it is said that Maleldil the Young came to Earth as a result of a commandment being broken and the introduction of bentness. As a result of his coming, bentness was contained in Earth awaiting future redemption. Although Earth became bent and sinful, Maleldil's love for his creation compelled him to rescue fallen Earth and ensure that it was not completely lost as the Bent One had planned. This story follows the same path as the biblical narrative, which starts with creation and the Fall and progresses towards the life, death, and resurrection of Christ to create a path to restoration and redemption. It was God's love for the world that prompted Him to send His Son to Earth to prevent the total loss of humankind.

The victory of Maleldil that was foreshadowed in the first two books of the Trilogy comes to fruition in *That Hideous Strength* as the N.I.C.E. is defeated and the company at St. Anne's prevails. Malacandra and Perelandra did not need Maleldil the Young to enter their world to redeem the planets from bentness, but these planets and their inhabitants serve to shift the reader's perspective from an earthly one to a heavenly one so that the salvation narrative becomes fresh and new. Likewise, the presence of these other unfallen worlds juxtaposed with Earth puts the salvific events on Earth in the perspective of a larger universe. Despite the plans of the Bent One and the actions of the bent humans, Maleldil's order and will prevail in the end because he has ultimate authority over his creation. Maleldil is the center of existence, and because of this, ultimate victory is his. The story of salvation appears in different ways in each of the three books in the Trilogy, and they work together to present the story of redemption.

The Trilogy is not a complete retelling of the story of Christ, but it communicates the general story and themes. Lewis assumes that his readers are familiar with the biblical narrative and repackages it within a cosmic context in order to tease out new perspectives. Presenting Earth within a progression of planets where Maleldil has revealed himself emphasizes the silence and fallenness of Earth but also the great love of Maleldil. Earth was not abandoned or rejected because of its failure. Instead, Earth's Fall allowed for a unique manifestation of love that leaves the rest of the heavens in wonder.[46] Similarly, Ransom's participation in the salvation of Perelandra may parallel Christ's action on Earth in some ways, but it also opens up the consideration of how God uses humans as a part of His ultimate plan for the salvation and restoration of humankind. Lewis's Trilogy includes the story of Christ as a part of Earth's history but focuses on the Christ-like works in the rest of the heavens to present a fresh perspective on the gift of redemption that is offered to all of us.

More than Myth

Although there is much more to be gained from the wealth of images and meaning revealed through myth within Lewis's science fiction trilogy, the examples that I have chosen highlight the basic elements of Christianity that make an appearance in the Trilogy. Lewis and Tolkien craved stories that could communicate myth, and their wager sparked a trio of books from Lewis that did just that. Lewis took advantage of myth's capacity to present readers with the ideas that he believed had been lost to his contemporaries. Not only does the Trilogy teach its readers about the power of myth, but it also presents them with the reality of God's presence, humanity's sin, and Christ's redemption. Lewis's story evokes a sense of the mythical and the divine that allows readers to glimpse divine truth unhindered by the assumptions and barriers of everyday experience, and these images and experiences affect readers long after the last page.

Endnotes

1 J. R. R. Tolkien to Charlotte and Denis Plimmer, February 8, 1967, in *The Letters of J. R. R. Tolkien*, ed. Humphrey Carpenter (New York: Houghton Mifflin, 2000), 29. For more on the wager, see the introduction by S. L. Jensen.

2 To clarify, Lewis does reference mythology in the Trilogy, for example, the reference to the Garden of the Hesperides and Cyclops in *Perelandra* when Ransom is trying to understand what world he has woken up on (*PER*, 40). However, an in-depth look at which mythological tales Lewis references and why is not the primary goal of this chapter. This chapter will use the word 'myth' or 'mythic' to describe a type of story that provides its reader with a taste of divine Reality. The word 'mythology' or 'mythological' will describe stories (like creation narratives) that help a culture convey their beliefs about the world and how to exist in it, but are not necessarily true. For more about this distinction, read the chapter "Miracles of the Old Creation" in Lewis's book *Miracles*.

3 I am using 'reality' and 'truth' here to indicate a sense of ultimate or divine Reality and Truth that is distinct from humankind's limited, finite understanding. Borrowing from A. W. Tozer's *The Pursuit of God*, reality is "that which has existence apart from any idea any mind may have of it, and would exist if there were no mind anywhere to entertain a thought of it." Going forward, divine reality or divine truth implies God's view, not humans'.

4 Many years after the Ransom Trilogy was completed, Lewis wrote *An Experiment in Criticism*. This work explores myth within the context of literary criticism and includes a list of qualities that a work should have in order to be called 'myth.' It is a very important work to consider when studying Lewis's thoughts on myth, but the content of *An Experiment in Criticism* falls outside of the scope of this chapter.

5 C. S. Lewis, "Religion Without Dogma?" in *God in the Dock: Essays on Theology and Ethics* (Grand Rapids, MI: Eerdmans, 2014), 138.

6 C. S. Lewis, *Surprised by Joy* (New York: HarperCollins, 2017), 18–19, 87. In the context of talking about Lewis's life, 'Joy' is capitalized because it is the word he used to indicate the feeling of longing he experienced before his conversion to Christianity. Some of his early experiences of Joy came from looking at a toy garden his brother Warren made, encountering *Siegfried & The Twilight of the Gods* by Richard Wagner, and gazing out onto the hills outside the nursery of his childhood home. After his conversion, Lewis recognized that this feeling of longing was connected to God and a sense of transcendence.

7 Charlie W. Starr, *The Faun's Bookshelf: C. S. Lewis on Why Myth Matters* (Kent, OH: Kent State University Press, 2018), 75.

8 C. S. Lewis, preface to *George MacDonald: An Anthology*, by George MacDonald, ed. C. S. Lewis (New York: HarperCollins, 2009), xxxviii.

9 Alister McGrath, *C. S. Lewis—A Life: Eccentric Genius, Reluctant Prophet* (Carol Stream, IL: Tyndale House, 2013); David C. Downing, *The Most Reluctant Convert: C. S. Lewis's Journey to Faith* (Downers Grove, IL: InterVarsity, 2002); Humphrey Carpenter, *The Inklings: C. S. Lewis, J. R. R. Tolkien, Charles Williams, and Their Friends* (New York: HarperCollins, 1997).

10 C. S. Lewis to Arthur Greeves, October 18, 1931, in *Letters of C. S. Lewis*, eds. Warren H. Lewis and Walter Hooper (New York: HarperCollins, 2017), 368.

11 Lewis, *Surprised by Joy*, 288.

12 Starr, 76.

13 Lewis, *Surprised by Joy*, 289.

14 Those interested in the full story of Lewis's conversion might read David Downing's *The Most Reluctant Convert*, Alister McGrath's *C. S. Lewis—A Life: Eccentric Genius, Reluctant Prophet*, or Andrew Lazo's "Did C. S. Lewis Get it Wrong?"

15 C. S. Lewis, *The Voyage of the Dawn Treader* (New York: HarperCollins, 2000), 247.

16 "Forms of Things Unknown" is another work by Lewis that incorporates the idea of figures from Greek mythology appearing as reality on other planets. Considering that Narnia also has mythical creatures in a world in the same reality as Earth, it is clear that Lewis continued to ponder the image of the mythical creatures existing in some part of reality.

17 It is interesting to note that Ares and Aphrodite become Mars and Venus, respectively, in their transition to Roman mythology. This strengthens their connection to the Oyéresu who reside over the planets humans would call Mars and Venus.

18 Maya Maley talks more about Ransom's experience of the reality of gender through Malacandra and Perelandra in Chapter 5. Evangeline also touches on this topic in Chapter 10.

19 C. S. Lewis, *Miracles: A Preliminary Study* (New York: HarperCollins, 2015), 218 footnote.

20 Genesis 1, John 1:14 (NIV).

21 Charles Moorman, "Space Ship and Grail: The Myths of C. S. Lewis," *College English 18*, no. 8 (1957): 405.

22 C. S. Lewis, "Myth Became Fact," in *God in the Dock: Essays on Theology and Ethics* (Grand Rapids, MI: Eerdmans, 2014), 57–58.

23 Lewis, "Myth Became Fact," 57.

24 Charlie W. Starr, phone conversation with the author, January 22, 2019.

25 C. S. Lewis to Arthur Greeves, October 18, 1931, in *Letters of C. S. Lewis*, eds. Warren H. Lewis and Walter Hooper (New York: HarperCollins, 2017), 368.

26 C. S. Lewis, "Sometimes Fairy Stories May Say Best What's to Be Said," in *Of Other Worlds* (New York: HarperCollins, 2017) 58.

27 C. S. Lewis, "On Stories," in *Of Other Worlds* (New York: HarperCollins, 2017), 15, 23.

28 C. S. Lewis to Sister Penelope, August 9, 1939, in *Letters of C. S. Lewis*, eds. Warren H. Lewis and Walter Hooper (New York: HarperCollins, 2017), 412.

29 C. S. Lewis to Sister Penelope, August 9, 1939, in *Letters of C. S. Lewis*, eds. Warren H. Lewis and Walter Hooper, 412. It is important to note that Lewis is using the word "romance" to describe popular adventure stories, not love stories.

30 Colin Duriez, *Bedeviled: Lewis, Tolkien, and the Shadow of Evil* (Downers Grove, IL: InterVarsity, 2015), 155.

31 C. S. Lewis, "Christian Apologetics," in *God in the Dock: Essays on Theology and Ethics* (Grand Rapids, MI: Eerdmans, 2014), 99.

32 Paul writes in Ephesians: "For our struggle is not against flesh and blood, but against the rulers, against the authorities, against the powers of this dark world and against the spiritual forces of evil in the heavenly realms" (Ephesians 6:12, NIV).

33 Duriez, 115.

34 Karen Mounts, "C. S. Lewis's Space Trilogy: A Study in Allegory" (Honors thesis, Ball State University, 1997), 13.

35 *Hnau* is the Old Solar word for a rational being that is made in the image of Maleldil.

36 Lewis, *Miracles*, 69.

37 Charles Moorman suggests a reason why the distinctness of the three aspects of the Trinity is obscured on Malacandra in his article, "Space Ship and Grail: The Myths of C. S. Lewis." Due to their unfallen state, "all the aspects of the Trinity which we on Earth normally see as separate qualities" are unified in their view (402). Since bentness has not been established on this planet, the inhabitants' concept of the Trinity appears differently than on Earth where redemption from bentness is necessary, and Maleldil the Young has a role that is distinct from Maleldil the Old.

38 Paul H. Brazier, *C. S. Lewis—On the Christ of a Religious Economy* (Eugene, OR: Pickwick, 2013), 173.

39 Jane also experiences a revelation of Maleldil's connection to the Christian God in *That Hideous Strength* when she says, "Maleldil might be, quite simply and crudely, God" (*THS*, 231).

40 Steven Paul Mueller, "Christology in the Writings of C. S. Lewis: A Lutheran's Evaluation" (PhD thesis, University of Durham, 1997), 62.

41 Mounts, 10–11.

42 Mounts, 17.

43 Genesis 3:15 (NIV).

44 There are more parallels between Ransom's fight with the Un-man and narrative of Christ that are present for the interested reader to explore. For example, Ransom crushes the Un-man's head (another facet of the Genesis 3:17 promise), the Un-man is thrown into a lake of fire (see Revelation 20:10), and Ransom spends several days underground before he returns to Perelandra's surface (similar to Christ's days in the grave).

45 Other allusions to scripture appear in the Trilogy as well, such as the enactment of the curse of Babel at the N.I.C.E. banquet at the end of *That Hideous Strength*.

46 Oyarsa of Malacandra asks Ransom for details about how Maleldil has saved Earth (similar to 1 Peter 1:11–12 where "even angels long to look into these things.") and Tinidril is fascinated when Maleldil reveals to her what has happened on Earth (*OSP*, 119–20; *PER*, 54).

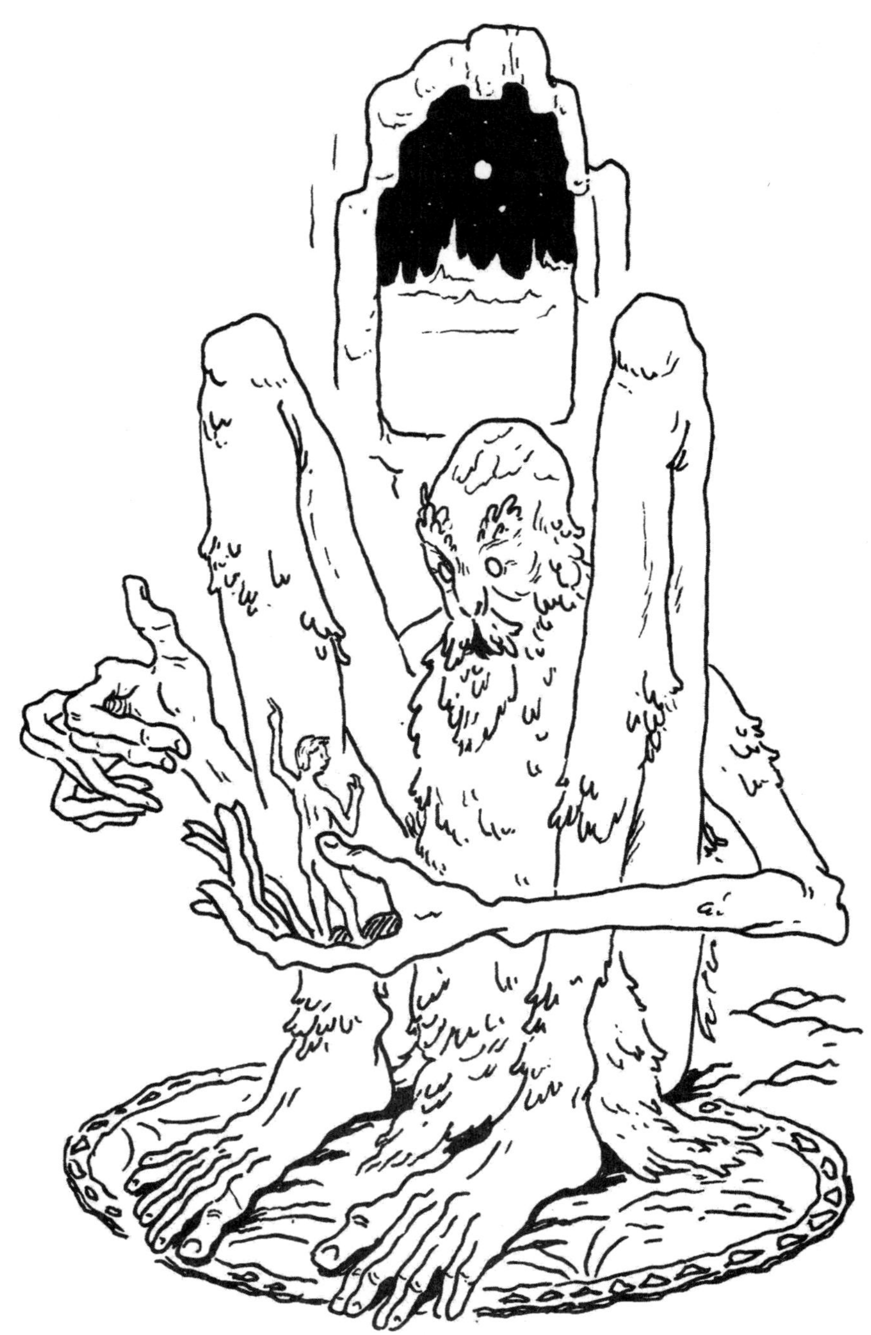

THE MONSTERS ARE DUE ON MALACANDRA

JACOB E. MEYER

If casual readers of *Mere Christianity* and The Chronicles of Narnia were told that C. S. Lewis wrote science fiction, they would most likely shrug the statement off in disbelief. The seven books of Narnia are cemented in the genre of fantasy. Four children fall magically through an old wardrobe into a land filled with fauns, talking animals, sword-wielding knights, and an evil witch. And yet, Lewis's earlier Ransom Trilogy is a massive epic awash with the influences and motifs of science fiction. Cosmic forces battle across the universe, with aliens and evil scientists around every corner. With that description, we could be gearing up for another episode of Star Wars. The average fan would hesitate to believe that they were about to read a Lewissian tale. While it was not necessarily the arena he would later spend most of his writing in, Lewis tapped into the science fiction genre to explore themes like alien monsters, evil scientists, and new worlds. For Lewis, science fiction became a battleground to combat dangerous ideas and to delve into the identity of humanity.

Science Fiction: The Genre

To help outline Lewis's impact and involvement, we shall begin by looking at the genre he chose to work in. When we hear the term 'science fiction' today, it evokes images of franchises and movies such as *Star Wars, Star Trek, Blade Runner, Doctor Who*; the list can go on and on. Science fiction currently encompasses a massive cadre of stories, but to better understand the Ransom trilogy, we need to shift our frame of reference. Much like how the term "rock" music currently has a general and diverse application, in its infancy "rock n' roll" specifically referred to a genre of music defined by a new and emerging technique. Similarly, our current view of science fiction offers a large lens through which to look at Lewis's trilogy, but to better understand the concepts he writes about, we need to tighten our focus to the science fiction of his time.

The proto-science fiction that evolved into the focus of Lewis's day has its roots in Gothic novels such as *Frankenstein,* but did not become a distinct genre until the work of Jules Verne. Verne's stories, like *20,000 Leagues Under the Sea* and *Journey to the Center of the Earth,* ventured into areas that previously had been physically unreachable. However, the advent of the Industrial Revolution provided technologies that quickly brought accessibility to the farthest dreams of the imagination. This industrialism, in turn, helped science fiction to grow. New technologies allowed for new frontiers and captured the imagination of the people.

Science fiction did not firmly establish itself as a literary force to be reckoned with until the British author H. G. Wells emerged onto the scene. Stories such as *The Time Machine, The Island of Dr. Moreau,* and *The War of the Worlds* opened the public's eyes to the imaginative possibilities science fiction offered its readers. Tales of time travel, mad scientists, and invading aliens became popular. These stories sparked Lewis's interest and eventually contributed to the wager mentioned in the introduction. Not only did Lewis challenge Tolkien to write good literature, Lewis tasked Tolkien with creating great science fiction. The genre of science fiction was dear to Lewis's heart, but he was left unsatisfied by his contemporary authors. Thus, *Out of the Silent Planet* was born. A story steeped in classic science fiction, *Out of the Silent Planet* did not serve as just another pulp novel made to hook the reader; Lewis used *Out of the Silent Planet* (and later, the rest of the Trilogy) as a platform to combat the dangerous ideas that were popular in the genre he loved.

Lewis's View of Science Fiction and its Authors

Looking at Lewis's view of the science fiction of his era and the people who wrote it helps to understand *Out of the Silent Planet*'s place and importance. In an essay titled "On Science Fiction," Lewis divides science fiction into five "sub-species," each focusing on a certain tendency he observed among science fiction writers. The first subspecies he lists consists of authors who use the expanded universe to create an already preexistent plot: he calls this the "Fiction of Displaced Persons." In such a story, "the author leaps forward into an imagined future when planetary, sidereal, or even galactic travel has become common," but all the author does is write yet another crime story, romance, or drama.[1] Lewis saw this trend as a waste of imaginative scenarios. Why write a story that takes place in space if it is merely a retelling of *Romeo and Juliet*? To Lewis, "the faintly imagined, and sometimes strictly unimaginable, scene and properties, only blur the real theme and distract us from any interest it might have had."[2] While a novel may feature a new environment or technology, if the story is a mere repetition of a tired theme, it ultimately does not affect the reader in a way that a new story should.[3] Lewis wanted stories to reflect the new nature of the world they explored, not just use outer space as a setting. If a story jumps to a new location, it must provide a new story. In an interview from 1962 between Lewis and two other science fiction writers, Lewis would explain that, in essence, the story must emerge from the location, not the location from the story.[4] A familiar tale may emerge out of the setting, but to start right off the bat with a goal in mind can congest and stunt a story's potential.

The second of Lewis's sub-species is what he refers to as the "Fiction of Engineers." These authors are mostly interested in the ways to reach the new possibilities afforded by technology. Lewis puts authors like Jules Verne and some of H. G. Wells's stories into this category: *20000 Leagues Under the Sea* and Wells's "Land Ironclads" propose new machines to explore previously unreached environments. While initially a fantastic concept, both the submarine and the tank were made real through the technological innovations of World War I.[5] This particular brand of science fiction is primarily focused on the *how*, trying in some way to logically reach the previously unreachable.

At this point, Lewis proceeds to define a third sub-species that is similar in style, but slightly different: while some authors are focused on making the *how* realistically achievable, the storytellers in the third style speculate imaginative methods to overcome unpassable problems and explain unseen locations. Using H. G. Wells's *The First Men in the Moon* as an example, Lewis writes about his use of a fictional substance, Cavorite, as a means of locomotion: "A man of [Wells's] ingenuity could easily have thought up something more plausible. But the more plausible, the worse. That would merely invite interest in actual possibilities of reaching the Moon, an interest foreign to his story."[6] To Lewis, the merit in this story lies not in trying to figure how to get to the moon. Instead, the story focuses primarily on the experience: What will it feel like? What will it be like to explore this new world, previously unreachable by humanity? While it can feel like there is too little detail in the development of the experience or character, Lewis actually supports this—if the author puts too much detail into the *how*, the reader can lose interest in the experience itself. The audience needs a character or environment that they can identify with in order to be successfully swept away by the story. In fact, this is how Lewis grabs the reader in *Out of the Silent Planet*. For the first two chapters, Ransom is an ordinary man in ordinary London. It is when this ordinary man is forcefully launched into space that the audience is hooked, and Lewis can explore his creation with gusto.

Lewis's fourth science fiction sub-species is "Eschatological" fiction, which imagines "the ultimate destiny of our species."[7] Prominent examples of this genre in Lewis's mind are H. G. Wells's *The Time Machine*, Olaf Stapledon's *Last and First Men* (which Lewis credits as partially inspiring some elements of *That Hideous Strength*), and J. B. S. Haldane's "The Last Judgement," which, as discussed in the next chapter, is a prime example of scientism (*THS*, 7–8).[8] When done well, this sub-species provides a fresh perspective on humanity's effect on history and its own development, but this was not Lewis's favorite type of science fiction.

The fifth and final sub-species (and Lewis's favorite) uses science fiction for a much simpler reason than the rest: outer space provides an unfamiliar territory in which the writer can explore and create new worlds. Lewis writes, "[T] he less known the real world is, the more plausibly your marvels can be located near at hand. As the area of knowledge spreads, you need to go further afield: like a man moving his house further and further out into the country as the new building estates catch him up."[9] There is more possibility for imaginative stories in space simply because we do not know much about it. It is less about the science of the story and more about what the science allows the writer to achieve.

The novel *A Voyage to Arcturus* by David Lindsay is a good example of this sub-species; Lindsay focuses very little on how his protagonist gets shot out into space and instead creates a whole new world to explore and ponder the human condition. Lewis absolutely loved *A Voyage to Arcturus*—in fact, he described it as "that shattering, intolerable, and irresistible work," an honor not bestowed on any other story.[10] Much of the storytelling behind *A Voyage to Arcturus* would become a useful influence in Lewis's own approach to writing the trilogy. In *Out of the Silent Planet*, Lewis is less concerned about the construction of the spacecraft that takes Ransom to Mars than about the fact that Ransom is journeying to an unknown world. Later, in *Perelandra*, Lewis uses angel-like beings to carry Ransom to Venus, separating him even further from the realm of familiarity. Science fiction takes the reader to something new, and the farther away from Earth the better. These unfamiliar environments provide new ways to look at the human spirit and the interactions one can have with a whole new world. Instead of offering a retelling of an old tale in space or getting lost in *how* to achieve space travel, Lewis saw the potential science fiction had to offer and set out to avoid the trap of so many before him.

Literary Influences in Science Fiction

While Lewis would soon create a story that has its own place in science fiction, he drew inspiration from several previous authors. In the entire Trilogy, Lewis mentions only a few authors by name, one of these being the previously mentioned H. G. Wells. Mentioned in both a note in the introduction and a few callouts later in the novel, Wells in particular provided a plethora of inspiration for *Out of the Silent Planet*. Throughout *Out of the Silent Planet*, Lewis subtly reworks many of Wells's themes to turn the tropes of his contemporaries' science fiction on their heads.

On the surface, *Out of the Silent Planet* shares many similarities with Wells's story, *The First Men in the Moon*. Both involve a spacefaring team consisting of a brilliant scientist and a greedy businessman travelling through space in a spherical craft powered by mysterious means. Little time is spent on the design and technicalities of the transportation. However, as mentioned earlier, both Wells and Lewis take less time to explain the *how* and instead focus on the literary environment they have spread before them. Likewise, the first glimpses of the new worlds are of a barren landscape that hides a diverse environment once explored.

Even the first reactions to extraterrestrial life in *The First Men in the Moon* and *Out of the Silent Planet* have strong similarities that play into Lewis's favor. When Lewis's trio lands on Malacandra, they encounter strange life-forms that they have little experience with. During Ransom's first encounter with an extraterrestrial, a *sorn*, he greets this new creature with apprehension and fear, without an investigation into its actual nature. The *sorns* appear frightening to Ransom, and he darts straight back towards the spacecraft (*OSP*, 46). In *The First Men in the Moon*, Bedford and Cavor become separated from their spacecraft and discover massive caverns below the surface of the Moon that house insect-like creatures they call Selenites. The Selenites appear to have their own society and evolutionary path, but a physiology devoid of any human conventions and their inability to communicate with the humans creates extreme dread for Bedford and Cavor. These first interactions with unknown creatures allow Lewis to bring to mind the human reaction of fear. A powerful emotion, fear drives some early decisions made by Ransom in *Out of the Silent Planet*.[11]

There are a significant number of similarities between *Out of the Silent Planet* and *The First Men in the Moon*. Wells inspired Lewis, and Lewis pays homage, in turn, by incorporating Wellsian references and motifs into his own story. However, *Out of the Silent Planet* is not a fan's imitation of another's work.

While *Out of the Silent Planet* features elements found in *The First Men in the Moon*, those elements prepare the reader to explore larger issues. The location, plot, and mechanics seem familiar, but when Lewis introduces the motivations and beliefs of his characters, his novel starts to dive deeper into analyzing the things that drive humanity. *Out of the Silent Planet* is not a retelling of *The First Men in the Moon*; rather, it is an analysis and retort to Wells's initial proposition.

Diving Deeper: The Characters and Their Flaws

The characters that Wells describes provide Lewis with a fertile bed in which to plant his ideas. While Wells's characters explore a new world, their actions are still superficial by nature (a trait often repeated by others in the genre). Lewis, on the other hand, elevates the significance of his characters by offering critique and insight on the nature and faults that drive each person.

The characters in *The First Men in the Moon* have fixed goals in mind, but Lewis adopts and twists these goals in his own way in *Out of the Silent Planet*. Richard Devine is Lewis's take on the character of Bedford, the businessman of the venture. While Cavor wants to explore the moon, Bedford can only imagine commercialization. As he dreams about the possibilities of their new compound, Bedford exclaims, "An extraordinary possibility came rushing into my mind. Suddenly I saw, as in a vision, the whole solar system threaded with Cavorite liners and spheres *de luxe*."[12] Bedford's mind is focused on the commercial benefits of what he can do with this new exploitable material. Once he is captured by the Selenites, he discovers that their shackles are made of gold, which provides further incentive for a return voyage. Upon losing the spacecraft, Bedford remarks,

> At one fateful blow all my vague resolutions of returning and recovery had vanished. My intention of going back to the moon, of getting a sphereful of gold, and afterwards having a fragment of Cavorite analyzed and so recovering that great secret—perhaps, finally, even of recovering Cavor's body—all these ideas vanished altogether.[13]

Bedford is first and foremost concerned with the commercial advantage the moon and Cavorite offer him and only lastly with the life of his business partner. This relative ruthlessness is actually a theme commonly seen throughout more modern science fiction. Later examples include the Weyland-Yutani Corporation of *Alien* and the RDA of James Cameron's *Avatar*, who focus exclusively on commercial gain, ignoring the sacrifice of others as a mere byproduct of the endeavor.

Dick Devine is likewise portrayed as a shallow man who focuses only on the monetary benefit he can receive from his voyage. When Devine is introduced for the first time in *Out of the Silent Planet,* he remarks to Ransom that while Weston is developing new technologies, he himself is eager to turn a profit wherever he can (*OSP*, 19). Devine views the interplanetary adventure first and foremost as a business investment. He is not concerned with progress or scientific advancement; instead, he is solely in it for the money. Later in the story, we see Devine rehash this belief when the three humans discourse with the Oyarsa; he expresses a simple desire to mine gold and avoid any conflict Weston may instigate (*OSP*, 133–134). Looking to avoid a conflict and get his money's worth out of the venture, Devine is perfectly content to leave Malacandra with a full cargo of precious metals and be done with the whole endeavor.

When Devine reappears as Lord Feverstone in *That Hideous Strength*, his goal remains much the same. He is more focused on his public image and personal success than on the severity of the situation. Right before the chaos erupts in the dining room at the N.I.C.E., Devine analyzes all of his possible escape routes from the failing organization (*THS*, 353). Self-preservation is the name of the game for Devine. This ultimately leads him to his doom, as he flees back to Edgestow and is swallowed by the earth in the town's destruction. No matter how much self-interest he expresses, he cannot escape his eventual end. Both Bedford and Devine embody the human traits of greed and egoism. However, Bedford is portrayed as a businessman guarding his ventures, while Devine elicits a feeling of disgust through his selfishness and worldly mindset.

Another character type Lewis adapts is that of the scientist. Weston is Lewis's own Cavor, twisted to disturbing levels. In *The First Men in the Moon* Cavor is as focused on scientific advancement as Bedford is on commercial gain. He is constantly on the prowl for new scientific discoveries. When the first large batch of Cavorite causes a massive explosion, he writes off the probable deaths of his three assistants as a "detail," caring little for their survival over the development of his new material.[14] When stranded on the moon, Cavor devises a way to communicate with the Selenites through reasoning and linguistic process while Bedford is more focused with a way to get back home.[15] Nothing is more important to Cavor than the scientific analysis of everything, including his own life and the possibility of returning to earth. He greets the new world with awe and wonder and looks forward to every new situation he encounters. Pure scientific discovery fuels him, while personal wealth and success are a secondary thought. He is very much like the archaeologist Belloq from *Indiana Jones*: while fame and wealth are options of success for him, the pursuit to go even farther and reach an almost "forbidden" knowledge is the real motivation for continuing.

Lewis's Weston is similar to Cavor, but Lewis heightens his fascination with science to an obsessive and dominating level. Weston is an impressive and accomplished scientist, as described by Devine (*OSP*, 15). He designed their spacecraft and provides the voice of scientific advancement throughout the story. He is not looking to make a cash grab out of the expedition and actually expresses disgust at Devine's fixation with economic gain. However, Weston has a shockingly different outlook on science than Cavor does. While Cavor is pursuing knowledge for science's sake, Weston is driven by the advancement of humankind. As he explains to Ransom, he is doing something completely unprecedented—leaving earth and journeying to other worlds (*OSP*, 29). Weston believes that if humanity can colonize other planets, the human species will fill the universe and never die out. For Weston, no price—even "the rights or life of an individual or of a million individuals"—is too high to pay in pursuit of this lofty goal (*OSP*, 29). Furthering humankind's place in the cosmos is Weston's driving motivation, no matter the consequences. He is fueled by humanity's conquering of mortality. While Cavor is a man in love with science and its potentialities, Weston shows how science can paint a harsh and cold picture of an otherwise idyllic scene. Lewis wants the reader to feel uncomfortable, to internally revolt at the way Weston conducts himself. Weston's drive is close to fanatical, and his outlook on the development of humanity is chilling.

Wells Versus Lewis: Evolutionism Through Weston

H. G. Wells championed something that Lewis termed "evolutionism," and Lewis was deathly afraid of it. Throughout many of Wells's stories, a theme of evolution and eugenics lies below the visible surface. Wells's first published story, *The Time Machine*, was written in 1895, a little over a decade after the death of Charles Darwin in 1882. Darwinism was reaching its height in Great Britain, and his theory provided a previously unheard-of perspective on life. Humanity was not divinely created by God; instead, humans were a result of a long line of gradual changes. The human race had evolved to its current state over a long period of time, unlike the instantaneous creation described in Genesis. While the battle of Darwinism and Creationism plagued the church and its followers, Lewis was not concerned by that aspect of Wells's ideology. His primary concerns revolved around evolutionism, or "Wellsianity"—the belief that humankind is not the final link in the chain but rather a mere prototype for unknown humanoids down the line.[16]

According to evolutionism, humans are a rung in the middle of the evolutionary ladder to move past when the time comes. Wells explored this concept in *The Time Machine*, where the Traveller journeys to a future Earth and encounters seemingly new lifeforms. He is greeted by the Eloi and the Morlocks: the first, a timid and frail humanoid and the latter, an aggressive and nocturnal ape. Throughout the novel, the Traveller slowly discovers that the ancestor of these new species is actually the current human race.[17] Over centuries, humanity evolved and two entirely distinct species emerged. By themselves, the Eloi and Morlocks provide a new creature to bring interest to the story. But, as soon as their connection to humanity is revealed, a much darker prediction emerges. As Robert Pasquini writes,

> *The Time Machine* destabilizes rather than verifies historical causality, and opens up the fossil record, that incomplete narrative of biotic existence, to future interventions. What seems at the outset as distinct entities—humans, Eloi, Morlocks, "grey things," tentacular monstrosities, protoplasmic ooze—eventually become linked by their affiliative markers within an evolutionary context.[18]

By connecting the Eloi and Morlocks to humanity, the individualism that defines humanity is slowly whittled away. Humanity is not unique among the creations of a loving God; it is just another step towards an uncertain future. Humans will eventually be replaced by another form, and we have no idea what the final outcome could be.

So, what was Wells to do about such a future? As far-fetched as it seems, Wells embraced the idea of change. The human race must "re-imagine" itself and accept the future of the species in order to survive and continue.[19] Instead of letting the whims of nature take the future of the species along, humanity could take the reins of its own evolution and design itself to overcome. Humanity would become less of a species designed and blessed by God and more of a line of organisms conquering any obstacle in its way. By leaving behind the physical forms that constrain their advancement, humans will conquer death and populate the universe. Humanity, in essence, will insert itself into divinity and immortality. Other authors like Olaf Stapledon and J. B. S. Haldane explored this strain of evolutionism further, but H. G. Wells provided the sturdy base and shocking takeaway that chilled Lewis to his core.

Lewis was strongly against this evolutionism, and he magnified its characteristics through Weston's exaggerated beliefs. When Weston comes into conflict with the Oyarsa of Malacandra, he explains his intention to spread humankind's domination throughout the universe, regardless of "whatever strange form and yet unguessed mentality they have assumed," killing off the other natural occupants when necessary (*OSP*, 136). Weston is devoted to the pursuit of science for the advancement of humanity, to the point that he will sacrifice anything for "the greater good." He does not even care if humanity will still be recognizably human—all that matters is the preservation of the human line of evolution. When we encounter him again in *Perelandra*, Weston has given so much of his life and soul to this idea that he becomes the warped Un-man. He leaves the idea of good far behind and looks only for progress. In his attempts to make humanity last forever, he loses his soul and becomes a revolting, inhuman husk that was once a man.

In a genre so fascinated with the development of science, Weston provides a frightening glimpse of the potential polarization that can occur. Weston is not open to the investigation of other life and a potential relationship with a new culture. Instead, he is solely focused on the development of the human race. Weston does not stop to think whether the order and structure of Malacandra is a better alternative to humankind conquering the universe. His mind is closed off to the classical idea of observing the world around him and is instead laser focused on a single, ruinous goal. He ignores the potential opportunities to learn about himself and humanity and how he possibly can save both. That job is left up to Elwin Ransom.

Ransom: The Third Man

The role of Ransom is that of a third party who has no previous history with the environments on Malacandra and Perelandra. Unlike Devine and Weston, Ransom does not have a literary counterpart in *The First Men in the Moon*. His character is actually similar to that of Maskull in David Lindsay's *A Voyage to Arcturus*, a man who travels to the planet Tormance and is thrust into a bizarre and wondrous new environment. Separated from the rest of his group upon landing, Maskull wanders across Tormance in a sort of extraterrestrial *Pilgrim's Progress*, interacting with and learning from the characters he encounters. A female extraterrestrial named Joiwind explains the sudden growth of new physical organs to help "understand and sympathise with all living creatures," to allow for "the advantage of not being cruel and selfish."[20] Maskull comes bearing an earthly mindset, but in his interactions with the inhabitants of Tormance, he is shown all of humanity's flaws and weaknesses. Each new being he encounters provides another perspective on the condition of humanity.

Ransom is Lewis's literary response to the inquisitive traveler found in Maskull. In a sense, Ransom is Lewis in the early chapters of *Out of the Silent Planet*.[21] A British professor who likes walking tours and identifies as a strong

Christian, Ransom could be considered a representation of the author or one of his other academic peers. Brought on an interstellar journey by accident, he has no premeditated desires or purposes for the experience. He is merely a bystander sucked into the whims and plans of his captors. Because of this, he has a very different approach to the new world when he arrives on Malacandra. While Weston and Devine already have specific plans and desires in mind as they go about their actions on the new planet, Ransom is able to approach his situation with an open mind for what may lie ahead. When approached by a *hrossa*, Ransom is at first afraid of the new encounter but soon revels in the opportunity to document a whole new language (*OSP*, 56).

Ransom's open mind, not plagued by preconceived notions or motives for being on Malacandra, enables him to approach this foreign planet with a sense of discovery and advancement. However, his sense of advancement is much different from Weston's. While Weston desires to make progress for the benefit of humanity and its posterity, Ransom echoes the mindset of Cavor: an interest in knowledge for knowledge's sake and a desire to learn all he can from this new world on which he has found himself. Ransom does not derive inspiration from a single goal of furthering humanity (at least not in the physical and technological frame). Ransom's goal is to learn, which in turn benefits humanity far more than Weston's pursuit of technological goals. This inquisitive traveler embodies constructive growth that allows for infinitely more good than Weston's closed-mindedness. By focusing on the sole goal of survival, Weston overlooks the positive growth of humanity's identity, spiritually and otherwise. Ransom is the only character to represent the good that humanity can achieve, and he ends up defending it in the cosmic battle that ensues in *Perelandra* and *That Hideous Strength*.

Wells Versus Lewis: "Bug-Eyed Monsters"

A larger science fiction trope that Lewis inverts is the idea of aliens as invading monsters. Wells's novel *The War of The Worlds* focuses on the invasion of Britain by Martians in impenetrable spacecraft. The British countryside is decimated by the invading foes, and the population is steadily captured by the Martians and used as food.[22] While the Martian invasion can be seen as a metaphor for colonialization's effect on developing countries, the image of an unbeatable and hideous alien attacking what humanity holds dear became a common theme among science fiction writers.[23] Similarly, in *The First Men in the Moon*, Wells portrays the native creatures on the moon as foreign and scary to the travelers, something instantly repulsive:

> It came to me as an absolute, for a moment an overwhelming shock. It seemed as though it wasn't a face, as though it must needs be a mask, a horror, a deformity, that would presently be disavowed or explained. There was no nose, and the thing had dull bulging eyes at the side—in the silhouette I had supposed they were ears.[24]

The Selenites are bug-like creatures that, during the initial encounter, display no human traits, emotions, or even an indication of intelligence. Wells refuses to call their facial features a face, instead resorting to terms like a "mask," a "horror," and a "deformity." The reaction Wells creates is one of fear and uncertainty at their new captor. There is nothing more foreign than this lifeform, and it is presented to the reader with trepidation. We do not know what will happen to Bedford and Cavor, but we are scared to find out.

Lewis takes this theme of monstrous alien invaders and turns it completely upside-down. Instead of aliens terrorizing the humans in his story, he presents the humans as the invading force, hostile to these new worlds. The inhabitants of Malacandra are peaceful, and though they are strange and foreign, they are not terrifying or inhumane. For example, on Malacandra, Ransom encounters the *pfifltriggi*, which at first glance seem similar to Wells's Selenites. The *pfifltriggi* are comparable to the emerging trope of "bug-eyed monsters," insect-like creatures that bear little-to-no resemblance to humans or mammals. However, Lewis describes them in a different way than Wells does: "It was rather like a grasshopper, rather like one of Arthur Rackham's dwarfs, rather like a frog, and rather like a little, old taxidermist whom Ransom knew in London" (OSP, 112). While the Selenites are compared with a lifeless mask and called horrors, Lewis compares his *pfifltriggi* to distinctly human counterparts. There is nothing scary about a small, old taxidermist or a dwarf. Both are human and much more familiar than an insectoid "deformity." Lewis flips this monster stereotype and presents a species that instantly becomes familiar without repulsing his readers. Life that is foreign to humanity does not need to be feared; in fact, it can help humans learn more about themselves in the process.

In ironic contrast, Weston and Devine become foreign characters to us later in *Out of the Silent Planet*. When Ransom is discoursing with Malacandra's Oyarsa, two foreign creatures are brought into the Oyarsa's court. Ransom describes them as stumpy, unrecognizable bipeds, but his attitude shortly changes when he realizes they are Weston and Devine. "He, for one privileged moment, had seen the human form with almost Malacandrian eyes" (*OSP*, 124). By the time Weston and Devine reenter Ransom's journey, their earthly actions seem foreign to the new system and world we have grown comfortable with. When the *hross* Hyoi is shot by Devine and Weston, Ransom confesses that his presence as a human on a foreign planet has brought pain and chaos to Malacandra (*OSP*, 82). Humanity is no longer the species to be protected; instead, it is the one to be watched carefully. Humanity is the destructive force in the ordered world of Malacandra. The revolt of humanity against order destroys that which is good in the worlds of Arbol, and this revolt must be dealt with.

Science Fiction on Earth

In the third book of the trilogy Lewis takes this cosmic adventure and sets it all on familiar turf, right in Lewis's backyard. Even though the story is anchored on an earthly plane, *That Hideous Strength* is a powerful science fiction narrative. In it, Lewis continues to push against the reign of cold scientism. To achieve this, he uses strategies and styles like that of his contemporaries, but instead of setting them far out in space, he places them in a very real and personal world.

One such theme in *That Hideous Strength* parallels the trend of contemporary dystopias, seen especially in *Brave New World* by Aldous Huxley. This theme deals with the modernization of society, going so far as to leave the human spirit behind in the interest of progress. In Huxley's society, humanity is genetically engineered to function as designated members in a fixed caste. All art and religion have been done away with; only pleasure seems to matter. The Controller Mustapha Mond states, "You can only be independent of God while you've got youth and prosperity; independence won't take you safely to the end. Well, we've now got youth and prosperity right up to the end."[25] The society is engineered to do away with all the afflictions of the natural world, which in turn does away with everything that makes human nature relevant. There is no need to solve problems when there are no problems to begin with. Society in Huxley's world has been modified to the point that the basic ideas of humanity are gone, and an almost robotic society remains.

Likewise, the National Institute of Coordinated Experiments (abbreviated N.I.C.E.) has plans to create their own society very similar to that of *Brave New World*. When Feverstone tries to convince Mark to join the N.I.C.E., he states, "Man has got to take charge of Man. Quite simple and obvious things, at first—sterilization of the unfit, liquidation of backward races, selective breeding . . . . A new type of man: and it's people like you who've got to begin to make him" (*THS*, 40). The goal of the N.I.C.E. is to remove nature from the equation and establish humans as above any other creature. Lewis shows the potentiality of a physically and spiritually sterile society and what can happen as a result. Selective breeding and education only foster this sterility by controlling the population and its influences. By training and conditioning humanity to follow a path devoid of all nature, humans become free—in a sense.

However, this path leads to the human race becoming free from human nature; humanity is no longer what we consider human and is something else entirely. Lewis warns that this is the end of all that is good. When we are shown the two human leaders of the N.I.C.E., we do not recognize the creatures they have become. Lewis portrays Wither and Frost's interactions as "animalistic" and inhuman, lacking any human emotion (*THS*, 240). Everything that roots their identity in humanity has been removed, leaving behind only a shell of their former selves.

Through his depiction of extreme scientism, Lewis creates tension. The N.I.C.E. is established as a scientific institution, but the reader cannot shake the uneasy feeling that the members of the N.I.C.E. are not actually concerned with beneficial scientific work. Fairy Hardcastle is forceful and abusive; Filostrato is purely focused on the scientific nature of the Head; Feverstone is involved only to turn another profit; and Wither and Frost are cold and unresponsive to the world around them, hinting at a lack of a spirit. It is not just the morality (or lack thereof) of the N.I.C.E. that creates this uneasy feeling; it is the varying degrees of scientism each character exhibits and the unified goal of furthering the human race, no matter the cost. Hardcastle kills unfaithful members. Feverstone leaves the N.I.C.E. to keep his money intact. Wither and Frost go so far as to make deals with the bent *eldila* of Thulcandra in order to try and achieve their dark goals. Each member renounces a part of their human spirit in order to pursue an earthly desire. When Mark and Jane, under the guidance of Ransom, emerge victorious in the end, Lewis shows his triumph over his old nemesis evolutionism and expresses a better way to engage with the world in which we live.

The Power of Science Fiction

Though he is critical of Wells and others, Lewis does not discredit the science fiction genre and its close ties with the growing science of the era. The point of his critique of science fiction is not to create rifts between faith and science, but rather to illustrate how science can be abused. Throughout all of the Ransom Trilogy, he combats and disarms the extreme polarization of scientific thought. Science fiction, in its very nature, provides a perfect ground in which to plant his ideas. While H. G. Wells wrote about the glorification of humanity through science, Lewis focused on the glorification of God through inquiry, with science serving as a vessel to bring the human race closer to the ultimate truth. Science fiction is not the only thing Lewis wrestles with, though. Many of the ideas and themes he reveals through his settings and characters stem from his analysis of scientism, which Rachel M. Roller fleshes out in the next chapter.

But, while scientism takes some of these themes to a whole new level, science fiction initiates it all. If a reader does not feel a sense of unease or questioning when reading science fiction, he or she could very well be missing key features of the genre he or she is engaging with. Science fiction by its very nature proposes a "what if?" and Lewis paints the biggest "what if" he possibly can across the Trilogy. He forces the reader to consider the essence of our humanity and makes us aware of what we must do to avoid a future in which the N.I.C.E. reigns supreme.

Endnotes

1 C. S. Lewis, "On Science Fiction," in *Of Other Worlds: Essays and Stories,* ed. Walter Hooper (New York: HarperCollins, 2017), 96–97.
2 Lewis, "On Science Fiction," 97.
3 Interestingly, *Star Wars* has escaped this harsh criticism; had more Americans been exposed to the 'samurai cinema' genre coming from Japan in the postwar era, *Star Wars* may have not become as big of a blockbuster as we know today.
4 Brian W. Aldiss, Kingsley Amis, and C. S. Lewis, "Unreal Estates," in *Of Other Worlds: Essays and Stories,* ed. Walter Hooper (New York: HarperCollins, 2017), 138.
5 Lewis, "On Science Fiction," 99.
6 Lewis, "On Science Fiction," 101.
7 Lewis, "On Science Fiction," 103.
8 Lewis, "On Science Fiction," 104.
9 Lewis, "On Science Fiction," 107.
10 Lewis, "On Science Fiction," 112.
11 Before we move on, it would be remiss to not mention Lewis's explicit reference to Wells when describing an interaction between the *hrossa* and Ransom: "He [Ransom] did not want to tell them too much of our human wars and industrialisms. He remembered how H. G. Wells's Cavor had met his end on the Moon; also he felt shy" (*OSP,* 71). Through the course of events in *The First Men,* Cavor is captured by the Selenites and cut off from communication with Earth when the Selenites learn of mankind's rough history and dispositions. Ransom himself is afraid of how the *hrossa* will act when informed of the barbarisms of humanity and does not want to be isolated on Malacandra if the *hrossa* decide to detain him to prevent further harm from occurring to the planet.
12 H. G. Wells, *The First Men in the Moon* (New York: Lancer Books, 1969), 45.
13 Wells, *First Men,* 221.
14 Wells, *First Men,* 37.
15 Wells, *First Men,* 125.
16 C. S. Lewis, "The Funeral of a Great Myth," in *Christian Reflections,* ed. Walter Hooper (Grand Rapids, MI: Eerdmans, 2014), 102.
17 H. G. Wells, *The Time Machine* (Rockville, MD: Phoenix Pick, 2009).
18 Robert Pasquini, "Evacuated Ecologies: H. G. Wells and the Evolutionary Aesthetics of Extinction," *Interdisciplinary Humanities 32,* no. 2 (2015): 56.
19 Pasquini, 60.
20 David Lindsay, *A Voyage to Arcturus* (Auckland, NZ: Floating Press, 2011), 64–65.
21 Many scholars also argue that Ransom is a representation of J. R. R. Tolkien, who embodied many of the same characteristics.
22 H. G. Wells, *The War of the Worlds* (New York: Scholastic Incorporated, 2005), 224–25.
23 Orson Scott Card, introduction to H. G. Wells, *The War of the Worlds* (New York: Scholastic Incorporated, 2005).
24 Wells, *First Men,* 119.
25 Aldous Huxley, *Brave New World* (New York: HarperCollins, 1998), 233.

SCIENCE ON THE SILENT PLANET

RACHEL M. ROLLER

"Lewis knew nothing about science except that he hated it."[1] This statement, taken from a 1979 review in the *New York Times*, sums up a common response to C. S. Lewis's science fiction trilogy. This reaction is understandable—Lewis's descriptions of space travel and life on other planets reveal that he was certainly no scientist, and his choice of a physicist and a scientific institute as his primary villains lends credence to the idea that he hated science. But is it true, as Philip Deasy claimed, that the Ransom Trilogy is a "total and unrelenting attack on science?"[2] A closer look at Lewis's writings suggests otherwise. Lewis's science fiction trilogy is not a warning against science itself, but rather against a worldview known as "scientism."[3] Before diving into Lewis's critique of scientism, let's examine what Lewis thought about science itself.

C.S. Lewis and Science

The first question to consider is whether Lewis even knew enough about science to critique it. After all, if it is in fact true that "Lewis knew nothing about science," he would have little or no credibility as a critic of the field. There is some evidence to support the notion that Lewis was ignorant about science—Lewis himself admitted that he had received "a philosophical rather than a scientific education," and those who knew him testified that he was far from scientifically erudite.[4] For example, when Lewis was preparing for university, his tutor, Professor Kirkpatrick, wrote that Lewis "knows nothing of science and loathes it and all its works."[5] Even Lewis's stepson, Douglas Gresham, reported that Lewis was "incredibly ignorant of things such as biology," to the point where he "thought that a slug was a reptile."[6] Clearly, Lewis was no scientist.

That being said, Lewis's writings reveal that he was at least conversant in scientific thought. For example, in *Miracles*, Lewis engages with scientific concepts ranging from Newton's laws and classical atomic theory to quantum physics and indeterminacy—something he certainly could not have done if he truly knew nothing about the field.[7] Indeed, a broader survey of Lewis's work indicates that he was familiar with the work of scientists such as Sir James Jeans, Sir Arthur Eddington, Sir Fred Hoyle, and even Erwin Schrödinger, who was his colleague at Magdalen College in Oxford.[8] In addition, Lewis's literary studies of the Copernican Revolution gave him significant insight into the foundations of science and the complex relationships between science, philosophy, and culture.[9] Thus, while Lewis was by no means a scientist, he was arguably more scientifically literate than the average reader, and he knew at least enough about scientific thought to insightfully engage with it.

If we grant that Lewis was not totally ignorant of science, however, we are left with another question: why is his science fiction so unscientific? After reading *Out of the Silent Planet*, J. B. S. Haldane, an eminent biochemist and harsh critic of Lewis's works, observed that the Trilogy's attempted scientific descriptions of space travel and other planets left much to be desired, and therefore concluded that Lewis's "accounts of supernatural intervention would have been more impressive had he known more of nature as it actually exists."[10] Haldane is correct in saying that the Trilogy contains a fair amount of inaccurate and incomplete science, but he is mistaken in implying that the scientific shortcomings of the Trilogy provide a reason to discount its messages. In his marvelously witty "Reply to Professor Haldane," Lewis defended himself against Haldane's accusations by clarifying that he was writing science *fiction*, not science. In his words,

> My science is usually wrong. Why, yes ... [but] my false science is produced in romances ... No one hopes, in such fantasies, to satisfy a real scientist, any more than the writer of a historical romance hopes to satisfy a real archeologist ... There is thus a great deal of scientific falsehood in my stories: some of it known to be false even by me when I wrote the books.[11]

Lewis claims that he was fully aware of the "scientific falsehood" in his fiction—he was not even trying to "satisfy a real scientist." For Lewis, the point of the Trilogy was not to give a plausible account of space travel, but to awaken the imagination. As he argues in his essay, "On Science Fiction," imaginative accounts of other planets need not be "at all tied to strictly scientific possibilities," because "it is their wonder, or beauty, or suggestiveness that matter."[12] Since Lewis was more focused on evoking wonder and beauty than on crafting a scientifically accurate space saga, he was convinced that the scientific inaccuracies in the Trilogy did not diminish the value of the Trilogy as a whole or discredit its deeper meaning.

A more serious issue is the accusation that Lewis was adamantly opposed to science and took every opportunity to attack it in his science fiction trilogy. A cursory reading of the Trilogy appears to support the notion that Lewis was anti-science: Weston, the villain of the first two books, is a physicist, while the unscrupulous National Institute for Co-ordinated Experiments (N.I.C.E.) in *That Hideous Strength* calls itself a scientific organization. It is easy to see how Deasy could read the Trilogy as a "total and unrelenting attack on science."[13] A deeper look at Lewis's writings, however, reveals that Lewis had no intention of attacking science itself.

Consider, for example, Lewis's portrayal of William Hingest, one of the unsung heroes of *That Hideous Strength.*[14] Hingest is an internationally renowned physical chemist who initially joins the N.I.C.E. because of its reputation as a credible scientific institute (*THS,* 55). When he discovers that the N.I.C.E. is really a political conspiracy that has little to do with actual science, Hingest attempts to leave the organization, with the result that he is promptly murdered by the N.I.C.E.'s secret police (*THS,* 68–9). Now, if Lewis meant to denounce science itself, why would he paint a scientist as a noble martyr or take such great pains to point out that the evil N.I.C.E. was only posing as a scientific organization? As Lewis explains in his "Reply to Professor Haldane," "the 'good' scientist is put in precisely to show that 'scientists' as such are not the target."[15] Lewis writes that he painted the N.I.C.E. as an insidious conspiracy precisely to show that the villains are "not scientists but *officials.*"[16] If this is not evidence enough, *That Hideous Strength* explicitly states that the physical sciences are inherently "good and innocent," clearly indicating that Lewis's Trilogy is not an attack on science (*THS,* 200).

Space Colonies and Scientism

If Lewis is not opposed to science, then what are the seemingly anti-scientific passages in the Trilogy critiquing? As the previous chapter pointed out, Lewis's science fiction trilogy was written as a response to the philosophies embodied in the science fiction of his time. In fact, much of Lewis's purported attack on science is actually a direct response to one short science fiction piece by Professor Haldane entitled "The Last Judgment." In this imaginative work, Haldane chronicles the destruction of our earth and the establishment of a human colony on Venus forty million years into the future.[17] The scientifically-minded rulers of Haldane's fictional society put the survival of the human race above all else, with the goal that "though men died, man should live forever."[18] They abandoned morality, declaring that "human ideals are the products of natural processes."[19] They stripped their people of pity, viewing it merely as "an unpleasant feeling aroused by the suffering of other individuals."[20] They rejected the pursuit of individual happiness, and believed that this sacrifice was "not a cause for great regret."[21] They eradicated freedom, treating people as disposable "members of a superorganism" rather than as independent, valuable individuals.[22] In sum, Haldane's imaginary Venus colony was the epitome of dehumanizing science.

This sort of dehumanizing science is exactly what the Trilogy is critiquing. In fact, in his "Reply to Professor Haldane," Lewis freely admitted that his Trilogy was an attack on the type of philosophy Haldane expressed in "The Last Judgment." After giving a brief summary of Haldane's story, Lewis writes, "It was against this outlook on life, this ethic, if you will, that I wrote my satiric fantasy."[23] This "ethic" or "outlook on life" is what Lewis called "scientism."[24] Lewis defines scientism as

> [T]he belief that the supreme moral end is the perpetuation of our own species, and that this is to be pursued even if, in the process of being fitted for our survival, our species has to be stripped of all those things for which we value it—of pity, of happiness, and of freedom.[25]

In this short definition, Lewis encapsulates Haldane's skewed system of morality that prioritizes human survival at all costs—even the cost of dehumanizing people by squelching their moral sense of pity, stealing everything that produces true happiness, and utterly destroying their freedom. In the next few pages, we will explore Lewis's definition of scientism in more depth and see how Lewis provides an alternative to Haldane's scientism.

Scientism and Naturalism

Science and scientism are two distinctly different things. The physical sciences—such as chemistry, biology, and physics—are simply ways of investigating the natural world through experiment and observation. They are a method of study, not an ideology. Scientism, on the other hand, is often defined as "extreme or excessive faith in science," or "the belief that only knowledge obtained from scientific research is valid."[26] Scientism is a system of belief—it could even be classified as a religion of sorts—that makes science the sole arbiter of truth. Lewis describes scientism as a "caricature of the true sciences" and remarks that it is "much less common among real scientists than among their readers."[27]

The main problem with making science the ultimate authority is that science is inherently limited in what it can study. Science's job is to observe and draw conclusions about the physical, material world. Lewis notes in *Mere Christianity* that all scientific statements boil down to something like "I put some of this stuff in a pot and heated it to such-and-such a temperature and it did so-and-so."[28] Science, by its very nature, cannot study things beyond the physical realm. Thus, when scientism declares that scientific research is the only way to truth, it almost inevitably leads to naturalism, or the belief that the natural world is all that exists.[29] According to reductionistic naturalism, there is nothing beyond the physical realm of matter and energy—in other words, if you cannot put it in a test tube or under a microscope, it does not exist.

When scientism reduces all of reality to matter and energy, it tends to abandon traditional morality. In *Mere Christianity*, Lewis maintains that the moral law found in every human heart is evidence of something beyond the physical realm, something that purely naturalistic science cannot explain.[30] Scientism, however, begins with the assumption that no such non-physical and scientifically unexplainable things exist. Therefore, under the strictly naturalistic paradigm of scientism, the moral law must be a human construct, a "mere subjective by-product" of circumstance and culture (*THS*, 200).[31] If science is the only source of knowledge, then the physical world is all there is, and intangibles such as morality can be dismissed as illusory. Scientism's insistence on reductionistic naturalism and its dismissal of transcendent morality set the stage for its focus on human survival as the "supreme moral end."[32]

Survival at All Costs

Scientism's preoccupation with "the perpetuation of our own species" ultimately flows from its naturalistic mindset.[33] When scientism declares that the natural, physical world is all that exists, it denies the reality of all non-physical and supernatural entities, including God and the immortal human soul. This includes the assumption that there is no life after death—when we die, we simply cease to exist. Under the paradigm of naturalism, then, death is the end of the story. Humans, however, seem to possess an insatiable longing to live forever, so when scientism squashes any religious hope of eternal life, we turn to science itself as an alternative route to immortality.[34] If there is no afterlife, then we are left with two primary options for gaining something akin to everlasting life: either we use science to ensure that our descendants will carry our genes into the foreseeable future, or we use science to conquer death, or at least extend the human lifespan for as long as possible.[35]

Lewis explores the first of these two scientistic approaches to immortality—ensuring the survival of the human race as a whole—primarily in *Out of the Silent Planet.*[36] Through the character of Weston, Lewis satirizes Haldane's ideal that "though men died, man should live forever."[37] Several times in the story, Lewis cleverly places fine-sounding scientistic arguments in the mouth of Weston, only to uncover their absurdity when Ransom "translates" them into the vernacular. For instance, when Weston attempts to justify kidnapping Ransom, he pompously asserts that individual rights or even individual lives are of miniscule importance compared to the possibility that "infinity, and therefore perhaps eternity, is being put into the hands of the human race" (*OSP*, 29). Here, Lewis is clearly parodying Haldane's vision that "The human race will prove that its destiny is in eternity and infinity, and that the value of the individual is negligible in comparison."[38] Weston's (and Haldane's) warped idealism sounds almost reasonable until Ransom observes that all of Weston's grandiose rhetoric about "infinity and eternity" just means that Weston believes he can do absolutely anything—even kill innocent people—under the pretext that it might promote human survival in the distant future (*OSP*, 29–30). When Weston replies that that is indeed what he means, Lewis has made his point: scientism's noble-sounding statements about sacrificing the individual for the survival of humanity are merely a thin veneer over a twisted scientistic mentality that places no value on individual lives.

Lewis dramatizes the consequences of this mindset by tracing Weston's gradual progression of being willing to sacrifice first a dog, then a "feeble-minded" boy, then an intellectual peer, and finally the entire population of Malacandra.[39] Sanford Schwartz highlights how Lewis uses this "chain of sacrificial substitutions" to reveal the treacherous "slippery slope" that begins when individual lives become disposable.[40] In a time when eugenics was growing popular among intellectuals and the horrors of Hitler's Reich were just beginning to loom on the horizon, Lewis's warnings about the danger of "liquidating" lower life forms were both sobering and prophetic.[41]

While *Out of the Silent Planet* reveals the peril of prioritizing, above all else, the survival of the human species as a whole, *That Hideous Strength* highlights the danger of turning to science as a source of individual immortality. In perhaps the most gruesome and haunting scene in the Trilogy, Lewis describes how the N.I.C.E. kept a disembodied Head alive artificially through science (*THS*, 177–79). It would be easy to dismiss the Head as a disturbing bit of science fiction horror thrown in for dramatic effect, but Lewis makes it clear that the image of the Head is packed with both literal and symbolic meaning. Filostrato views the maintenance of the Head as the beginning of "the conquest of death," and Straik sees the Head as the first step toward placing humanity on the "throne of the universe" (*THS*, 173–75). Both Straik and Filostrato speak of the Head in explicitly religious terms, even comparing the never-dying Head to the resurrected Christ (*THS*, 174). For Filostrato and Straik, science offers humankind eternal life and limitless power. Science, for them, has become both a god in itself and a way for them to become immortal and omnipotent.

Through the story of Weston and the image of the Head, Lewis prompts us to ask ourselves whether we, like Straik and Filostrato, view science as our source of immortality, but he also invites us to consider whether the type of immortality that science offers is worth the price. For Lewis, a long life—whether for an individual or for humanity as a whole—is not nearly as important a goal as a life filled with joy and goodness. In his essay "Is Progress Possible?" Lewis explains, "Progress, for me, means increasing goodness and happiness of individual lives. For the species, as for each man, mere longevity seems to be a contemptible ideal."[42] Aslan's declaration in *The Magician's Nephew* that "length of days with an evil heart is only length of misery" underscores Lewis's conviction that humanity should be wary of making immortality our chief moral end.[43]

The Final Conquest of Nature

Through the stories of Weston and the Head of the N.I.C.E., Lewis warns us about the dangers of turning to science as an alternate source of immortality. Yet this preoccupation with using science to conquer death is only one aspect of a deeper issue: the idea that science can conquer nature itself. Lewis explores this idea in *That Hideous Strength* mainly through the character of Filostrato. According to Filostrato, the ultimate goal of science is not to improve life through better medicine and technology but rather to conquer nature and free humankind from their reliance on the natural world (*THS*, 173–74). Filostrato took this idea so far that he believed in completely abolishing organic life—making a "clean" world where the human mind was freed from its dependence on the body, where forests were replaced with the metal "art tree," and where the earth was stark and barren like the moon (*THS*, 169–74). The Head, which represented the triumph over death, was merely the first step in this campaign to increase "Man's power over Nature" (*THS*, 174–75).

Filostrato's ideas about conquering nature clearly echo Lewis's critique of scientific power in *The Abolition of Man*. Lewis was profoundly concerned that "Man's conquest of Nature" would turn out to be "Nature's conquest of Man"—in other words, that the quest for scientific power would ultimately destroy everything that makes us human.[44] To be clear, Lewis did not believe scientific power in and of itself was evil. Rather, he feared a certain type of scientific power—power that was separated from transcendent truth and morality. In *That Hideous Strength*, Lewis writes that the sciences began to go wrong when "despair of objective truth" was "insinuated into the scientists" until they became indifferent to truth and concentrated on "mere power" (*THS*, 200). In this passage, Lewis warns that science becomes scientism when it abandons the quest for objective truth and begins to lust after mere power. Mere power, uncoupled from truth, is the type of scientific power that turns "Man's conquest of Nature" into "Nature's conquest of Man."[45]

What exactly does Lewis mean when he speaks of "Nature's conquest of Man"? Ultimately, the answer goes back to the problem of reductionistic naturalism. Lewis notes that "conquering nature" usually involves reducing everything to the level of the purely natural, that is, treating it as if it is nothing more than matter in motion. In Lewis's words, "the price of conquest is to treat a thing as mere Nature."[46] Treating a thing as "mere Nature" means that we analyze it in terms of measurable qualities, such as its mass or its usefulness to us.[47] According to Lewis, this scientific way of analyzing an object is valid and often necessary, but it somehow misses a part of the object's reality. In his words, "The great minds know very well that the object, so treated, is an artificial abstraction, that something of its reality has been lost."[48]

As long as the objects that we analyze in this way are, in fact, merely objects, this loss of reality is fairly minimal. For example, viewing a sample of copper(II) sulfate as a purely natural entity does not do it much harm. The real problem arises when we begin to treat *ourselves* as purely natural objects, that is, when we "take the final step of reducing our own species to the level of mere Nature."[49] When we take this final step of reducing ourselves to merely natural objects, we forget that we are far more than a sample of carbon, hydrogen, nitrogen, and oxygen. We begin to treat ourselves and our fellow humans as "raw material for scientific manipulation."[50] In essence, we forget the non-physical things that make us human. In our quest to conquer nature, we reduce ourselves to mere nature and thus abolish the essence of our humanity.

Lewis's ultimate concern, then, is that scientism will reduce, redefine, and, ultimately, dehumanize the human race. This is why he warns that scientism, if we let it, will strip the human species of "all those things for which we value it—of pity, of happiness, and of freedom."[51]

Pity

One of the most horrifying consequences of scientism is that, in reducing everything to mere matter, it strips humanity of the ability to feel compassion or pity. Pity, in its highest form, restrains us from inflicting unnecessary pain on others and drives us to alleviate the suffering of those around us. If, however, as Haldane's imagined space colony believed, pity is merely "an unpleasant feeling aroused by the suffering of other individuals," scientism can easily explain it away as a chemical response to an external stimulus.[52] A sense of pity prevents us from abusing animals or experimenting on humans without their full knowledge and consent, so if scientism's quest for power demands such actions, scientism must diligently work to squelch pity and compassion. This is exactly the goal of the N.I.C.E., which is convinced that "the stifling of all deep-set repugnances was the first essential for progress" (*THS*, 200). The N.I.C.E. promotes a skewed version of "objectivity" that systematically kills off every wholesome and normal human reaction, including tenderness, compassion, and pity (*THS*, 296).[53]

Frost, a psychologist at the N.I.C.E., attempts to initiate Mark into the N.I.C.E.'s inner circle by training him in this sort of "objectivity." Frost holds that all emotions, motives, and ethical conceptions are merely "chemical phenomena," and therefore tells Mark that he must utterly destroy every vestige of ethics, aesthetics, logic, preference, and will in his mind (*THS*, 252, 293–94). This warped version of "objectivity" is tantamount to destroying one's humanity—it is killing the part of the self that instinctively gravitates toward goodness, beauty, and truth and recoils from cruel or unethical practices. False "objectivity" utterly destroys the basis of pity and begins the slow process of stripping away everything that makes us human.

Happiness

Scientism destroys not only pity but also happiness—recall Haldane's society that discarded all thought of individual happiness without a qualm. This loss of happiness is the logical consequence of the N.I.C.E.'s skewed "objectivity," which insists on analyzing objects, experiences, and people rather than enjoying them. In "Meditation in a Toolshed," Lewis discusses several examples of this, such as a young man experiencing being "in love" versus a scientist describing the young man's reaction to a "biological stimulus."[54] Lewis believed that it is impossible to experience love and analyze it at the same time. Thus, if the N.I.C.E. is right in that we must view the world solely through an "objective," analytical lens, there is effectively no room for the experience of love. It is important to note here that Lewis is not criticizing the "scientific" way of looking at life (he specifically says that these two ways of looking at love may be "equally correct in different ways") but he is critiquing the modern scientistic tendency to assume that the scientific, analytical method of observing phenomena is inherently better or more accurate than personal experience.[55]

Focusing exclusively on the analytical view robs people of the ability to experience beauty and joy. For example, Mark, who has not yet succumbed to the N.I.C.E.'s "objectivity," hears birds singing and feels as if they were calling "Wake! Wake!," while Cosser, who is steeped in the culture of the N.I.C.E., merely curses at the noise, and Filostrato, who has fallen so far into scientism that he advocates abolishing all organic life, dreams of the day when one will turn artificial birdsong on and off with the flip of a switch (*THS,* 85, 170). Similarly, Mark is still able to enjoy the sunshine on a lovely morning and the drinks at a local pub, but Cosser can think only of the effect of sunlight and "stimulants" on one's health (*THS,* 86). Cosser and others at the N.I.C.E. grow so accustomed to considering everything from a purely "objective" standpoint that they can no longer enjoy the simple joys of sunshine, birdsong, or a trip to the pub. By "objectively" reducing reality to mere matter in motion, scientism strips humanity of happiness.

Freedom

J. D. Wunderly points out in Chapter 4 that as Lewis witnessed the horrific abuses of scientific power in Nazi Germany, he grew increasingly concerned about scientism's tendency to demolish freedom. Lewis repeatedly warns in both *The Abolition of Man* and *That Hideous Strength* that "Man's power over Nature turns out to be a power exercised by some men over other men with Nature as its instrument."[56] This is why he was incredibly skeptical of Haldane's claim that "social problems can only be solved in the long run by the application of scientific method."[57] Lewis dreaded a technocracy, or a rule of the scientific experts, because scientific training does not prepare specialists to answer the central questions of government, "questions about the good for man, and justice, and what things are worth having at what price."[58] The N.I.C.E. is a perfect example of such a freedom-destroying technocracy—they combine the latest science with the power of the state in order to dominate and recondition the human race (*THS*, 21; *THS*, 37–39). In their quest to conquer and reform society, they were willing to resort to sterilizing and "liquidating" those they deemed unfit, experimenting on criminals and the mentally ill, conditioning children, spreading propaganda, and even engineering riots—all in the name of science and the good of society.[59] They promised progress but brought only tyranny. The N.I.C.E. powerfully illustrates Lewis's point that "'under modern conditions any effective invitation to Hell will certainly appear in the guise of scientific planning'—as Hitler's regime in fact did."[60]

A New Natural Philosophy

Lewis's warning is clear: when scientism declares that science is the only source of truth, it abandons objective morality, sets up human survival as the supreme goal, and systematically robs humanity of pity, happiness, and freedom. However, a question remains. What is the solution to this problem of scientism? According to Deasy, the author who alleged that the Trilogy is a "total and unrelenting attack on science," it is not enough to say that Lewis was attacking scientism rather than science, because if Lewis only portrays the "godless and dehumanizing" side of science and never casts a vision for how science can be redeemed, he is effectively calling for a return to the dark ages.[61] This problem plagued Deasy so much that he asked, "Can a popular Christian apologist continue to be effective and relevant in our Space Age without such a vision?"[62]

Fortunately, Lewis did cast such a vision. In fact, according to Lewis, science itself may provide the best solution to scientism. As he writes in *The Abolition of Man*, "I even suggest that from Science herself the cure may come."[63] The final section of *The Abolition of Man* contains Lewis's vision for a "regenerate science" that would provide the cure for scientism.[64] Lewis calls this redeemed science a "new Natural Philosophy," a term that literally means the "love of wisdom of natural things."[65] The name "Natural Philosophy" comes from the days before the scientific revolution, when science was considered a branch of philosophy and those who studied it were called natural philosophers. While modern scientism views science as the only way to truth, the ancients thought that science, philosophy, and theology (which was called "queen of the sciences") could work in harmony to discover the nature of reality.[66] By calling his regenerate science "Natural Philosophy," then, Lewis implies that we should recapture the ancients' integrated view of reality. Yet, by calling the regenerate science a "*new* Natural Philosophy," Lewis makes clear that he is not calling for a return to the dark ages but rather for a reimagined science that combines the wisdom of the past with the scientific knowledge of the present.

How does Lewis describe this new Natural Philosophy? Lewis explains that the new Natural Philosophy would constantly remember that the objective, analytical view used in the laboratory is only a partial picture of reality. As Lewis puts it, the regenerate science would recognize that "the 'natural object' produced by analysis and abstraction is not reality but only a view."[67] Essentially, this means that the new Natural Philosophy would reclaim the true meaning of objectivity. The N.I.C.E.'s perverted version of "objectivity" focused exclusively on the abstract, analytical way of viewing the world and thus declared that nothing beyond the material world exists. This is why Frost and the N.I.C.E. declared that everything was merely "chemical phenomena" and therefore discarded morality, pity, happiness, and freedom. The genius of the new Natural Philosophy is that it retains the ability to study "chemical phenomena" while remembering that reality is not reducible to the random movement of atoms. In Lewis's terminology, the regenerate science explains phenomena without explaining them away.[68] To return to Lewis's example in "Meditation in a Toolshed," true objectivity would mean that a new Natural Philosopher could explain the smitten young man's response to the young woman in terms of a "biological stimulus" while at the same time refusing to simply explain away love as nothing more than a cocktail of hormones.[69] True objectivity does not hesitate to view things analytically, but it keeps in mind that there is more to reality than the analytical view can uncover. As Lewis expresses it, it carefully considers individual aspects of reality without forgetting the whole.[70]

When philosophers of science discuss the difference between false "objectivity" and true objectivity, they sometimes use the terms "ontological naturalism" and "methodological naturalism."[71] Ontological naturalism declares that ontologically—that is, in the very essence of reality—there is nothing beyond the natural world. Like the N.I.C.E's false "objectivity," ontological naturalism springs from the idea that science is the only way to truth, and says that if science can't measure something, it cannot be real. Ontological naturalism reduces everything to chemical and physical phenomena and leaves no room for God, objective morality, or an afterlife. In contrast, methodological naturalism uses naturalism as a tool—that is, as a *method* of looking at the world—without declaring that naturalism is, in fact, true. To the methodological naturalist, naturalism (the assumption that the natural world is all that exists) is just a helpful simplification, like ignoring air resistance in a physics problem. Methodological naturalism focuses exclusively on the natural, physical world while practicing science, but it never dismisses the possibility that there may be something beyond the physical. It achieves true objectivity by remaining conscious of the whole of reality. To hearken back to Lewis's terms, methodological naturalism uses the objective, analytical view in the laboratory without losing the experiential view in the rest of life.

At this point, one might ask, why is methodological naturalism a good thing? Why not discard naturalism altogether rather than leaving God at the door of the laboratory? The answer lies in the fact that methodological naturalism recognizes the inherent limitations of science. Science is not designed to adequately investigate things beyond the physical world—it has no way to satisfactorily study the full scope of reality. Methodological naturalism acknowledges the limits of scientific inquiry by narrowing science's focus to natural, observable causes. This narrow focus means that when scientists are faced with a question like, "Why did it rain this morning?" they can explain the weather in terms of humidity, temperature, and condensation rather than trying to determine whether or not God was responding to a farmer's prayer to end a drought. Essentially methodological naturalism lets science do what it does well—investigating natural causes—while leaving other questions to disciplines such as theology and philosophy, which are better equipped to explore supernatural reality. In this way, methodological naturalism allows science to investigate parts of reality without forgetting the whole.[72]

How does methodological naturalism or true objectivity affect the practice of the new Natural Philosophy? For one thing, true objectivity means that science must respect the dignity and personhood of the humans it studies. When the regenerate science studies human beings, it never reduces people to the level of "mere nature" or treats them as objects. As Lewis puts it in his vision for the new Natural Philosophy, the regenerate science investigates the *It* without forgetting the *Thou*.[73]

Lewis borrowed this concept of *It* and *Thou* from Martin Buber, a renowned Jewish philosopher. Buber posited that humans have two ways of relating to the world: "*I-It*" and "*I-Thou*."[74] The *I-It* experience applies to objects we sense, think, or feel, but the *I-Thou* relationship applies to how we ought to relate to God and human beings.[75] The *I-Thou* relationship acknowledges the transcendent immortal soul in the other person, and treats them with love and respect. The *I-It* relationship, on the other hand, treats the other as an object rather than a person. According to Buber, the "exalted melancholy of our time" is that we treat every *Thou* as an *It*, reducing the *Thou* to "an object among objects."[76] This objectification of the *Thou* to an *It* is indeed tragic, because it fails to recognize the transcendent dignity and worth of the human person who is made in God's image.

Lewis highlights this concept of *It* and *Thou* in his science fiction trilogy by juxtaposing the examples of Mark Studdock and Ransom. Mark, in his pursuit of sociology, becomes so accustomed to studying humanity in the abstract—in statistics and social trends—that he almost forgets that the populations he studies are made up of individual men and women (*THS*, 85). He reduces individual *Thous* to a depersonalized, faceless, conglomerate *It*. When William Hingest observes Mark's skewed perspective of reality, he grows concerned and attempts to correct Mark, saying, "You can't study men; you can only get to know them" (*THS*, 69). In essence, Hingest encourages Mark to step away from his sociological study of the *It* so that he can get to know the *Thou*.

If we take Hingest's statement that "you can't study men; you can only get to know them" by itself, we could get the impression that Lewis was completely opposed to the scientific study of humans. The story of Ransom in *Out of the Silent Planet*, however, provides an example of how science can study persons without objectifying them. Ransom investigates Malacandra in a scientific manner, making detailed observations about the landscape, the flora and fauna, the strength of gravity, the linguistics and cultures of the three species of *hnau*, and even the body temperature of a *hross* (103°F, according to the postscript). As a philologist, Ransom is thrilled about the opportunity to learn the language of Malacandra—his passion for the science of linguistics drives him to overcome his fear of the *hrossa* in order to discover the secrets of their extraterrestrial tongue (*OSP*, 56). In the midst of this scientific inquiry, however, Ransom takes the time to live among the *hrossa* and build relationships with them as individuals. In the postscript, he passionately declares that he knows the *hrossa* in such a deep way that he cannot communicate it in a mere story (*OSP*, 154). The fascinating thing is that by getting to know the *hrossa* personally, Ransom is able to study them more accurately than Weston could. Unlike Weston, who holds on to his mistaken scientific theories about the "natives" despite mounting evidence that the Malacandrians are far more than primitive, tribal, near-animals, Ransom is able to overcome his preconceived notions of extraterrestrial life because he knows the *hnau* of Malacandra personally.[77]

Thus far, Lewis's vision for regenerate science is relatively straightforward: scientists should strive for true objectivity in the laboratory, remember that there is more to reality than what fits in a test tube, and study the *It* without forgetting the *Thou*. The remainder of Lewis's vision, however, is slightly more controversial. When Lewis says that the regenerate science "would not do even to minerals and vegetables what modern science threatens to do to man himself," he implicitly challenges the assumption that the "natural object" is purely natural.[78] Think of the scene in *The Voyage of the Dawn Treader*, when Ramandu (himself a "retired star") responds to Eustace's assertion that stars in our world are nothing more than "huge ball[s] of flaming gas" by saying, "Even in your world, my son, that is not what a star is but only what it is made of."[79] In Lewis's mind, nothing—leaf or animal, stone or star—can be treated as a disposable lump of matter. Everything is more than the sum of its parts, because all of creation is the gift of God.

A look at a few examples in the Trilogy may help clarify what Lewis is trying to say about treating even "minerals and vegetables" with respect. Both of the Trilogy's chief villains indiscriminately abuse non-human life—the Un-Man constantly tortures animals and mutilates plants, while the N.I.C.E. practices vivisection, wastefully razes gardens, pollutes the river that runs through Edgestow, and destroys Bragdon Wood.[80] The heroes, on the other hand, view all of creation as a gift from Maleldil and thus treat it with respect. Ransom and the Green Lady take only the fruit they need to satisfy their hunger, the Green Lady rules over the animals as valued subjects rather than slaves, and the people at St. Anne's lovingly cultivate a garden and care for Mr. Bultitude the bear.[81] Where the villains exploit nature, the heroes treat the created world with dignity, care, and gratitude.

Lewis makes this contrast between the two attitudes toward creation explicit when he describes the difference between Merlin's Natural Philosophy and modern scientism.[82] Merlin knew the flora and fauna of his land intimately and reverenced all life—so much so that he refrained from harming any growing thing (*THS*, 282–83). In contrast, modern naturalistic scientism views nature as a dead object to be manipulated (*THS*, 282–83). When Lewis draws this contrast, of course, he is not arguing that scientists should become magicians like Merlin or that it is wrong to use a sharp tool on a plant. One of the characters in *That Hideous Strength* clearly says that we need to return to Merlin's principles, but in "some *different* way" (*THS*, 283). Essentially, Lewis is arguing that the new Natural Philosophy needs to glean wisdom from the Natural Philosophers of old—and even from magicians like Merlin—without becoming like them in every respect.

Perelandra offers a glimpse of how we can respect creation without reverting to the way of Merlin. The Green Lady shows us that one does not have to see a spirit in every tree to value a beautiful forest; one simply has to recognize that every part of the natural world—even a speck of dust—has intrinsic worth because it is God's creation. As Lewis expresses poetically in the Great Dance at the conclusion of *Perelandra*, each grain of dust is at the center of creation because Maleldil endows it with the "unmixed image of His energy" (*PER*, 185). If the scientists of today learned to see "the unmixed image of His energy" in each grain of dust, the new Natural Philosophy would treat even "minerals and vegetables" as valuable gifts from God to be appreciated rather than wasted, exploited, and abused. If science can truly study humans without reducing them to the level of "mere nature" and study objects without abusing God's creation, it will in fact "conquer nature without being conquered by her and buy knowledge at a lower cost than that of life."[83]

A Warning and a Vision

Although Lewis's Trilogy is too often portrayed as an uninformed and inaccurate attack on science, a closer look reveals that it is, in fact, a prophetic warning against scientism and an inspiring vision for a regenerate science. Lewis warns that scientism—a caricature of science that rejects all moral goods except survival and abandons objective truth in favor of power—will dehumanize us by stripping us of pity, happiness, and freedom. If we follow the route of scientism, Lewis warns that "Man's final conquest of Nature" will lead to "Nature's final conquest of Man."[84] This warning, however, is not the end of the story—there is still hope for a regenerate science to reverse the evils of scientism. Lewis casts a vision for a new Natural Philosophy that reclaims true objectivity, explains without explaining away, treats humans as persons rather than as objects, views all of nature as a valuable creation of God, and pursues scientific knowledge and power without discarding everything that makes us human.

Lewis's warnings are not the theoretical, ivory-tower musings of an Oxford don; rather, they reflect real dangers that Lewis witnessed in the world around him. Nor were Lewis's concerns about scientism merely a product of his era; if anything, the menace of scientism has only grown since Lewis's time. Yet, the danger of scientism is not unconquerable—the vision of a new Natural Philosophy offers a promising solution to scientism. If we take Lewis's warning and vision to heart, perhaps there will be hope for the redemption of science here on the Silent Planet.

Endnotes

1 Samuel Hynes, "Guardian of the Old Ways," review of *C. S. Lewis at the Breakfast Table: And Other Reminiscences*, edited by James T. Como, *New York Times*, July 8, 1979, https://www.nytimes.com/1979/07/08/archives/guardian-of-the-old-ways-guardian.html.

2 Philip Deasy, "God, Science, and C. S. Lewis," *Commonweal 68* (July 25, 1958): 422.

3 C. S. Lewis, "A Reply to Professor Haldane," in *Of Other Worlds: Essays and Stories,* ed. Walter Hooper (New York: HarperCollins, 2017), 121.

4 C. S. Lewis, *Miracles: A Preliminary Study* (New York: HarperCollins, 2015), 20.

5 George Sayer, *Jack: A Life of C. S. Lewis* (Wheaton, IL: Crossway, 1988), 14. It may be worth noting here that loathing science as a subject in school is not the same thing as hating science as a field.

6 Chad Walsh, *The Literary Legacy of C. S. Lewis* (New York: Harcourt Brace Jovanovich, 1979), 15.

7 Lewis, *Miracles*, 18–19, 41, 88–89, 134.

8 Michael Ward, "Science and Religion in the Writings of C. S. Lewis," *Science & Christian Belief 25*, no. 1 (April 2013): 3–4.

9 Ward, "Science and Religion," 3–4; Margo Lee Simpson, "The Anti-Modern Imagination: C. S. Lewis and 'The Cosmic Trilogy'" (thesis, University of Ottawa, 1999), 4–5.

10 J. B. S. Haldane, "Auld Hornie, F. R. S.," in *Everything Has a History* (London, UK: Allen & Unwin, 1951), 249–258, http://www.lewisiana.nl/haldane/.

11 Lewis, "Reply to Professor Haldane," 119–20.

12 C. S. Lewis, "On Science Fiction," in *Of Other Worlds: Essays and Stories,* ed. Walter Hooper (New York: HarperCollins, 2017), 108–9. Much of modern science fiction seems to support this idea—fans have little trouble suspending disbelief to enjoy lightsabers, Psychohistory, warp speed, sentient robots, time-traveling DeLoreans, and the like.

13 Deasy, 422.

14 Henry F. Schaefer, III, "C. S. Lewis: Science and Scientism," in *Science and Christianity: Conflict or Coherence?* (Athens, GA: The Apollos Trust, 2003), 124. Hingest is far from the only 'good scientist' in the Trilogy—Dr. Humphrey, Ransom's trusted friend, is described as a scientist, and the *séroni* of Malacandra appear to be scientists or natural philosophers of some sort. See Robert Boenig, "The Face of the Materialist Magician: Lewis, Tolkien, and the Art of Crossing Perilous Streets," *Mythlore 35*, no. 1 (2016): 8.

15 Lewis, "Reply to Professor Haldane," 123.

16 Lewis, "Reply to Professor Haldane," 124.

17 J. B. S. Haldane, "The Last Judgment," in *Possible Worlds and Other Essays* (London, UK: Chatto and Windus, 1927), 292.

18 Haldane, "Last Judgment," 302.

19 Haldane, "Last Judgment," 310.

20 Haldane, "Last Judgment," 303.

21 Haldane, "Last Judgment," 307.

22 Haldane, "Last Judgment," 304.

23 Lewis, "Reply to Professor Haldane," 122.

24 Lewis, "Reply to Professor Haldane," 121.

25 Lewis, "Reply to Professor Haldane," 121.

26 *Oxford English Dictionary*, 3rd ed., s.v. "Scientism," accessed February 25, 2019, www.oed.com/view/Entry/172696.

27 C. S. Lewis, *The Discarded Image* (Cambridge, UK: Cambridge University Press, 1964), 17; Lewis, "Reply to Professor Haldane," 121.

28 C. S. Lewis, *Mere Christianity: A revised and amplified edition, with a new introduction, of the three books, Broadcast Talks, Christian Behavior, and Beyond Personality* (New York: HarperCollins, 2015), 22.

29 As noted later in this chapter, this type of naturalism is more properly termed ontological naturalism. It can also be described as materialism (the belief that nothing beyond matter exists) or reductionism (the belief that everything can be reduced to natural causes). A full discussion of naturalism is beyond the scope of this chapter, but it is a subject well worth exploring. For Lewis's most developed thoughts on naturalism and supernaturalism, see *Miracles*, and for a discussion of how naturalism is incompatible with science, see Alvin Plantinga's *Where the Conflict Really Lies*.

30 Lewis, *Mere Christianity*, 22–24.

31 See Chapter 9 for Daniel J. Friend's more in-depth exploration of subjectivism.

32 Lewis, "Reply to Professor Haldane," 121.

33 Lewis, "Reply to Professor Haldane," 121.

34 See Chapter 6 for Nolan Andrew's discussion of the desire for immortality as a symptom of pride.

35 A third common attempt to achieve immortality through science is to make such an important contribution to the field that one will be remembered by one's work after death. (I owe this thought to Diana Pavlac Glyer, personal interview, Azusa, CA, March 15, 2019). Lewis offers a nod to this approach when he has Ransom engrave Weston's tombstone on a cliff in Perelandra. Ransom reflects that "there ought to be some record" of Weston's death because he was "a great physicist," but, ironically, the epigraph is located where "no one will ever read it" (*PER*, 161).

36 The word "scientistic" is simply the adjective form of the noun "scientism."

37 Haldane, "Last Judgment," 302.

38 Haldane, "Last Judgment," 312.

39 These ideas are found throughout *Out of the Silent Planet*. See, for example, pages 14, 21, 29, and 134–46.

40 Sanford Schwartz, *C. S. Lewis on the Final Frontier: Science and the Supernatural in the Space Trilogy* (New York: Oxford University Press, 2009), 27.

41 J. D. Wunderly explores the influence of World War II on Lewis's Trilogy in Chapter 4.

42 C. S. Lewis, "Is Progress Possible?: Willing Slaves of the Welfare State," in *God in the Dock: Essays on Theology and Ethics*, ed. Walter Hooper (Grand Rapids, MI: Eerdmans, 2014), 347.

43 C. S. Lewis, *The Magician's Nephew* (New York: HarperCollins, 2000), 190.

44 C. S. Lewis, *The Abolition of Man* (New York: HarperCollins, 2015), 39. Lewis's exposition of "Nature's conquest of Man" is multifaceted—see Daniel J. Friend's discussion of the topic in Chapter 9.

45 Lewis, *Abolition of Man*, 39.

46 Lewis, *Abolition of Man*, 71.

47 Lewis, *Abolition of Man*, 69.

48 Lewis, *Abolition of Man*, 71.

49 Lewis, *Abolition of Man*, 71.

50 Lewis, *Abolition of Man*, 72.

51 Lewis, "Reply to Professor Haldane," 121.

52 Haldane, "Last Judgment," 303.

53 In the rest of this chapter, I will distinguish true objectivity, which is the scientific skill of impartially evaluating data, from the N.I.C.E.'s perversion by enclosing the N.I.C.E.'s false form of "objectivity" in quotation marks.

54 C. S. Lewis, "Meditation in a Toolshed," in *God in the Dock: Essays on Theology and Ethics*, ed. Walter Hooper (Grand Rapids, MI: Eerdmans, 2014), 230–31.

55 Lewis, "Meditation in a Toolshed," 234.

56 Lewis, *Abolition of Man*, 55.

57 J. B. S. Haldane, "Science and Politics," in *Possible Worlds and Other Essays* (London, UK: Chatto and Windus, 1927), 183.

58 Lewis, "Is Progress Possible?", 351.
59 See *That Hideous Strength,* 40–41, 126–27, and 184.
60 Lewis, "Reply to Professor Haldane," 126.
61 Deasy, 422.
62 Deasy, 423.
63 Lewis, *Abolition of Man*, 76.
64 Lewis, *Abolition of Man*, 79.
65 Lewis, *Abolition of Man*, 78; Tom McLeish, *Faith and Wisdom in Science* (Oxford, UK: Oxford University Press, 2014), 25.
66 See Peter Kreeft's annotations on Thomas Aquinas, *Summa of the Summa*, trans. The Fathers of the English Dominican Province, ed. Peter Kreeft (San Francisco: Ignatius, 2012), 42.
67 Lewis, *Abolition of Man*, 78–79.
68 Lewis, *Abolition of Man*, 79.
69 Lewis, "Meditation in a Toolshed," 230–31.
70 Lewis, *Abolition of Man*, 79.
71 Alvin Plantinga, *Where the Conflict Really Lies* (New York: Oxford University Press, 2011), 169.
72 Lewis, *Abolition of Man*, 79.
73 Lewis, *Abolition of Man*, 79.
74 Martin Buber, *I and Thou*, trans. Ronald Gregor Smith (New York: Scribner Classics, 1986), 19.
75 Buber, 19–24, 77.
76 Buber, 30.
77 Margo Lee Simpson, "The Anti-Modern Imagination: C. S. Lewis and 'The Cosmic Trilogy'" (Thesis, University of Ottawa, 1999), 29–33.
78 Lewis, *Abolition of Man*, 79.
79 C. S. Lewis, *The Voyage of the Dawn Treader* (New York: HarperCollins, 2000), 209.
80 See, for example, *Perelandra,* 110; *That Hideous Strength*, 72–73; and *That Hideous Strength,* 118–19.
81 See *Perelandra,* 38; *Perelandra,* 56; *That Hideous Strength*, 60; *That Hideous Strength,* 161–62.
82 Daniel Z. Hsieh discusses Merlin as a symbol of reconciliation with the natural world more fully in Chapters 7 and 8.
83 Lewis, *Abolition of Man*, 79.
84 Lewis, *Abolition of Man*, 39.

THE WARS OF OUR WORLD

J. D. WUNDERLY

When Lewis began writing his Trilogy, he was not crafting a story based purely upon imagination; the imagery and themes of his work are informed by his experiences as a war survivor. He did not just hear of a war from the distant past or know that it was occurring on a far-off continent. War came to Lewis's door, dropped bombs upon his cities, and forced him to crouch in the trenches. Survivors of WWI and WWII knew what it was like to experience an invasion, not just to read about it. We cannot afford to lose this perspective. If we forget that Lewis wrote the Trilogy in the midst of an enemy marching on his home, we lose sight of what is really at stake.

The warnings that Lewis shares in his Trilogy were not crafted from thin air. They were heard in the rumble of explosions through the streets. But the evils Lewis warned against were not always immediately obvious. Just as the German Reich did not begin with the Holocaust or the invasion of Poland, neither did the N.I.C.E. immediately send their enforcers to take over Edgestow. Through the stories of the Trilogy, Lewis equips his readers with an understanding of the danger of evil and impresses them with the responsibility to take action against it, lest we be doomed to repeat the horrors of the past.

A War Story

Although Britain's enemies never made landfall, the British public did face the destruction of war both at home and abroad. During German bombing campaigns, the wail of air raid sirens and the following concussive blasts became regular sounds of the city. These bombings occurred in both wars, but they were much more devastating in the second. The Blitz, as it was called by the British people, brought WWII to the front doors of British civilians and consisted of a bombing campaign conducted by the Germans over a period of eight months. The Blitz involved regular air raids on towns, industrial sites, and, notably, a bombing of London for fifty-six days. The intention of the bombings was to destroy Britain's means to wage war and break the morale of its civilians.

Ironically, the bombings only strengthened the resolve of the British people. The stress of war and the restrictions it caused served to break down the barriers between citizens. Simply living in Britain became a stance against the Axis powers.[1] It did not matter who your British neighbors were as long as they were able to help you put out the fire in your garden.

Lewis illustrates this British unity and the perils that led to it through the company at St. Anne's. The members of this fellowship are brought together by extreme circumstances. Their town is literally being torn apart by aggressive foreigners, disrupting their lives and the usual social order. In this context, it is not important that Ivy Maggs used to be Jane Studdock's lowly housekeeper. They are brought together on equal footing in the company at St. Anne's to survive the takeover of their town. Lewis uses these and many other circumstances in *That Hideous Strength* to recall the imagery of war. Just as Mother Dimble laments the tearing up of her beautiful garden, many of Lewis's readers would have mourned the destruction of their own.

Although Lewis himself was not physically harmed by the bombings, he certainly faced the dangers of these attacks. Lewis spent many nights on watch, armed with a heavy rifle and scouting for signs of German paratroopers.[2] Lewis's home, the Kilns, had a dugout entrenched in its garden and blackout curtains draped over its windows. Children were sent to live there after being evacuated from vulnerable cities.[3]

The war, however, was not fought primarily on British soil. Instead, it took place over the greater landmass of continental Europe as well as Africa and Asia. In these arenas, the march of an approaching army was far more literal and the need to flee from such a force much more prevalent. In *That Hideous Strength*, Mark Studdock views a procession of families, with their possessions loaded up onto wagons, carts, and cars, in retreat from the town of Edgestow. Mark had never seen a war, and thus did not recognize that the signs of a flight were written clearly on the caravan, inscribed, "Enemy behind" (*THS*, 211). This was the sight present for many soldiers in France as the Axis powers completed their six-week campaign against the nation, ending in France's surrender and the retreat of the remaining French forces. Lewis's depiction of the N.I.C.E.'s advance upon Edgestow is not intended to be viewed merely as an unfortunate bureaucratic decision. It is specifically representative of a takeover and is intentionally crafted to remind its readers of this historic invasion. This is what was at stake for Lewis and, thus, what is at stake for us should we neglect the warnings and truths that his Trilogy has to share.

The N.I.C.E. and Germany

It would be remiss to address the impact of the Second World War on the Trilogy without addressing key aspects of Nazi Germany. The dangers that Lewis wrote of in *That Hideous Strength* were originally intended to serve as theoretical extremes of evil tendencies Lewis had perceived in his world. However, the combination of Germany's eugenics ideology and fascist control during this period served as the very incarnation of Lewis's "evil tendencies" taken to their logical end.[4]

The military might of Germany was certainly a threat during WWII, but Lewis's main concerns about the Nazi powers settled on a different danger, one that was far quieter than the approach of an army. Carole J. Lambert shares the following:

> Tyranny comes in many forms, most of which are more subtle than Stalin's gulag or Hitler's death camps. Lewis knew this, and his most compelling writings on tyranny for us today focus on these more subtle forms of oppression . . . . The tyranny that could result from the union of modern science and the modern state. Such tyranny is, of course, exemplified in [Lewis's] novel *That Hideous Strength*, the final work in his space trilogy, which vividly demonstrates bureaucratic power and the linguistic gibberish that accompanies it.[5]

Although the military strength of Germany facilitated its power, it was the infusion of scientistic thought into their government that produced the truest horrors of the war. The main representation of this disastrous union in *That Hideous Strength* is the organization ironically named the N.I.C.E. It is described as a "constructive fusion" between state and laboratory that promises to produce great advancement and circumvent the red tape typically surrounding scientific institutions (*THS*, 21).

Especially when it comes to their ideologies, the N.I.C.E. represents the kind of insidious power that Lewis warned of—a force that creeps in and takes over, only recognized for what it is when it is too late to stop it. The N.I.C.E. reflects the ideology of the Nazis, a group that also rose to power through the promise of a superior humanity. The end result of Nazi control is all too well known. Their dehumanization of citizens and scientifically-backed experimentation upon those deemed lesser made a mark upon history that humanity ought never to forget.

The Good of Evil

A wise approach to combating a great threat like scientism is recognizing the danger that it poses. Just as it is easier to treat a disease that is caught early, it is easier to avert a great danger if it is recognized in its first stages. Thus, the best warnings communicate how a danger begins and what it looks like before it becomes a full-fledged threat. This is not always an easy task; just as the N.I.C.E. was not immediately discernible as evil in *That Hideous Strength*, neither were the Nazis originally seen as potential perpetrators of genocide. The inability to perceive evil in both these instances came from the fact that the evil present was not entirely separate from good. The N.I.C.E. was a research organization, promoting scientific progress and promising hope for a better world (*THS*, 21). Similarly, Lewis indicated in a letter to his friend Dom Bede Griffiths that fascism and communism are powerful because they imitate good things. They are particularly popular because they meet a need brought about by failures of government and leadership that leave people starved and open to receiving help wherever they can find it.[6]

After WWI, Germany was in exactly such a desperate situation. In its negotiations for peace after the war, Germany was forced to pay reparations to France and Great Britain. These war reparations eventually resulted in a massive economic failure as the war-torn German economy was unable to keep up with its own needs alongside the sizable payments. Germany was also forced to relinquish thirteen percent of its land.[7] These terms, mandated as a part of the Treaty of Versailles, not only crippled the German economy but also humiliated its people by taking their territory and insisting that the nation owed reparations to their opponents. In short, the treaty left the Germans seeking any way out of their dire situation, and this paved the way for Adolf Hitler to take power.

Hitler offered the German people a restoration to glory and freedom from terrible economic suffering and shame. Most importantly, he offered a scapegoat, in the form of the Jewish people and others upon whom to place the blame of Germany's previous failures: their defeat in war and inability to restore their economy. Hitler did not initially gain power through a show of military force. In fact, his original attempt to do so during the failed Beer Hall Putsch led only to his imprisonment. Instead, through charismatic speeches, Hitler garnered support and the backing of a people in desperate need of a strong leader. Similarly, the Soviets in Russia gained power after both the Russian monarchy and an attempted democratic government fell in the wake of WWI. The Soviet Union rose by promising peace, land, and bread to a starving populace tired of war.

Wrong and right are not as easily recognised as we might want them to be, and believing that any progress is better than none is an extremely dangerous yet tempting path. The danger of the evil embodied by the N.I.C.E. is not the kind of pure evil seen in the Un-man from *Perelandra* but is, instead, an offer of something good in a time when so much bad is apparent. The Un-man, although terrifying, quickly stirs a desire to fight. Its very existence and demeanor cries out to those who have seen it that it needs to be resisted and destroyed. Groups like the N.I.C.E., in contrast, create unity among people; they present a purpose and a sense of community. It is because of this difference that groups such as the Nazis can be far more dangerous than any demon man.

Test Subjects

As history has shown, when groups like the N.I.C.E. take power, they are prone to divide those they control based on perceived value. Such division usually comes under the guise of science and can lead to the ideology of scientism. Genocide sounds cruel and inhumane when proposed plainly, but when purported to restore the health and prosperity of the human race and coming from the mouths of beloved public servants, it can sway even the staunchest adversaries. This is especially true when the idea comes through the voice of an expert—someone whom we are expected to trust on issues we do not understand. When such experts obtain the capacity to make decisions, rather than just influence them, their hypotheses can become the laws of a nation.

Lewis shares these concerns in his article "Is Progress Possible?" when he says that he dreads government in the name of "science." He explains that this is how tyrannies gain access to power, by preying upon the greatest hopes and fears of their age. Tyrants have used magic and religion for such ends in the past; today, it is common to appeal to science. Even if their so-called science is not supported by real scientists, those dissenting opinions can be smothered. After all, many scientists did not approve of Hitler's theories of racial supremacy, but they were silenced.[8] The Nazis deemed some people scientifically sub-human and regarded handicapped citizens as disposable because of their disabilities.

This kind of wrongly applied science is at the very heart of the N.I.C.E., as evident in the goals of Filostrato, Straik, and Frost. All of these individuals are proponents of scientism and believe that they can become superior to the rest of humanity. Filostrato wants to obtain a "clean" world where bodies and interaction with nature are unnecessary (*THS,* 173). Straik wants to become a new god by freeing himself from the threat of death (*THS,* 175). Frost desires "objectivity": an escape from truth and an ability to determine his own reality (*THS,* 296). Despite the differences in the particulars of their goals, each desires to place himself above the natural state of humanity. This inevitably means that those who do not choose this path are perceived to become lesser, not only in status but also in intrinsic value.

It is only logical, therefore, that the criminals under the control of the N.I.C.E. are treated as if they have no rights, literally being locked up alongside animals and used for experimental purposes. The Nazis took very similar actions, experimenting on Jews, homosexuals, and invalids, and allowing them to die in horrific ways. In *Out of the Silent Planet,* Weston echoes this practice when he tries to use a mentally disabled boy as what amounts to a human sacrifice for the benefit of his scientific projects. It is clear that in such scientistic thinking, the failure of any groups to be "useful" to society renders them mere test subjects in the eyes of the scientist. In "Is Progress Possible?", Lewis writes:

> Thus the criminal ceases to be a person, a subject of rights and duties, and becomes merely an object on which society can work. And this is, in principle, how Hitler treated the Jews. They were objects; killed not for ill desert but because, on his theories, they were a disease in society. If society can mend, remake, and unmake men at its pleasure, its pleasure may, of course, be humane or homicidal. The difference is important. But, either way, rulers have become owners.[9]

The danger of governments forgetting their place as protectors of the people and, instead, becoming their keepers is a threat that cannot be overlooked. It is a danger that looms in *That Hideous Strength* just as it did in Hitler's Third Reich, and it is a danger that must be combated.

A Growing Power

The potential for tyranny in our world presents a threat of utmost importance. It is perhaps too easy to brush off tyranny as the extreme end of some distant and terrible *other*, something that our societies would never fall into. This rationalization could not be further from the truth. In fact, Lewis feared that the danger of tyrannical governments was growing. Even his own country of Britain began to reflect some of the tyrannical qualities that characterized Nazi Germany and by extension the N.I.C.E. In the same way that the N.I.C.E. is granted emergency powers over Edgestow, Winston Churchill and the British government were granted extensive wartime powers over Great Britain. While the N.I.C.E. and Nazi Germany were rendered powerless by their defeat, other governments around the world retained many of the powers they had been granted during the war. For example, Britain moved towards a government-run welfare state, while the United States government gained more economic control and executive authority.

Lewis warns against the danger of such consolidated power, reminding us that, "two wars necessitated vast curtailments of liberty, and we have grown, though grumblingly, accustomed to our chains. The increasing complexity and precariousness of our economic life have forced Government to take over many spheres of activity once left to choice or chance."[10] This greater government control is not inherently evil. Governments, after all, are intended to serve the people. But the more power given to governing bodies, the greater the danger a misuse of that power can pose. Depending on who gains control and how much power they wield, it is always possible that the dangerous ideologies that took hold of Germany could do the same in Britain or the United States.

Once the rights of individuals have been handed over to the state, the leaders' beliefs about science and humanity can determine what will be done to their citizens. If governments and authorities of all kinds are not watched carefully, history can and will repeat itself. Lewis's warnings help us to recognize the dangers rising in our world, but recognition is not enough; it must be accompanied by action.

Violence: A Powerful Tool

When great dangers arise, there must be a response. One potential answer is to turn to violence. Living through not one but both of the world wars certainly influenced Lewis's view of the option of violence, both in terms of its usage and its restraint. Lewis endured the horrors of WWI as a soldier. He arrived at the front line trenches on his nineteenth birthday and left duty after being hit by shrapnel from a shell that killed his compatriots right in front of him.[11] Lewis wrote that he experienced the destruction of war, "the frights, the cold, the smell of H.E., the horribly smashed men still moving like half-crushed beetles, the sitting or standing corpses, the landscape of sheer earth without a blade of grass, the boots worn day and night till they seemed to grow to your feet."[12] There can be little doubt that Lewis knew what advocating for violent action entailed.

However, Lewis also witnessed the ineffectiveness of appeasement, compromise, and treaties as means to stop the rise of Nazi Germany or to prevent it from committing atrocities. Although the violence Lewis experienced in WWI was horrific, it was violence that succeeded against the Axis powers in WWII where peaceful means had failed. It is likely due to these experiences that Lewis affirmed the necessity of violent action in war, although he certainly did not see it as a good in itself.

This view is exemplified in the relationship Lewis creates between the *hrossa* and the *hnéraki* in *Out of the Silent Planet.* The two share a relationship of natural violence in which the *hrossa* kill the *hnéraki* that come too close to their homes and threaten their children. Hyoi mentions specifically that it would be wrong of the *hrossa* to allow the *hnakra* to come so close without seeking it out and killing it (*OSP*, 76). Even on an unfallen planet such as Malacandra, the *hrossa* have a duty to kill the *hnéraki*; it is a rightful defense of their homes and children to do so. Lewis makes the point that killing is not *inherently* evil. However, violence is not always the answer. Immediately after the celebrated death of the *hnakra* comes the shocking death of Hyoi. Violence and killing has a place even on a planet without sin, but Weston and Devine's murder is unacceptable.

A Time to Tarry

Although violence is sometimes a necessity, it should rarely be the first course of action. Just as there is ground to cover before any force reaches its target, many options must be considered and tried before the point of combat is reached. In many cases, violence could have been avoided if more time had been spent deliberating instead of rushing onto the battlefield. This is exemplified in *Perelandra* when Ransom tries to stop the Un-man from corrupting the Green Lady. At first, Ransom has an opportunity to use Weston's gun to end the dilemma right then and there. Instead, he throws the weapon into the ocean, confident that the conflict can be resolved as it was on Malacandra, with the natural good of the planet's inhabitants overwhelming the childish proposals of Weston's scientistic views. When Weston, now the Un-man, begins talking with the Green Lady, Ransom does not even intervene in their conversation. He hears the Un-man speaking with the Green Lady and recognizes a potential for great harm, but waits, serving only as a spectator for this first encounter. This scene exemplifies that if violence is to be considered, the situation in which it is employed must be understood. In this instance, the Lady rejects the Un-man on her own, and a path to a peaceful resolution seems viable; no violence is necessary.

Soon after this, however, Ransom realizes that the situation on Perelandra is far different from the one he faced on Malacandra. His enemy is not a pair of men twisted by greed and skewed altruism but a being practicing whole-hearted evil that will not stop until Perelandra falls. Ransom takes up the next course of action and becomes a participant in the discussions between the Un-man and the Lady, attempting at every turn to overcome its corruptive influence through the use of reason. He counters his enemy's deceptions and works to uncover the truth of the Un-man's temptations and the horrible cost of the actions that are being suggested. Ransom's goal is not to defeat the Un-man but to preserve the world and the innocence of the Green Lady; thus, there is still no need to physically assault it. Sometimes, Ransom wins these battles of words, and other times he loses, but it is only after many, many attempts at this strategy that he realizes the assaults of the Un-man will never stop. Slowly but surely, the enemy is pressing its advantage, and should this conflict continue, the Un-man will win. It is only after exhausting all of his other options that Ransom accepts the responsibility of turning to violence.

Refusal of Duty

When Ransom realizes that the demon incarnated in Weston must be fought physically if the world is to be saved, he does not immediately jump to action. Instead, he resists in fear of what he perceives as a diabolical and superhuman entity. He denies his purpose, although he does so only temporarily (*PER*, 122–25). Ransom eventually realizes he must act and fight this evil, even if he must kill it with his bare hands. The world would not be entirely lost if Ransom refused his duty at this moment, but saving a fallen Perelandra would have extracted a terrible price, a price that did not have to be paid because Ransom took action.

Just as Ransom was able to stop a great tragedy, Britain and France had the opportunity to step in and stop the rise of fascist power in Germany. Although the rise of fascism could have been hindered in a variety of ways, one particularly poignant example is the failure of the Allies to stop Germany from remilitarizing the Rhineland. The Rhineland was a demilitarized zone, intended to serve as a buffer between Germany and France and prevent a swift attack on French territory. On March 7, 1936, Adolf Hitler ordered German troops to occupy the Rhineland. Unbeknownst to the Allies, the German forces had orders to retreat if they faced resistance, which the Allies failed to provide. Instead, Britain and France stood by and allowed this breach of the Treaty of Versailles, just as they had allowed many trespasses before.

The dangers that Lewis—and, in fact, the world—faced from the Nazi powers did not fall from the sky unannounced as Weston did in *Perelandra*; they rose slowly and without opposition. Germany had been defeated in WWI only twenty years prior; they had lost great amounts of men and material, were saddled with a massive amount of debt, and were banned from rebuilding military power. Despite these restrictions, however, Hitler began to raise German military might and refused to pay the debt imposed upon the country. The rest of the world stood back and allowed this because they were tired of war and were unwilling to risk stepping into a brutal conflict like WWI again.

Although stopping the rise of German power would have likely necessitated the threat of violence, there were many opportunities where such actions would have ended the conflict peacefully. The Allies could have demanded the continued payments, stood against the rebuilding of the German military, or even refused Germany's annexation of Austria and other key territories. Should the Allies have acted sooner, perhaps fascism would have been defeated without such drastic losses. Instead, violence was reserved, greater violence became necessary, and a greater evil was allowed to occur. This battle was always necessary in some capacity. There was an enemy that had to be stopped, whether by politics or force. Thus, when the necessity of conflict was realized, even after France fell to the German Blitzkrieg in 1940, Britain did not surrender. They realized the great danger their enemy posed to the world. They had to stand against it, just as Ransom has to stand against the evil invading Perelandra.

A Time to Fight

This is not an easy battle; no fight is. Ransom knows first-hand the realities of war and the horrible necessities that violence forces upon men. Such horrors would be especially terrible on Perelandra, a place so pure and unmarred that even the sight of one of its frog-like creatures mutilated by the Un-man brings about a sense of horror and disgust. Earlier, Ransom decides that this frog creature must be killed to end its pain but soon realizes that the arduous and drawn-out act of ending its life was the wrong choice and only increased its suffering. He compares the horrible act of killing the creature to the Battle of the Somme, saying that he would have thought himself better equipped to handle the task after enduring such a conflict (*PER*, 94).

Comparing the violence on Perelandra with this then-recent conflict drives home the gut-wrenching nature of the act. The Battle of the Somme, which Lewis himself fought in at the age of nineteen, occurred during WWI. The nearly five-month onslaught caused the death of one million combatants—a third of those participating. It was a brutal and long struggle, filled with the ear-shattering roar of artillery shells and a mixture of blood and turned earth. Its mention connects violence on Perelandra to the violence of war, making sure that the cost of the task Ransom is about to undertake does not go unrecognized.

The battle against the Un-man is certainly justified, but it is not a clean or easy strike against Ransom's enemy. He fights a drawn-out battle of fists and will, both sides being battered and cut in a messy brawl. The conflict does not even end at this, but transforms into an exhausting chase on land and sea, stretching from minutes into hours and ending after a false peace and another brutal struggle in the dark. This is the nature of violence: cruel and painful. It always necessitates a loss, yet it is still required when called upon, for the cost of refusing violence can be much greater than that of pursuing it.

On Perelandra, Ransom manages to avert a crisis. He suffers in his battle and Weston is eventually killed, but Ransom is victorious and averts much greater suffering for the inhabitants of the planet. On Earth, 1940s London was being bombed by the enemy they had refused to resist. There is, perhaps, no better showcase than this to reveal the necessity of taking action against evil. Lewis's warning is not intended to be read once and forgotten; it is to be remembered. We are to stand vigil: willing to recognize when dangers are growing too large and committed to doing what we can to stop them. The stakes are clear, and the consequences are written both in Lewis's science fiction and in human history.

Endnotes

1 John Baxendale, review of *Half the Battle: Civilian Morale in Britain during the Second World War*, by Robert Mackay, *Reviews in History*, June 2003, https://www.history.ac.uk/reviews/review/332#author-response.

2 George Sayer, *Jack: A Life of C. S. Lewis* (Wheaton, IL: Crossway, 1988), 268.

3 Sayer, *Jack*, 268.

4 C. S. Lewis to Marg-riette Montgomery, June 10, 1952, in *The Collected Letters of C. S. Lewis, Volume 3: Narnia, Cambridge and Joy (1950–1963)*, ed. Walter Hooper (New York: HarperCollins, 2009), 199.

5 Carole J. Lambert, *Against Indifference* (New York: Peter Lang Publishing, 2015), 21.

6 C. S. Lewis to Dom Bede Griffiths, January 17, 1940, in *The Collected Letters of C. S. Lewis, Volume 2: Books, Broadcasts and War (1931–1949)*, ed. Walter Hooper (New York: HarperCollins, 2004), 327.

7 Daniel Castillo, "German Economy in the 1920s" Dec. 2003, http://www.history.ucsb.edu/faculty/marcuse/classes/33d/projects/1920s/Econ20s.

8 C. S. Lewis, "Is Progress Possible?: Willing Slaves of the Welfare State," in *God in the Dock: Essays on Theology and Ethics*, ed. Walter Hooper (Grand Rapids: Eerdmans, 2014), 351.

9 Lewis, "Is Progress Possible," 348–49.

10 Lewis, "Is Progress Possible," 349.

11 C. S. Lewis, *Surprised by Joy* (New York: HarperCollins, 2017), 238–40.

12 Lewis, *Surprised by Joy*, 240.

TRAVERSING THE MEDIEVAL COSMOS

MAYA MALEY

We have spent the last few chapters considering the realities of Lewis's world and how, through his Trilogy, he warns his audience of the dangerous ideologies that had taken root in his society. Lewis does so by making the truth of the matter—whether that be the grotesqueness of scientism or the evil of totalitarian regimes—compelling to his audience. At the same time, Lewis also makes the beauty of the truth enticing by giving the audience a chance to be captivated by the beauty and glory of creation through Ransom's experiences. For instance, we experience with Ransom the awe of the heavens while aboard the spaceship. As we will soon discover, this specific scene from *Out of the Silent Planet* is the first of many that harkens back to ancient perspectives of our cosmos and is one where Lewis's love of medieval cosmology is on display. Lewis, like philosophers of the past, believed that the heavens were created by God as bright, beautiful, and orderly. Yet, in Lewis's society, astronomical advancements drove modern scientists and science fiction writers alike to create a new cosmos: a cold, formidable, and chaotic darkness that was void of God's presence. Lewis feared that society's acceptance of this modern philosophy of the universe would strip the heavens of their grandeur, their order, and their Maker. In order to revive the images that had been discarded by his society, Lewis evoked a medieval cosmology within the Trilogy, reclaiming the wisdom of a time almost forgotten.

From Outer Space to the Heavens

Aboard Weston's spaceship en route to Malacandra, Ransom is struck by the sunlight that is beaming into the ship. He makes use of tinted glasses in order to walk and eat without being blinded by the "the tyranny of heat and light" (*OSP*, 31). Even the darker parts of the spaceship appear to be too bright to look at directly, and Ransom reflects, "'I always thought space was dark and cold'" (*OSP*, 31). Ransom had been held captive by the belief that outer space is cold and dark until he literally sees the light.

Ransom, like many in Lewis's society, held to a narrative that had roots in the work of Giovanni Schiaparelli, who published his findings of the planet Mars in the late nineteenth century. Schiaparelli had studied what appeared to be lines across Mars's surface, and his works, such as *Life on Mars*, began a world-wide obsession with the planet and its make-believe inhabitants. This Martian obsession continued with Percival Lowell, who published *Mars and Its Canals* in 1906 in an attempt to present his discoveries about Mars to the scientific community. As the scientific world continued to turn its focus toward the stars, astronomers and physicists continued to shape the popular understanding of the universe with their discoveries. Astronomers such as Yakov Perelman and Edwin Hubble made the universes seem even more distant and overwhelming with their discoveries and theories. Scientists like Albert Einstein, Edward Emerson Barnard, and Harlow Shapley overturned previously-held beliefs about the universe. These scientific discoveries created a new framework for outer space, and society went on to fill in the gaps through imaginative storytelling. That is why Ransom, who serves as our lens into this mindset, cannot help anticipating the ghastly images drawn from the works of H. G. Wells and other writers as he begins to fear what may await him on Malacandra.

However, throughout his time aboard the spaceship, Ransom begins to reconsider his preconceived notions about the universe. As he sits and contemplates the light that shines like noon at every hour in the ship, he awakes from the "nightmare" that had been kept alive in his modern mind (*OSP*, 34). Science had named this brightness "space" and convinced Ransom and his society that space was "the black, cold vacuity, the utter deadness, which was supposed to separate the worlds" (*OSP*, 34). With evidence to the contrary, Ransom decides that space is not the right name for the universe. Ransom then recalls the wisdom of those who had come before him and decides to again refer to this radiance as "the heavens" (*OSP*, 34). This realization leads Ransom to declare the words of Psalm 19: "The heavens declare the glory of God; the skies proclaim the work of his hands."[1]

Here, Lewis begins to unveil his perspective and invites his audience to take a leap of faith with Ransom to dare to consider a new perspective on the cosmos. At this point, Lewis hands the reader a pair of untinted glasses to look through for the remainder of Ransom's story.

The Medieval Model

Continuing with the metaphor, the reader may ask, "How did Lewis receive these glasses?" In short, his glasses were formed in the fashion and from the material of the medievals. In a collection of lectures known as *The Discarded Image*, Lewis coined the term "the Medieval Model," a model in which he personally and professionally delighted. He recognizes how his society took the opportunity to discard this model as a relic, a falsity, or "a work of art" at best, but he argues that "there is abundant evidence that it gave profound satisfaction while it was still believed in" (*OSP*, 34). He argues that society has specifically lost the cosmological model of the medievals—or discarded the image—that was formed by those "older thinkers [who] had been wiser" by referring to space as the heavens (*OSP*, 34). In his lecture on "The Heavens," he argues that "nothing is more deeply impressed on the cosmic imaginings of a modern than the idea that the heavenly bodies move in a pitch-black and dead-cold vacuity. It was not so in the Medieval Model."[2] He explains the contrast: the medievals' model for the cosmos was "the whole organization of their theology, science, and history [formed] into a single, complex, harmonious mental Model of the Universe."[3] The model included the voices of scientists, theologians, and historians alike who wove together a harmonious portrait of the heavens.

Lewis collected a number of medieval artifacts to, in a sense, reconstruct the medieval model. In *The Discarded Image,* he first turns to Ptolemy's work as the fundamental piece of medieval cosmology. Ptolemy, a first-century astronomer, theorized that the earth was the center of the solar system and that the sun, moon, and other planets orbited around the earth. The earth remained in a fixed location at the center while the other heavenly bodies moved across the heavens in circular revolutions around the earth. Philosophers and astronomers who followed Ptolemy built upon the Ptolemaic model by considering the paths of the heavenly bodies and referring to them as spheres. The spheres, like Russian nesting dolls, served as shells that increased in size as they were located farther away from the earth.[4] As this model persisted into the medieval period, it became increasingly popular to believe that God, the Creator of the cosmos, inhabited the largest and most removed sphere from the earth. This outermost sphere was referred to as the Primum Mobile, and from the Primum Mobile, God orchestrated and moved the heavenly spheres according to His plan. It was this grand image—God orchestrating the movement of the universe—that Lewis hoped to revive in his Trilogy.

This image eventually faded from popular thought as Galileo's scientific work legitimized the Copernican model. Copernicus and Galileo's observations caused a cosmic shift as they revealed the sun, not the earth, as the center of the solar system. They posited that the sun holds a fixed location in space and that the earth and planets revolve in elliptical motion around the sun. Copernicus and Galileo sought to glorify God through their scientific observation of His universe, but their work initiated a tidal wave of scientific discoveries that would soon push God out of the cosmic picture. Philosophy and theology were slowly removed from astronomy, and astronomers steadily altered the picture of the heavens until it became unrecognizable to the medieval thinker. By the time *Out of the Silent Planet* was published in 1938, scientists and astrophysicists were far along in their purely naturalistic rendering of outer space. Modern astronomy had brought with it more scientific—and less religious—images about the final frontier.

Lewis did not discredit modern astronomy and its advances, but he believed that there was far more to the cosmos than what we could observe through a telescope, as Rachel M. Roller notes in Chapter 3. Lewis argues in *The Discarded Image* that there are those in modern society who believe that through scientific progress, they have learned much more about the universe than the medievals and have, therefore, surpassed them in knowing the truth. In response to this belief, he explains that they "could 'know' the ultimate physical reality more or less as, by maps, pictures, and travel books, a man can 'know' a country he has not visited."[5] Their observations can only provide them with a portion of the truth of our universe, and his attempt to reacquaint readers with the medieval model was an attempt to rediscover abandoned truths.

Lewis held tightly to deeply religious images of the cosmos, especially those found in Dante Alighieri's *Divine Comedy*. What Ptolemy had theorized, Dante depicted. Dante masterfully and beautifully displayed the Ptolemaic model in his *Paradiso*, in which the character Dante rises from Earth through the heavenly spheres to arrive at the Primum Mobile. In *Paradiso*, Dante took the liberty of changing his audience's perspective on the Ptolemaic model: though Earth is technically in the center of Ptolemy's solar system, Dante places Earth at the bottom of a kind of cosmic ladder. In Dante's depiction, God in the Primum Mobile inhabits the top of the cosmic ladder. With God at the top and humanity at the bottom, humanity is cosmically positioned far removed from God.

Lewis takes these images with him as he sets the cosmological landscape of the Trilogy. As Dante in *Paradiso* encounters light and music as he moves up through the spheres toward God, Ransom also encounters the light of the universe once he leaves Earth, the Silent Planet. Ransom is overwhelmed by the light of the heavens just as Dante the character becomes overwhelmed by all the glory that he witnesses while traveling through the heavens. With every sphere, Dante is overtaken by its beauty and majesty; in the same way, Lewis spends a great deal of time illustrating the natural beauty of the worlds of Malacandra and Perelandra. On Malacandra, Lewis places his hero on a pristine beach surrounded by crystal-blue waters and tall green mountains. On Perelandra, Lewis drops Ransom into a golden sea with islands of fantastic bubble trees and curious creatures. The heavens of the Trilogy are not a dark vacuum dotted with lifeless, floating orbs; the heavens are full of light, and the planets are more beautiful than we could have ever imagined. This is why scholars have long observed that Lewis is "without doubt following Dante."[6]

Unlike those who lived in Dante's time, Lewis's audience assumed a cosmology that was devoid of this wonder and praise. From Lewis's perspective, they had lost the wonder that filled the souls of Dante's readers over the centuries. The awe-inspiring nature of Dante's images of creation pointed the reader back to the Creator, His greatness, and His creativity in reigning over the universe. Now, space "looked" vastly different from the heavens of the medieval period. Lewis believed creation had lost sight of its place in the cosmos; his society was losing sight of the Creator and the purpose of creation. Without strong cosmological bearings based on theological and philosophical truths, society could not fight against the emerging anxiety that Lewis writes about in *The Discarded Image*:

> Such a man today often, perhaps usually, feels himself confronted with a reality whose significance he cannot know, or a reality that has no significance; or even a reality such that the very question whether it has a meaning is itself a meaningless question. It is for him, by his own sensibility, to discover a meaning, or, out of his own subjectivity, to give a meaning—or at least a shape—to what in itself had neither. But the Model universe of our ancestors had a built-in significance.[7]

It was this significance that Lewis returns to in his Trilogy. Through it, Lewis offers us a glimpse into a medieval worldview that can rid society of the problems central to a modern cosmology and gives us a second chance to see God's glorious order and purpose for His creation.

A Cosmic Hierarchy and Order

Lewis did not revive the medieval model to rival the scientific theories of his time; instead, he saw value and importance in the model's hierarchy and order as a remedy to society's anxieties. From Lewis's arguments in *The Discarded Image*, it is evident that Lewis, like those in the medieval period, saw that the heavens and all of creation are intended to be a place of perfect order. In the Ptolemaic model, there is a definite, perfect order in the planets and in their spheres around the earth. As depicted in Dante's work, God set the heavens in perfect order and maintains them to glorify Himself. Because of these attributes, Lewis argues that the medieval universe is to be admired like "a great building... overwhelming in its greatness but satisfying in its harmony."[8] Here, Lewis admits to the overwhelming nature of God's entire creation, but he does not allow his audience to be distracted by the idea that the great expanse of the heavens must be inherently chaotic. For Lewis, the heavens should be a source of joy and satisfaction because they are ordered by God's hand.

As we find Ransom anxious for what awaits him in the expanse of space, Lewis argues that the heavens should not be a source of fear for those who consider them. Lewis explains that, when the medievals looked into the night sky, they believed that they were looking up into the bright and beautiful heavens toward the dwelling place of God.[9] The medievals could look up and believe that they had a glimpse of the higher rungs of the ladder. Lewis contrasts this medieval belief with the modern concept of looking out into space, the dark void. With a modern cosmology, "Earth is now just one of many planets, endlessly revolving around a not-very-special star that we call the Sun."[10] Lewis explains that looking out into the night sky can fill the modern man or woman with terror because of how limitless and lifeless the expanse of space seems to be.

In taking Dante's order of the cosmos, Lewis sets his literary version of Earth, Thulcandra, at the bottom of the Trilogy's cosmic ladder. Ransom's story begins on Earth, and in his ascension to Malacandra, Ransom must rise above the atmosphere of Earth before he can see the beauty of the cosmos (*OSP*, 33). Later in the story, Ransom is confronted with an unfamiliar glimpse of Earth when he is awaiting the Oyarsa of Malacandra. In Meldilorn, Ransom walks along the stone monoliths and examines the artistic representations of the planets in the solar system. He observes monolith after monolith, anticipating the depiction of Earth. To his surprise, he finds Earth to be the most dejected of the depictions, lacking the flame (representing an Oyarsa) that was present in the other carvings (*OSP*, 111). Earth is clearly not the focal point nor the most beautiful of the images. Here, Lewis draws the audience into this moment to consider a new perspective of Earth that does not place prideful importance on us as the focal point of the universe.

The idea that humanity is not the center of the universe seems to run counter to the Ptolemaic, Earth-centric system, yet knowing that Lewis is borrowing from Dante's perspective helps us marry these two ideas together. If the Earth is at the bottom of the cosmic ladder, humanity should not think too highly of itself. It should especially not think itself higher than God, and the Trilogy depicts the fall of characters who attempt to place themselves at the top of the cosmic ladder. Dante's perspective places humanity in a position where it can feel important in its rightful position in comparison to God's Primum Mobile, free from the anxiety of trying to forcefully move up the cosmic ladder.

This concept of hierarchy was not found in the modern cosmology, and that is why Ransom is confused when he learns that the species of Malacandra willingly submit to higher authority. The hrossa tell him that the three species, the *hrossa, séroni,* and *pfifltriggi,* live in harmony with one another as equals. They exist alongside the *eldila,* and the three species honor them. Above them all presides the Oyarsa of Malacandra who lives in harmony with the other Oyéresu, and the Oyéresu collectively submit to the ultimate authority of Maleldil. All of creation, in its glorious hierarchy and order, honors Maleldil.

The souls in Malacandra and in Perelandra offer Maleldil glorious praises throughout the first two books, and the beautiful image continues into the third with the company at St. Anne's. The company reflects the order that should exist when humans take their proper place within creation under their Creator. Like the races of Malacandra, those at St. Anne's live in harmony with one another while serving under the Director, Ransom, who serves Maleldil. By submitting themselves to the cosmic order they experience peace despite the chaotic circumstances they live through.

The chaos in *That Hideous Strength* is provoked by those who seek to overturn the cosmic hierarchy; their story therefore contains images of extreme disorder, chaos, and anxiety. The N.I.C.E. is characterized by a lack of true order with "leaders" who do not actually have a say in the institute's doings. The "scientists" of the N.I.C.E. did not want to conform themselves to the ethical or moral standards of the past because they believed that their breakthrough studies in science had given them the higher authority to throw off old regulations. The members of the N.I.C.E. repeatedly place themselves above each other and everyone else. They feel that they are deserving of power and political standing, to the extent that they murder one another to maintain their positions. They each have a blatant disregard for their neighbor, for nature, and for God.

Slowly, chaos builds up within the *That Hideous Strength* until it is unleashed in the dining room scene where many members of the N.I.C.E. meet their bloody end. Likewise, *in Perelandra,* Weston places himself as the sole arbiter of the fate of the human race and meets a violent end. The deaths of these characters are gruesome illustrations of what can happen when individuals reject the wisdom of old. In this, Lewis warns that attempting to overthrow the cosmic order will spell disaster; to think oneself powerful and entitled enough to exploit creation or reject God as authority is an invitation for one's own destruction.

Planetary Spirits and Gender

Looking over the entirety of the Trilogy, we can see some layers of the cosmic order may seem unfamiliar to us, the modern reader. As the reader journeys with Ransom to meet new characters, settings, and languages, the reader must also become acquainted with the Trilogy's supernatural beings: the *eldila*, Oyéresu, and the planetary spirits that descend on Earth in *That Hideous Strength*. As Julianne Johnson discusses in Chapter 1, the reality of the supernatural is key for both Ransom and the reader to grasp as we both move through the Trilogy. While the first two supernatural beings I have listed might feel rooted in Christian tradition, the third kind of beings, the planetary spirits, feel strange and, perhaps, out of place. For some, the planetary spirits are reminiscent of pagan traditions that are seemingly incompatible with Christianity. If Lewis's intent was to draw us closer to the truth of the universe and its Maker, why did Lewis include pagan imagery?

In *The Discarded Image*, Lewis explains that, from antiquity, great thinkers and theologians considered the spirits of the planets and believed in their effect on earthly life. Lewis states: "Orthodox theologians could accept the theory that the planets had an effect on events and on psychology, and, much more, on plants and minerals. It was not against this that the Church fought."[11] The medieval church fought against the idea that the planets themselves should be worshipped, yet, nonetheless, believed that this was a way to understand and glorify God through His creation. Lewis begins by introducing us to the first planetary spirit, the Malacandrian spirit, as he exists on his home planet. Malacandra is laden with imagery similar to that of the pagan god Mars. Ransom finds on Malacandra strong and tall mountain peaks that tower over the land, and he soon meets the *hrossa* who introduce him to their weaponry. At one point, he is even caught up in a heated battle between the *hrossa* and their enemy, the *hnakra*. As Ransom slowly encounters the Malacandrian language and geography, he becomes influenced by the Malacandrian spirit of strength, dutifulness, and courage.

Ransom recognizes these influences when they occur, but his moment of full recognition comes on Perelandra when he first sees the Malacandrian spirit himself next to the spirit of Perelandra. In this scene, the two spirits display themselves in human-like forms to honor the King and Queen of Perelandra. Their forms reveal to Ransom that the two are somehow similar yet somehow distinguished. Malacandra is "cold and morning colours, a little metallic—pure, hard, and bracing," like a rhythm to which Perelandra, a Venus-like spirit, is the melody (*PER*, 171). In a kind of beautiful contrast and complement, Perelandra "glowed with a warm splendour, full of the suggestion of teeming vegetable life," just like the planet itself (*PER*, 171).

It was in this instance that Ransom thinks, "Gender is a reality" (*PER*, 172). He finds that the human forms on Earth that held masculine and feminine qualities were only reflections of these forms that existed as realities within the cosmos. One of the forms before him was simply masculine, the other clearly feminine, yet, neither was male or female. Ransom realizes that the old myths and pagan stories of Earth held a few pieces of truth to this puzzle. For Lewis, the all-encompassing cosmic order contains gender, and for this reason, he viewed the concept of gender as being objective and concrete. To him, it brought glory to God to meditate on the realities that God had set into the cosmos and into our very beings. Though the idea of gender may stand as a mystery, it does not negate the fact for Lewis that the genders exist as transcendent ideas above incomplete, terrestrial manifestations of them.

The Cosmic Order of Marriage

The story of Jane and Mark comes at the heels of the love story that came before: the unification of the Lady and Lord of Perelandra. The Lady patiently and longingly waits for her husband and king, and she is blessed for her faithfulness by his presence and love in the end. As they come together as one, all of creation sings praises to Maleldil. Their marriage is a reason to glorify God, and it serves as a reflection of the ultimate and eternal marriage between the Lamb of God and the Church as His bride. The marriage of the King and Queen of Perelandra is untouched by sin, so we are given a conjectural image of marriage as God intended and ordered it to be.

From the onset of Jane and Mark's story, Lewis describes their state as two individuals, legally married but living outside the order of marriage. Unknowingly, they are then in a kind of rebellion against the cosmic order. They live, at best, with misunderstandings and a cold indifference toward each other. Jane is unhappy and bitter, and Mark stays far from home as long as possible. It is not until their individual encounters with a planetary influence that they have the chance to take hold of the truth that awaits them both.

As Jane and Mark submit themselves to the great cosmic hierarchy and order, the couple find joy and fulfillment as never before. They stand as an example, a symbol of hope for humanity to find peace and rest within the cosmos. This is by no means tangential to the medieval story Lewis has woven up to this point; the reunification of the couple is a symbol of the end of the medieval cosmology by which all is made peaceful and right in the universe. If humanity may accept its rightful and joyful place within the realms of marriage and gender, there is hope that one day it may take again its rightful place in the cosmic marriage between God and His bride, the church.

A New Cosmology

Looking to his present day, Lewis watched as many in society lived with fear, doubts, and anxieties because they, in their pride, had removed themselves from the influence of ancient wisdom. Learning from his friend and fellow Inkling, Owen Barfield, Lewis observed that modern society tended to believe that the mere passage of time brought progress. They believed that they had progressed morally, scientifically, or otherwise past the wisdom of the preceding centuries. Barfield called this "chronological snobbery," an act of rejecting the old simply because it was old and believing that the new was superior simply because it was new.[12] Through his Trilogy, Lewis sought to offer his society a set of new cosmological bearings as well as the peace found in the wisdom of old. He "found in the medieval world a potent antidote to the malaises of the modern," so he penned these beautiful stories to remind us of the power of the medieval model.[13] Still, Lewis writes in *The Discarded Image:*

> I hope no one will think that I am recommending a return to the Medieval Model. I am only suggesting considerations that may induce us to regard all Models in the right way, respecting each and idolising none . . . We can no longer dismiss the change of Models as a simple progress from error to truth. No Model is a catalogue of ultimate realities, and none is a mere fantasy. Each is a serious attempt to get in all the phenomena known at a given period, and each succeeds in getting in a great many.[14]

As we seek to uncover more about the universe we live in, we must recognize that it is in the synthesis of the truth in our history's models, not the rejection of all models that came before, that we will bring ourselves closer to the truth. The models of the ancients and medievals still contain truths that are too valuable for us in our modern society to lose. For this reason, Lewis offers us a chance to step into the world of the medievals and to sense awe and wonder as we look up into the night sky toward our Creator. As we reflect on our place in the cosmos, may we lovingly submit to our gracious God so that we, too, may declare the glory of the heavens.

Endnotes

1 Psalm 19:1 (NIV).
2 C. S. Lewis, *The Discarded Image* (Cambridge, UK: Cambridge University Press, 1964), 111.
3 Lewis, *Discarded Image,* 11.
4 Michael Ward, *The Narnia Code: C. S. Lewis and the Secret of the Seven Heavens* (Carol Stream, IL: Tyndale House, 2010), 33.
5 Lewis, *Discarded Image,* 216.
6 Chris R. Armstrong, *Medieval Wisdom for Modern Christians* (Grand Rapids, MI: Brazos, 2016), 103.
7 Lewis, *Discarded Image,* 203–04.
8 Lewis, *Discarded Image,* 203–04.
9 Ward, *Narnia Code*, 32.
10 Ward, *Narnia Code*, 32.
11 Lewis, *Discarded Image*, 103.
12 Armstrong, 30.
13 Armstrong, 29.
14 Lewis, *Discarded Image,* 222.

THE PERILOUS PROBLEM OF PRIDE

NOLAN ANDREW

The Ransom Trilogy is an exciting story of a man swept away into a cosmic adventure. On this journey, he encounters fantastical creatures, mystical planets, and the vilest of villains. In the end, the bad guys lose and the good guys win—and the story is over. Or is it? From a theological perspective, the Trilogy contains implications that sit with the reader long after the book has been closed. It is an exploration of a celestial and terrestrial battle between good and evil that influences not only the characters but the reader as well. Underneath the story, Lewis shines a light on problems that are far more real and sinister than fictional organizations and mad scientists.

Defined by Lewis as a "complete anti-God state of mind," pride is an underlying issue in all three books, becoming the centerpiece of a warning in both the imaginary and real worlds.[1] Pride can appear in a variety of forms, as outright opposition of the divine or even disguised as the pursuit of societal good. It can be difficult to detect, but its poison is potent enough to misdirect souls and take down nations. Lewis recognized the danger of this vice both within himself and in the world around him, and as a result, pride became a recurring area of concern in many of his works. In light of this emphasis, pride is one of the most important topics in not only study of the Trilogy but in Lewis studies in general.

The previous chapter explored Lewis's belief in the power and truth of the medieval mindset, a subject that is essential for understanding his writing more completely. Medieval thought places an emphasis on theological vice, virtue, and hierarchy—themes discussed by theologians for centuries. Pride is the primary vice that disrupts divine order and separates people from God. Lewis, who was steeped in both the medieval mindset and modern Christianity, views pride as the most perilous problem Christians face on their spiritual journeys. Before we look at how Lewis wove a warning against pride into the Trilogy, let us venture into how Lewis understood pride itself.

Defining Pride

After Lewis's conversion, nearly all of his writings focused on Christianity or were informed by Christian language and imagery. In *C. S. Lewis: A Guide to His Theology*, David G. Clark insists that a background in Christian thought is necessary for the reader to fully appreciate Lewis's writing because "the Bible is by far [his] most influential source."[2] Clark adds that readers of the Ransom Trilogy need to be particularly aware of orthodox (widely accepted) Christian beliefs, due to the subtlety of religious themes in the books.

The topic of pride appears in Lewis's writing as early as 1930, two years before his conversion to Christianity, when he wrote to his friend Arthur Greeves explaining that he believed pride to be a persistent problem in his life. In the letter, Lewis describes himself as "an instrument strung but preferring to play itself because it thinks it knows the tune better than the Musician."[3] As any guitarist knows, the person playing the guitar is fully in control of the strings. Notes and chords come into existence because the musician knows the frets intimately and strums the instrument precisely. Through metaphor, Lewis artistically and eloquently reveals his struggle with pride. He had been behaving like he was superior to God and grappling with submission to a Higher Power. In this case, pride is not a distant idea studied by a theologian in a library full of ancient books. Pride, for Lewis, has a personal nature. This reality is the foundation for the rest of Lewis's writing on pride and the platform for its inclusion in many of his works including (but not limited to) *The Screwtape Letters*, *A Preface to Paradise Lost*, *Mere Christianity*, and the Ransom Trilogy.

There are several places in his writing where Lewis stresses the severity of pride. Beginning in his letter to Greeves, Lewis calls pride the "mother of all sins."[4] In *The Screwtape Letters*, the demon Screwtape describes pride as "the strongest and most beautiful of the vices."[5] In *Mere Christianity*, Lewis says, "the essential vice, the utmost evil, is Pride."[6] The repeated emphasis of the point that pride is the root of evil makes its importance to Lewis easy to see. It is no coincidence that this idea is also stressed in orthodox Christianity. After all, pride is considered to be at the forefront of the seven deadly sins, a list that has its origins in the teachings of early church fathers. Therefore, a proper understanding of pride is an invaluable tool for interpreting Lewis's works.

To say Lewis was familiar with the Bible is an understatement. His stepson Douglas Gresham remembers seeing him read the Bible every day.[7] Clark insists, "Whether the subject was the history of the world, human nature, modern science, space travel, whether major or minor topics, the Bible provided the lens through which [Lewis] understood everything."[8] To fully understand Lewis's definition of pride, his readers must also view it through this biblical lens.

In the Bible, the word "pride" is found sixty-three times, and the word "proud" is found forty-four times.[9] Psalm 10:4 defines a proud person as someone who does not seek God or think about God. According to this verse, pride is not so much an active behavior as it is a lack of attention given to God caused by disinterest or distraction. Because it is a mindset rather than a behavior, pride can be incredibly difficult to detect. However, the biblical stakes are immense; it is a blameworthy offense in the eyes of God. Proverbs 16:5 warns that the proud are detestable and will be punished, and Proverbs 16:18 says that pride will eventually lead to destruction. We see Lewis's incorporation of these biblical warnings about pride in many of his writings, especially *Mere Christianity*.

Adapted from a collection of radio talk show appearances between the years 1941 and 1944 (around the same time Lewis wrote the Trilogy), *Mere Christianity* is Lewis's explanatory defense of the Christian faith. While pride is mentioned several times throughout the text, it is most heavily discussed in the chapter "The Great Sin," where, in accordance with orthodox Christian theology, Lewis asserts that pride is the root of all other evils—the greatest sin.[10] Due to its magnitude, the misery "in every nation and every family since the world began" can be connected to pride as its chief cause.[11] These miseries include war, interpersonal strife, and every other issue associated with human affairs.[12] Lewis's claim has massive implications. If one is able to narrow in on the cause of misery, which Lewis asserts as pride, one may be able to figure out how to stop misery from occurring.

Knowing now the nature and consequences of pride, one must turn to the outward fruits by which pride can be recognized. Unlike the other vices, such as gluttony and lust, which affect our physical beings or what Lewis calls our "animal nature," pride affects our spiritual selves.[13] It is something entirely internal that appeals to the innermost desire to be in control. The unseen, spiritual nature of pride is what makes it the most deadly of all the sins. Just as the snake in the Garden of Eden tempted Eve with forbidden knowledge, pride is subtle and sly. Despite its subtle appearance, it has the most severe consequence—as demonstrated in the Genesis account when Adam and Eve are cast out of the Garden. Pride has the power to separate humankind from God.

From a Christian perspective, this separation is the worst thing that can happen to a human. Since the soul's status is at stake, it is a matter of spiritual life and death. For this reason, Lewis argues, the devil uses pride as his ultimate weapon, since his concern is not with our physical states but the conditions of our souls.[14] Satan, a paragon of pride, is prominently featured in all three books of the Trilogy and is a point of interest in Lewis's other works.

Space Satan, or the Bent One

Known by names such as Lucifer, the Prince of Darkness, and the devil, Satan plays a significant role in Christian theology as the force opposing God and His followers. He is the embodiment of pride. While featured as a character in numerous literary works such as Milton's *Paradise Lost*, Dante's *Divine Comedy*, and even Lewis's Ransom Trilogy, Satan is a real, existing entity to Lewis. He is not solely a character in a book but an actual threat to a person's spiritual well-being. Lewis's belief in the existence of this dark power is a foundational narrative element throughout his fiction writing, his nonfiction works, and even his personal interviews.[15]

In *Mere Theology*, Will Vaus explains that Lewis first encountered the occult when he attended Cherbourg School, where the school's matron spoke of communicating with the dead.[16] Later, he met practicing Spiritualists—those who believe communication with a spiritual realm is possible—at Oxford, but eventually turned away from spirituality and declared himself an atheist. His denial of the existence of angels and demons lasted until his conversion to Christianity, when he took on the orthodox belief that "certain angels, by the abuse of their free will, became enemies of God and therefore enemies of humanity as well."[17] Lewis's understanding that Satan and his demons were the enemies of humanity is reflected in the writing of Ransom Trilogy where the Bent One and the bent *eldila* act as the antagonistic force.

The first reference to Satan is made in *Out of the Silent Planet* during the Oyarsa's telling of the fall of the Bent One. According to the Oyarsa of Malacandra, each planet was assigned a ruling *eldil* upon creation by Maleldil. The ruler of Earth was the brightest and greatest of all the Oyéresu. For an unspoken reason, the Oyarsa of Earth "became bent... It was in his mind to spoil other worlds besides his own" (*OSP*, 120). After a thwarted attack on Malacandra, the Bent One was forced to remain on his assigned planet, ruling over it in darkness. The similarity between Satan and the Bent One is further reinforced by Lewis in a letter to Sister Penelope shortly after the publication of *Out of the Silent Planet*, where he explains that the resemblance of the fall of the

Bent One to the traditional tale of the fall of Satan is intentional.[18] This parallel connects pride to the Trilogy; if pride is the sin of Satan, it is also the sin of the Bent One.

Further elaboration on Satan's affiliation with pride is found in Lewis's *Preface to Paradise Lost* and *Mere Christianity*. *Preface to Paradise Lost* is a literary analysis of John Milton's epic poem, which is perhaps the most famous retelling of the fall of humankind as depicted in Genesis.[19] Lewis's *Preface* includes a chapter on the character of Satan. He argues that Milton did not intend to glorify Satan or paint him in a positive light, despite the popular opinion that Satan is the protagonist of the poem. Instead, Satan is painted as a supreme egotist, someone whom the reader should empathize with but not want to imitate.[20] Satan's sin and the cause of his downfall is the desire to disrupt hierarchy, to become equal with or greater than God—in other words, to reign. According to Lewis, readers of Milton's poem are able to understand this desire because they share characteristics with Satan.[21] We all have the capacity to indulge the sin of pride.

Lewis further expands on the idea of a relatable Satan in *Mere Christianity*. The mindset Lewis describes is pride: putting oneself first and wanting to be God.[22] Because Satan taught this skewed perspective to Adam and Eve, who in turn passed the sin onward, it can be argued that Satan's pride is in some way responsible for every skewed aspect of humanity, whether that be "money, poverty, ambition, war, prostitution, classes, empires, slavery—the long terrible story of many trying to find something other than God which will make him happy."[23] From Satan comes pride, and from pride comes a multitude of evils, including several evils that Lewis depicts throughout the Ransom Trilogy such as idolatry, immortality, power, and selfishness.

Being God vs. Receiving the Gift of Godhood

David C. Downing, author of *Into the Region of Awe: Mysticism in C. S. Lewis*, comments on how the world Lewis builds in *Out of the Silent Planet* is "certainly the stuff of science fiction... [but] it is also orthodox Christian theology, as it might be understood in an unfallen, hierarchical world."[24] While the settings and characters used are unique to the Trilogy, the idea of hierarchy is not.[25] Christian theology positions an all-powerful, all-knowing God above humans. Church fathers such as St. Augustine, Theodoret, and Lactantius echo that humans are to submit to God as an acknowledgment of their proper place in the divine hierarchy.[26] Certain characters in the Trilogy reject the divine hierarchy and display an impulse to create their own order, placing themselves above all others, even God.

The planet Ransom explores in *Out of the Silent Planet* is an unfamiliar world where the inhabitants adhere to a clearly structured society. Unlike the war-stricken Earth, Malacandra is a place of peace; its inhabitants work together to ensure the wellbeing of all (*OSP,* 73). During his time spent living among the natives, Ransom is able to learn about the way the planet operates, specifically how its hierarchy functions. The three species of *hnau* are of equal status. Among the *hnau* dwell the invisible *eldila*. These beings are all ruled by Oyarsa, a more powerful *eldil*. Above Oyarsa is Maleldil the Young, creator of the planet, and Maleldil the Old, both of whom are spirits who reside everywhere at all times (*OSP*, 69). Because of the planet's unfallen nature, the sin of pride does not disrupt its inhabitants' respect for order and for each other. The creatures acknowledge their role as *hnau* and respect Maleldil as supreme authority. Throughout the Trilogy, Lewis emphasizes how this attitude of equality is different from the human mindset of self-promotion and idolatry.

Beginning with *Out of the Silent Planet*, Ransom informs the curious *sorns* of some heinous acts committed by humans on Thulcandra such as "war, slavery, and prostitution" (*OSP*, 102). In an attempt to understand why these things occur, the *sorns* suggest it is because humans have no Oyarsa, or ruler. Augray, an older and wiser *sorn*, says it is because humans each want to be their own Oyarsa, their own god. At the end of the book, during the questioning of Weston and Devine, the Oyarsa of Malacandra repeats the same notion, concluding that humankind is bent and obeys a "blind Oyarsa" in each soul (*OSP*, 137). This allegation is supported in *Perelandra* when Weston completes his transformation into the Un-man after declaring, "'I *am* the Universe. I, Weston, am your God and your Devil'" (*PER*, 82). Just as the *sorn* and Oyarsa suggested, Weston is a bent human who chooses to become his own god.

Another example of humans seeking godhood through pride is found in the actions of the N.I.C.E. in *That Hideous Strength* when Filostrato and Straik convey to Mark their goal to create their own god out of Francois Alcasan's talking head (*THS*, 176). The N.I.C.E.'s attempts at creating a god worthy of worship are ironic because, according to Lewis, each of us is actually called to be a "god or goddess, a dazzling, radiant, immortal creature, pulsating all through with such energy and joy and wisdom and love as we cannot now imagine."[27] Following Lewis's logic, humans are intended to reign on Earth, but not by their own power and authority. Instead, humans receive the gift from a divine ruler. This is portrayed at the end of *Perelandra* when the Oyarsa of Perelandra bestows authority on the humanlike King and Queen, giving them the title of Oyarsa (*PER*, 177). In a sense, these characters become gods of their planet, but only after maturing in their understanding of divine hierarchy. These characters stand in direct contrast to those of Weston and Devine who rely on their own power to become great, rather than receiving the gift of power rightfully bestowed. As Lewis points out, it is not through our own greatness that this royal bestowing occurs; we become mighty by choosing to reflect God's power, thus adhering to the biblical command to "clothe [ourselves] with the Lord Jesus Christ."[28]

Immortality

Multiple characters in the Trilogy seek after immortality. This search is rooted in pride, but it need not be so. Just as Lewis argues in regards to pursuing godhood, eternal life is already ours to partake in—it is a part of our nature, given to us by God.[29] The way in which we view immortality must not come from a place of pride but from a perspective that credits our Creator. Too often, this desire for immortality comes from a mindset of supremacy, which threatens the well-being of our relationship with God.

From the beginning of the Trilogy, it is clear that eternal life is one of the scientists' goals. Weston reveals to Ransom that his primary objective in traveling through space is to set up a space colony that will allow humans to survive forever (*OSP*, 29). He believes their potential discovery of immortality is so magnificent that they are justified in assaulting and kidnapping Ransom. Similarly, in *That Hideous Strength*, Filostrato tells Mark that one of the N.I.C.E.'s goals is to eliminate death (*THS*, 171).[30] Rather than bow to the natural course of life as created by Maleldil, these characters attempt to subdue death and become immortal gods.

Lewis critiques this search for immortality in "Cross Examination," saying, "I find it difficult to keep from laughing when I find people worrying about future destruction of some kind or other. Didn't they know they were going to die anyway?"[31] To Lewis, spending energy on attempts to further our longevity is wasteful, for death is inevitable.[32] Lewis expands on this conviction further in "Is Progress Possible?" by critiquing a search for immortality motivated solely by survival. Our efforts should instead be fixed on "increasing goodness and happiness," because it is not how long we live that matters but how we live.[33] The material world will die, but our souls will live on forever. Therefore, our attention needs to be devoted to our spiritual health.

The Center

At the University of London in 1944, one year before the release of *That Hideous Strength*, Lewis delivered a lecture called "The Inner Ring." In it, he describes an inner circle of people one tends to envy or desire to associate with.

According to Lewis, no matter how appealing or delightful these inner rings appear, one "will reach no 'inside' that is worth reaching. The true road lies in quite another direction."[34] In *That Hideous Strength*, Mark makes a similar discovery. For a majority of the book, he longs to be in the inner ring of the N.I.C.E. but later recognizes that the group he so desperately wanted to belong to is in reality villainous and evil.

The desire to be at the center of something is a component of pride that most, if not all, people can relate to; wanting to belong is an innate aspect of human nature. While this part of us is not inherently bad, it can become a hindrance to our spiritual well-being if we let it consume us. When we place self-interest at the center, we leave no room for God.

In *Mere Christianity*, Lewis maintains that "the natural life in each of us is something self-centered, something that wants to be petted and admired, to take advantage of other lives, to exploit the whole universe."[35] In our desire to belong, we long to be at the center of everything, blinding ourselves to the reality that no human is truly the center of anything. Lewis wants his audience to learn that the true center, the place of ultimate belonging, is found in God.

This belief is found in the Trilogy, specifically in *Perelandra* when Weston becomes the Un-man and declares himself "the conductor of the central forward pressure of the universe" (*PER*, 82). His declaration is an example of extreme self-centeredness which, in his case, leads to terrifying possession and a brutal death. Weston's mindset is contrasted by the praises of the *eldila* during the Great Dance at the end of the book. The voices sing that Maleldil is the center, those who follow Maleldil are at the center with Him, and those who follow the Bent One are out of the center (*PER*, 185–86). Because of Weston's self-centered attitude, the *eldila* indicate that he was never in the true center, for his allegiance resided with the Bent One. Fortunately, the *eldila* explain that there is a way to be in the true center: voluntary obedience to Maleldil.

In *The Weight of Glory*, Lewis expresses his wish for all people to eventually find their way to the center. In order to experience the glory that comes from being at the center with God, one must have a mindset of complete submission.[36] Once this happens, all self-centeredness vanishes and the joy of belonging ensues. It is only in this state that one's spirit is healthy. Lewis believes the alignment of self determines the soul's final destination; placing ourselves at the center puts us on a path to Hell, while laying ourselves down directs us toward Heaven.[37] This belief plays out in the Trilogy through the destruction of Weston and the joining of Ransom with the heavenly *eldila* in the Great Dance. While the thought of being included in an "inner ring" is alluring, the opportunity to reside in the true center with God is infinitely better. Like Ransom, we can dance with the divine.

Battle of the Will: Self-Love and Self

One of the most brilliant aspects of the Trilogy is its simultaneous inclusion of external and internal battles. On a cosmic scale, Maleldil is at war with the Bent One, but on a personal scale, a battle rages in the characters' wills. Lewis argues that this battle of the will is the most important fight an individual faces, for it is not until we choose to align our wills with God that we become our true selves. Self-love, a component of pride, is the foe on the front line determined to prevent us from achieving wholeness. The battle of the will is a recurring theme in the Trilogy, as all of the human characters encounter choices that align their wills with Maleldil or the Bent One.

In *Out of the Silent Planet,* Weston attests to aligning his will with the Bent One when he childishly tells the Oyarsa of Malacandra, "Me no care Maleldil. Like Bent One better: me on his side" (*OSP*, 139). His transformation into the Un-man in *Perelandra* is the final confirmation that the battle over his will has been lost. Tinidril experiences the same battle when the Un-man tempts her to disobey Maleldil and join the Bent One. Unlike Weston, Tinidril emerges from the battle victorious. The book's heavy incorporation of dialogue among the three characters supports the idea that the main conflict is internal; the Un-man does not want to harm Tinidril's physical being but rather to skew the direction of her will. Jane and Mark go through similar trials in *That Hideous Strength.* At first, Jane's will is pulled towards Maleldil, and Mark's will is unknowingly drawn towards the Bent One. By the end of the story, both characters successfully fight internal (and at times, external) battles to overcome the Bent One's pull and align their wills with Maleldil.

The most traceable battle of the will, however, occurs in the character of Ransom.[38] He is introduced to the cosmic battle between Maleldil and the Bent One in *Out of the Silent Planet.* In *Perelandra,* he casts his whole force of will toward Maleldil once he decides to defeat the Un-man no matter the cost.[39] Finally, in *That Hideous Strength,* Ransom's character provides a picture of what it looks like to be in complete alignment with God. As Downing puts it, Ransom "has become a unitive mystic, someone whose I-will has been utterly subdued."[40] The "I-will" is the part of ourselves that wants to become god; it is the voice in our heads that tells us we know best. In the previous books, Ransom operated under his "I-will" and as a result lived in fear and uncertainty. Once his will becomes one with Maleldil's, the fear subsides and he gains a new wisdom, power, and confidence. Lewis believes that, just as Ransom submitted his will to Maleldil, readers need to submit their wills to God in order to thrive. This is most clearly seen in *Mere Christianity,* where he states that we become our true selves once we let go of personal desire and conform to God's will.[41] Pride hinders the sacrifice of self when we choose to place a greater emphasis on love of self versus love of who we will become when we let God take over.

In "Two Ways With the Self," Lewis wants his readers to understand that the self is neither to be adored nor hated. Instead, we must love ourselves and others with impartiality, knowing that all are wonderfully made, all are tragically flawed, and it is only God who deserves total adoration.[42] Since God is perfect, submitting our wills to Him transforms and unites us with His perfection. However, loving ourselves to the point of wanting to pursue our individual will over God's will—as Weston does—sets us up for failure and causes us to miss out on experiencing what Ransom has in *That Hideous Strength*: peace. Therefore, we must fight without ceasing to overcome pride and win the battle of the will.

The destruction of the antagonists at the end of the Trilogy is a visualization of what can happen when pride becomes all-consuming. In contrast, the victorious arc of Ransom is an example of what happens to those who win the battle of the will by overcoming pride and clothing themselves in humility. It is at this point that I transition from the topic of pride to discuss its counterpart, for Lewis was not satisfied with merely recognizing our pitfalls and maladies but offering a prescription as well. If pride is the problem, humility is the solution.

Humility

It is clear from the biblical perspective that, simply put, pride is bad and humility is good. According to the Bible, prideful people are opposed by God, disgraced, and destined to fall, but those with humble spirits are lifted up, granted wisdom, and honored.[43] Psalm 149:4 says the Lord "crowns the humble with victory." This verse's imagery closely parallels the experiences of Ransom who, after two books of toil, becomes quite literally crowned. The similarity between the rewards of humility in the Trilogy and Scripture is no coincidence; Lewis was well-acquainted with the biblical call to live in humility.

Chapter XIV of *The Screwtape Letters* focuses on the subjects of pride and humility. Lewis uses the voice of Screwtape to convey what God desires of His followers regarding this topic: "to be so free from any bias in [their] own favour that [they] can rejoice in [their] own talents as frankly and gratefully as in [their] neighbour's talents."[44] In other words, having humility means understanding that all humans are equally valuable in the eyes of God. To maintain this perspective, we must not fixate on personal merit but on the worth of all of humanity. With that said, Lewis reminds us that God created us to do great things, so being humble does not require us to abstain from greatness. As a character, Ransom embodies this ideal. By the end of the Trilogy, Ransom has traveled through space, defeated the Un-man, built a community at St. Anne's, and become the Pendragon. Even Tor and Tinidril honor him by calling him "Lord and Father," while he bows at their feet (*PER*, 178). Lewis asserts in *Mere Christianity* that rejecting God's plans is not humility but cowardice.[45] Therefore, those who practice humility may be some of the most accomplished people, just as Ransom becomes the regal Pendragon.[46] The ultimate example of harmony between humility and greatness, however, is Jesus.

Just as Satan is the embodiment of pride, Jesus is the incarnation of humility. He is the Son of God, the most powerful King, yet he lowered himself by taking on human form and communing with His servants.[47] It is Jesus who redeems us from the perilous problem of pride. Concurrently, it is Jesus whom Lewis desires his reader to encounter through his writing.[48] Lewis relays this conviction in "Cross Examination" when he declares that we "need to believe in the one who saves us from our sins."[49] Not only is Jesus our savior, He is the living example of who we become once we swallow our pride and clothe ourselves in humility.[50] This act of embracing humility and submitting one's will to a divine power is exactly what saves Ransom and his companions in the Trilogy.

A Critical Reminder

Despite its alluring pull, Lewis warns his readers that a mindset of pride leads to peril. When we try to be like God, we become like devils. When we pursue immortal life, we create monsters instead. When we long to enter an inner ring, we find ourselves on the outside of the true center. Pride is destructive, but it is not an incurable, inseparable part of human nature. By cultivating habits of humility, we achieve those things we only thought possible through prideful ambition. We receive the gift of godhood, live eternally, and dance in the true center with God.

The journey towards the true center is not easy—it may take an equivalent of three books to get there—but once we arrive, Lewis believes we will find happiness and peace like no other.[51] We must be like Jane, Mark, and Ransom who fight to align their wills with the Creator. We must put our selfish inclinations aside, stomp out the serpent, and look past the grand facade of the "inner ring" towards the promising future that awaits us. As we navigate away from the false pretenses and selfish ambitions that pride presents, Lewis provides the redemption of the Ransom Trilogy as a compass to guide his readers toward spiritual well-being at the true center.

Endnotes

1 C. S. Lewis, *Mere Christianity: A revised and amplified edition, with a new introduction, of the three books, Broadcast Talks, Christian Behavior, and Beyond Personality* (New York: HarperCollins, 2015), 122.
2 David G. Clark, *C. S. Lewis: A Guide to His Theology* (Malden, MA: Blackwell Pub., 2007), 2.
3 C. S. Lewis, *Yours, Jack: Spiritual Direction from C. S. Lewis*, ed. Paul F. Ford (New York: HarperCollins, 2008), 11.
4 Lewis, *Yours, Jack*, 11.
5 C. S. Lewis, *The Screwtape Letters* (New York: HarperCollins, 2015), 130.
6 Lewis, *Mere Christianity*, 121.
7 Clark, *C. S. Lewis: A Guide to his Theology*, 2.
8 Clark, *C. S. Lewis: A Guide to his Theology*, 2.
9 Data from the Bible Gateway online database, New International Version.
10 Lewis, *Mere Christianity*, 121.
11 Lewis, *Mere Christianity*, 123–24.
12 Lewis, *Mere Christianity*, 123–24.
13 Lewis, *Mere Christianity*, 125.
14 Lewis, *Mere Christianity*, 124.
15 C. S. Lewis, "Answers to Questions on Christianity," in *God in the Dock: Essays on Theology and Ethics*, ed. Walter Hooper (Grand Rapids: Eerdmans, 2014), 46.
16 Will Vaus, *Mere Theology: A Guide to the Thought of C. S. Lewis*, (Downers Grove, IL: InterVarsity, 2004), 109.
17 Vaus, *Mere Theology*, 109.
18 C. S. Lewis to Sister Penelope, August 9, 1939, in *Letters of C. S. Lewis*, eds. Warren H. Lewis and Walter Hooper (New York: HarperCollins, 2017), 412.
19 It should be noted that the plot of *Paradise Lost*, the fall of humankind due to the temptation of pride, is the main focus of *Perelandra*.
20 Colin Duriez, *Bedeviled: Lewis, Tolkien, and the Shadow of Evil* (Downers Grove, IL: InterVarsity, 2015), 192.
21 C. S. Lewis, *A Preface to Paradise Lost* (London, UK: Oxford University Press, 1969), 101.
22 Lewis, *Mere Christianity*, 49.
23 Lewis, *Mere Christianity*, 49.
24 David C. Downing, *Into the Region of Awe: Mysticism in C. S. Lewis* (Downers Grove, IL: InterVarsity, 2005), 88.
25 See Maya Maley's contribution in Chapter 5 for more information on hierarchy in the Trilogy.
26 Leslie Walker, "Divine Providence," *The Catholic Encyclopedia*, Vol. 12 (New York: Robert Appleton Company, 1911), http://www.newadvent.org/cathen/12510a.htm.
27 Lewis, *Mere Christianity*, 206.
28 Lewis, *Mere Christianity*, 205; Romans 13:14 (NIV).
29 Rachel M. Roller discusses the topic of immortality in Chapter 3. My focus here is on how the desire for longevity is a symptom of pride.
30 How ironic that the scientists who aim to abolish the natural function of death end up getting killed by nature in the form of animals.
31 C. S. Lewis, "Cross-Examination" in *God in the Dock: Essays on Theology and Ethics*, ed. Walter Hooper (Grand Rapids: Eerdmans, 2014), 295.
32 Similarly, Augray explains to Ransom that Maleldil does not make worlds or races to last forever (*OSP*, 100).
33 C. S. Lewis, "Is Progress Possible?: Willing Slaves of the Welfare State" *God in the Dock: Essays on Theology and Ethics*, ed. Walter Hooper (Grand Rapids: Eerdmans, 2014), 347.

34 C. S. Lewis, "The Inner Ring," in *The Weight of Glory: And Other Addresses* (New York: HarperCollins, 2009), 157.
35 Lewis, *Mere Christianity*, 178.
36 C. S. Lewis, "The Weight of Glory," in *The Weight of Glory: And Other Addresses* (New York: HarperCollins, 2009), 36–39.
37 Duriez, 162–63.
38 Downing, *Into the Region of Awe*, 97.
39 Downing, *Into the Region of Awe*, 98.
40 Downing, *Into the Region of Awe*, 103.
41 Lewis, *Mere Christianity*, 203.
42 C. S. Lewis, "Two Ways with the Self," in *God in the Dock: Essays on Theology and Ethics*, ed. Walter Hooper (Grand Rapids: Eerdmans, 2014), 211.
43 James 4:6, James 4:10, Proverbs 11:2, Proverbs 15:33, Proverbs 18:12.
44 Lewis, *Screwtape Letters*, 71.
45 Lewis, *Mere Christianity*, 204.
46 For more information on Ransom as Pendragon, see Daniel Z. Hsieh's contribution in Chapter 7.
47 Philippians 2:5–8 (NIV) says, "In your relationships with one another, have the same mindset as Christ Jesus: Who, being in very nature God, did not consider equality with God something to be used to his own advantage; rather, he made himself nothing by taking the very nature of a servant, being made in human likeness. And being found in appearance as a man, he humbled himself by becoming obedient to death—even death on a cross!"
48 Lewis, "Cross Examination," 290.
49 Lewis, "Cross Examination," 288.
50 "Rather, clothe yourselves with the Lord Jesus Christ, and do not think about how to gratify the desires of the flesh." Romans 13:14 (NIV); Lewis, *Mere Christianity*, 181.
51 Lewis, *Mere Christianity*, 50.

ARTHURIAN LEGEND IN DEEP HEAVEN

DANIEL Z. HSIEH

We read the first two books of the Ransom Trilogy in delight—and then ... *That Hideous Strength.* A broken marriage, Merlin coming back to life, a head started up like a car, a bloody stampede through a banquet hall, and the book goes on and on. The dystopian world of *That Hideous Strength* is a composite one, and it seems equally haunted by things of the past and things of the future. We are left with many questions. A central one is this: What are we to make of all the Arthurian Legend in the story?

Arthurian Legend is "a mass of legends in several languages" originating in Welsh literature around the Sixth Century.[1] Some historical accounts suggest the existence of an actual King Arthur who fought the Saxons when they invaded the Britons. Other accounts are clearly parts of an imaginative corpus of romances, epics, and novels written in Latin, English, French, and German that constitute in themselves a distinct literary tradition. *That Hideous Strength* exists inside this stream of "Arthuriana."

As a professor of medieval and Renaissance literature, Lewis was steeped in "The Matter of Britain." Outside the academy, his love for the Legends was just as strong. From his first reading of Malory in 1915 to the plans he made with Walter Hooper to study the "old French sources" behind Malory, Lewis was endlessly fascinated with King Arthur and the adventures that constellate around him.[2] Things that are esoteric and obscure for us were common knowledge for him. And unfortunately for us, some of his characters in *That Hideous Strength* are as knowledgeable as he is when it comes to the Legends. We are told that Ransom, Dr. Dimble, and the Dennistons share among themselves an understanding of Arthurian Britain that "orthodox scholarship will probably not reach for some centuries" (*THS*, 197). If Lewis knew Arthurian Legend as a professional and his characters know it even more intimately, what is to become of us?

An exhaustive study of Arthurian Legend in *That Hideous Strength* would take a lifetime—perhaps more. There is, nevertheless, a key sequence of insights that unlocks some of the meaning of *That Hideous Strength* in a profound way. The present chapter is dedicated to exploring this sequence of insights. Once it is discussed, the warning that it forms will become clear. This warning, to never neglect how we *ought* to live in our zeal to identify how *not* to live, will be discussed at length in the next chapter. The project of this chapter is to uncover what the Arthurian elements mean; the project of the following one is to uncover what they mean for us. In view of this goal, I will present four individual Arthurian elements encountered in *That Hideous Strength*, highlighting their meanings in both Arthuriana and the development of the Trilogy. These elements are Merlin, the Pendragon and Fisher-King, Logres, and Avalon.

Merlin

Merlin is the most original and authentic Arthurian piece in *That Hideous Strength*. He is presented in a pure form, cut straight from accounts written in the medieval era and pasted into the novel. The first description of Merlin (before we are even told it is him) establishes his ancient character. Jane is said to have seen people digging up an "ancient British, druidical kind of man, in a long mantle" (*THS*, 13). He returns to earth replete with old garb and everything. The next time we see him, he is mentioned in the context of Dr. Dimble's discussion of Arthurian Legend, which is concerned with medieval accounts like Malory's and Layamon's (the first English version of the Legend).[3] Dimble even takes time to clarify Merlin's historically ambiguous identity as one who is magical, yet not evil (*THS*, 29). It is as if Lewis knows his readers will need to be familiar with Merlin in order to understand the story and, thus, he graciously briefs us about him, reminding us of his powers and his original place in medieval Arthurian literature.

There are many other descriptions of Merlin which show his almost untouched character. His Latin, for example, is said to be a very early one (*THS*, 276). At one point, after Merlin suggests beheading Jane for not bearing the long-awaited child destined for rulership of Logres, Ransom admits that they should not assume Merlin's legal standards or "penal code would be that of the Nineteenth Century" (*THS*, 277). When speaking to his wife, Dr. Dimble remarks that the company at St. Anne's were foolish for expecting that Merlin would "be a Twentieth Century man" simply because he came back in the Twentieth Century (*THS*, 279). In the midst of Lewis's dystopian world, where technology is reaching frightful capabilities at Belbury, Merlin is brought in unchanged, still riding a horse, still wearing a long mantle. He serves as a stark contrast to the modern world, yet there is a sort of boldness about him that he shares with the N.I.C.E. Perhaps they are two sides of the same coin. As Dimble says, "Merlin is the reverse of Belbury. He's the opposite extreme" (*THS*, 282).

Merlin as the opposite extreme of Belbury succinctly describes his role in *That Hideous Strength* and is an example of how, in the novel, Earth is described through antitheses. There are binaries everywhere: a very good Director and a very bad one, a love of literature with strong morals and a submission to scientism with no morals, a weak-minded husband and an independently-spirited wife. Additionally, the world is not simply modern or contemporary. It is a battleground between the future and the past. If the N.I.C.E. is the future gone wrong, then Merlin is the past gone right.

We see Merlin's old magic as an antidote to the N.I.C.E.'s new technology with particular clarity when we examine the literary significance associated with his exhumation from the ground near the woods at Bracton College. When Jane first dreams about Merlin's underground enclosure, Ransom describes the place as being a tunnel under a lot of stones (*THS*, 223). When Mr. Stone (aptly named) of the N.I.C.E. finds the place from which Merlin had broken free and reports back to the Deputy Director, he says the place is a crypt, composed of "Stonework and some Roman brick" (*THS*, 248). Then, when depicting the scene of Merlin's escape, Stone says that something had been "smashed-up" as if with explosives (*THS*, 248). While this might seem like a mere hint at Merlin's command over natural elements, a glance at medieval Arthuriana reveals its deeper and older significance.

In Geoffrey Monmouth's *Historia Regnum Brittanniae*, the first known text to give Arthur and Merlin lengthy consideration, there is a scene in which Merlin tells the King, who is consulting him about making a burial site, to fetch stones from a certain mountain in Ireland. Merlin says these stones contain "a mystery, and a healing virtue against many ailments."[4] He then goes on to describe the history of the stones, which were brought to Ireland from Africa by giants who used them to make baths containing healing water. Once Merlin and his men arrive at Killare in Ireland to bring the large stones, Merlin challenges them, saying, "Now, my men, try what ye can do to fetch me down these stones! Then may ye know whether strength avail more than skill, or skill than strength."[5] The men are unable to move them, so Merlin comes and lays "the stones down so lightly as none would believe."[6]

As we can see from this example, Merlin being encased in stone and surrounded by water at some burial site in *That Hideous Strength* is far more than a simple nod to Arthurian details. Lewis is invoking the Legend's old magic, highlighting those things pertaining to Merlin that foreshadow the triumph and healing of Britain through supernatural power. The mention of the stones and Merlin blasting his way through them sets up, symbolically and literally, the battle between the N.I.C.E.'s modern technology and Logres's spiritual authority. Merlin is asked once again to show how skill aided by supernatural power is more effective than brute strength—as powerful and hideous as that strength might be.

Throughout the whole novel, then, Merlin embodies a past mode of interacting with the world, one which views reality as visible and invisible, physical and magical. As Ransom believes, Merlin's magic is a sort of psychological artifact, "the last survival" of an openness between humanity and nature that, if pursued today, would either be demonic or divine (*THS*, 198). Merlin's magic is "*magia*," the older kind, which loves and reverences Nature, knowing it from within (*THS*, 283). The N.I.C.E. on the other hand, practices "*goeteia* – the brutal surgery from without" (*THS*, 283).

While Merlin's control over nature comes from the perspective of a trusting relationship with nature, Belbury's control comes from knowing external means of manipulation. And their goal is not a relationship with nature but "power exercised by some men over other men with Nature as its instrument."[7] As Lewis says, science, in the time of Merlin, "had not yet tasted man's blood."[8] In the era of Belbury, science is thirsting for it. Merlin comes in to ensure they drink no one else's blood but their own.

The Pendragon and Fisher-King

Another important Arthurian element is Ransom as Pendragon and Fisher-King. These titles, likely foreign to most general readers, are derived from particular strands of Arthurian Legend. Their importance to the Ransom Trilogy is, at least, twofold. First, they are closely bound to Ransom, the uniting character of the Trilogy; and second, they are a converging point for many myths, an intersection through which one can see the many narrative layers at play within the Trilogy as a whole and *That Hideous Strength* in particular. If none of the Arthurian elements in *That Hideous Strength* were closely tied to Ransom, they might feel extraneous and distracting. As they are, however, designations like "Pendragon" and "Fisher-King" continue Ransom's journey and function both as a means through which new things can be introduced and as a glue that holds previously established things together.

"Pendragon" means "chief dragon," and in medieval Arthurian Legend, it is a title for the king and spiritual leader of the Britons.[9] The first time Ransom is clearly given this regal designation occurs rather late in the text. Though chapter 7 is entitled "The Pendragon" and contains Jane's first impression of Ransom, it is in chapter 9 where we learn, through Camilla's dramatic conversation with Jane under an ominous moon, that Ransom *is* the Pendragon and that what they see at St. Anne's is all that is left of Logres (*THS*, 192).

Even after this, however, we hear Ransom referred to by a whole host of other titles—Director, Lord of the House, Master—as well as Pendragon. Only when he faces off with Merlin do we see plainly the heavy meaning and power of his office. When Ransom answers Merlin's three questions and proclaims himself as the Pendragon, the large and rather obstinate Merlin kneels on the ground in submission to Ransom and reverence toward the heavy mantle he carries (*THS*, 271).

Following this encounter, we learn that Ransom is now the spiritual leader of Britain, that he is the King of Logres, and that his office traces all the way back to King Arthur, Uther (Arthur's father), and Cassibelaun (*THS*, 367). Ransom is the seventy-ninth Pendragon from Arthur; the novel ends in anticipation of who will be the eightieth (*THS*, 367). Furthermore, according to sources like Monmouth, the Pendragon is part of a line of kings that goes past Arthur himself, all the way back to Aeneas of Troy.[10] This is a connection Lewis would appreciate, since *The Aeneid*, according to Walter Hooper, was Lewis's "favorite of all books" and one he read repeatedly throughout his life.[11]

By including the office of Pendragon in *That Hideous Strength*, Lewis not only links his universe to the Arthurian Legends, but also refreshes the link between the Arthurian Legends of Britain and the Roman hero Aeneas. This decision significantly broadens the scope of the Trilogy. By means of cutting-edge science, Ransom travels through outer space, only to come back and become a bridge to antiquity. The farther away he goes from human civilization, the deeper he finds himself in human history.

That Hideous Strength continues Ransom's journey by leading him from other-worldly experiences to that which is very much of this world and entwined with the heritage of western civilization. "The Pendragon" is an office rich in meanings and associations from the past. But this is only one of two offices Ransom is given. Lewis balances Ransom's character by making him not only the chief dragon but also the Fisher-King. The two titles function together to create one of the most complex and densely-layered characters in literature.

Although he explicitly ties "Pendragon" back to its Arthurian roots in *That Hideous Strength*, Lewis makes no such attempts with "the Fisher-King." The explanation for Ransom assuming the title is simply that his wealthy sister, Mrs. Fisher-King, bequeathed her fortune to Ransom under the condition that he take on her name and keep watch against "a great danger" hanging over the human race (*THS*, 112). This danger, according to an Indian mystic named Sura (a friend of Mrs. Fisher-King), is said to descend on Britain. The whole episode seems out of place. Perhaps its seeming randomness is what caused Lewis scholar Margaret Hannay to find the explanation weak and unconvincing.[12]

Whatever the strength of its explanation in the text, however, Ransom as Fisher-King clearly has a unique role in *That Hideous Strength*, one which Lewis finds worthy enough to risk the possibility of narrative contrived-ness. The key to understanding this role is, I believe, to always associate "Fisher-King" with a sense of waiting. Ransom takes on the name "Fisher-King" from someone entrusting him with a fortune and a responsibility to wait, "watch for… danger, and to strike when it [comes]" (*THS*, 112). When we look back at Arthurian source material, we find that a waiting Fisher-King is a key figure in "the Grail Quest," a sub-plot of Arthurian romances, emphasized in French versions of the Legend. In Chrétien de Troyes's *Arthurian Romances*, for example, we learn that the Fisher-King is a "very wise and courtly" man whose exact background is rather mysterious, but whose constant waiting for an undefined "benefit" is rather well-known.[13]

In addition to the act of waiting, other key characteristics of the traditional Fisher-King include the two *reasons* why he must wait. The first is that the Fisher-King is nearly always portrayed as being badly wounded. Although the wound is presented differently in different accounts, "it is often the work of a spear, and often in the high groin area."[14] The cause of the wound differs among accounts as well, though the most famous one can be found in Malory, in which the Fisher-King is said to have received his wound by the Dolorous Stroke, stabbed by the very spear used to pierce Christ's side.[15] Because of this wound and its continual bleeding, the Fisher King has, at times, been associated with menstruation and, thereby, with femininity. Ransom's wound is on his heel, and its bleeding is also continuous. In this sense, he resembles the traditional Fisher-King and his gendered association.

The second reason why the Fisher-King must wait is that, according to medieval sources, he "is kept alive by the power of the Grail."[16] His knights search for it as he waits at his castle. He is often seen "reclining on a couch by a fire surrounded by his people" or sitting in his boat and fishing (hence his title, Fisher-King), because he is in too much pain to go hunting.[17] This also fits the description of Ransom, as he is almost always depicted as being sustained by other-worldly life, surrounded by the company at St. Anne's, and waiting on a throne-like dais.

Lewis loved the Grail Quest. The idea of knights searching for something like the Holy Grail, an object imbued with deep spiritual meaning, enchanted him from an early age. In his teens, we find him calling his friend Arthur

Greeves "the spotless knight of the Grail."[18] Later in life, Lewis befriended Charles Williams, whose "purpose in his own Arthurian poetry was to unite the episodic, knightly tales of King Arthur and his court with the spiritual quest for the Holy Grail in a relationship closer than had ever been done in literature."[19] Thus, while layering the title "Fisher-King" on Ransom's character might feel like a stretch for the reader, it was not much of a stretch for the author. And as we have seen, the Fisher-King as a man, one who is wounded and waiting, fits rather seamlessly with certain aspects of Ransom's role.

Yet, I believe the significance of Ransom as Fisher-King is truly unleashed, not when it is considered in isolation, but when it is explored in conjunction with Ransom as Pendragon. The two titles work in tandem to make Ransom a balanced character and, therefore, a more empathetic one. He is a noble king—yet severely wounded. He is a space-traveler—yet has difficulty moving about his own house. As the Pendragon, Ransom is a sort of warrior, akin to Solomon of Israel or Arthur of the Britons, having muscular arms and broad shoulders (*THS*, 139). As the Fisher-King, he is a vulnerable figure, always in pain and therefore limited to his house and domestic affairs. Jane begins the novel by wanting to leave her house in a spirit of independence; Ransom, in the course of the whole story, never once leaves his.

Furthermore, Ransom, unlike perhaps the traditional King Arthur, does not make his most intimate circle a group of men with an abundance of "ladies" and "maidens" in the background. Rather, men and women are equally part of his inner circle. As Benjamin Shogren points out, both genders are represented in him. If chapter 16 of *Perelandra* were not complicated enough, Ransom's thoughts on gender throughout *That Hideous Strength* become even more nuanced when we understand him as someone displaying both masculine *and* feminine traits, each corresponding to the titles Pendragon and Fisher-King respectively.

Shogren takes this a step further and asserts that Ransom as Pendragon and Fisher-King—Pendragon as masculinity and Fisher-King as femininity—are earthly expressions of his interactions with the *eldila*, Malacandra and Perelandra. There is a compelling case to be made for this, particularly in the way Malacandra is described as "one standing armed . . . in ceaseless vigilance, his eyes ever roaming the earth-ward horizon" and Perelandra as one whose eyes "were the curtained gateway to a world of waves and murmurings and wandering airs, of life that rocked in winds" (*PER*, 172). When he speaks with them before the coronation of Tor and Tinidril, Ransom explicitly says that "he of Malacandra was masculine . . . she of Perelandra was feminine" (*PER*, 172). Having visited both Mars and Venus, Ransom, in *That Hideous Strength*, carries within himself the spirits of both Malacandra and Perelandra. In the words of Shogren,

> As Pendragon and Fisher-King, Ransom achieved in the measure due him the opposite virtues of the fundamental polarity of the universe, the ruling iron scepter and the welcoming open hand of Malacandra and Perelandra, of the Father and the Son, of the Masculine and the Feminine.[20]

This has massive implications for the novel. For one, the whole book can be seen as a discussion about the interaction between Masculine and Feminine in the universe. It reinforces the idea that the Trilogy is composed of a structure of opposites. Furthermore, Ransom carrying both the spirits and titles of masculinity and femininity explains why he has such keen insights on gender and its roles in marriage, the home, and faith.

In summary, then, Lewis's use of the Pendragon and Fisher-King might, at first, be a point of confusion. But when the two titles are examined more carefully, it is evident that they contribute substantially to Ransom's identity and to the Trilogy's layered complexity. They bring together in one person at least three overarching myths, which I will restate here for clarity:

First, through "Pendragon," Lewis makes Ransom a representative of King Arthur, whose rulership can be traced back to Aeneas. All of Arthurian Legend is opened up. This explains, for example, why Merlin can feature so prominently. Merlin, traditionally, worked closely with King Arthur.

Second, through "Fisher-King," Lewis loops in the Grail Quest, which is essential to the life and work of one of the biggest influences on the novel, Charles Williams. The Grail Quest also explains, among many things, Ransom's constant waiting and his wound, which he received in the previous book.

Third, by ascribing Pendragon and Fisher-King to the same person (something not normally done in Arthurian Legend), Lewis suggests that the titles are representative of Masculine and Feminine, which in turn are representative of Malacandra and Perelandra.[21] In other words, gendering the titles integrates them into the cosmology of the Trilogy.

Britain and Logres

By including a Pendragon, Lewis carves out a way for there to be a Logres—that is, an Arthurian kingdom, a remnant of Britain that still submits to the spiritual ruler of the land. Yet Lewis keeps the fact of Logres residing in St. Anne's a secret from the reader for quite a while. The first mention we have of the gathering at St. Anne's comes when Denniston describes it as "little household, or company, or society" (*THS*, 111). Later, the word "Logres" is explicitly used when Camilla attributes a quote to Williams's *Taliessin through Logres*, and soon after, when at the top of the garden in St. Anne's, she says that what they see is all that remains of Logres—the rest is "merely Britain" (*THS*, 192). Even in these first two instances, the meaning and function of Logres in the novel begins to emerge. Unlike the Arthurian elements we just discussed, which are concerned with large concepts and overarching mythologies, Lewis's use of Logres highlights the ways in which Arthurian Legend can help redeem Britain in particular. In addition to this particularity, Lewis does not draw from the broad realms of medieval Arthurian Legend for the literary grounding of Logres, but from the "totalizing myth" of his friend and fellow Inkling, Charles Williams.[22]

The notion of Logres and the condition of Britain in particular have, traditionally, been closely tied. Speaking of Logres in relation to many names and places (fictitious though some may be) in Britain is unique to Arthurian Legend, not necessarily to Lewis. What is unique to Lewis is his appropriation of Williams's specific interpretation of Logres. As Brenton D. G. Dickieson puts it, the Company at St. Anne's ties directly back to "Williams' understanding of 'the company' and to his own person."[23] Charles A. Huttar claims that Logres is the *only* element that can be "traced with any certainty to Williams' influence."[24] So what is Williams's Logres? And what does it mean when placed in the Trilogy? As with anything pertaining to Williams, the answer to these questions is not simple. We will need to take a brief detour into his "Arthuriad."

Considered "the most serious Arthurian author" of the Inklings, Williams wrote poetry about the Legends all his life.[25] He published single lyrics in various periodicals throughout his career and, eventually, longer works like *Taliessin through Logres* (1938) and *The Region of the Summer Stars* (1944), both of which Lewis praised as being some of the greatest works of verse written in the century and which undoubtedly influenced his writing of *That Hideous Strength*. What we will be concerned with here, though, is the bit of Arthurian nonfiction he wrote, but never finished, and the comments Lewis made on it before publishing it posthumously as *Arthurian Torso*.

Originally intended to paint a historical and literary picture of the figure of King Arthur, *Arthurian Torso* is Williams's only attempt at writing a scholarly work on Arthurian Legend. The sections on Logres and Lewis's remarks about it are, for our purpose, of special importance. Williams first mentions Logres in relation to the poem, *Lancelot*: "It is here that the name Logres seems to be first used for King Arthur's land; its derivation said to be from the Welsh Lloeger, a land of faerie which was also Britain or within Britain."[26] Right from the start we see Logres connected to King Arthur and imbued with some spiritual, or at least supernatural, presence. It is also used as a name for a region within Britain or for Britain itself. Evidently, Lewis does not change these aspects of Logres in *That Hideous Strength*, as Ransom's Logres sits at the heart of Britain and is continually visited by planetary spirits.

The next development Williams writes of regarding Logres is connected with the Holy Grail. Williams says, "Logres and the Grail are to come together, and the king is to preside at the union."[27] Though there is no "holy object" in *That Hideous Strength*, we have discussed how "the Fisher-King" is a title associated with the Grail Quest; and, by the end of the novel, Ransom can be said to "preside" over the union between Mark and Jane. But this does not strike at the heart of Williams's Logres.

What makes Williams's Logres unique and particularly profound is his portrayal of it as a point of light in the darkness, a seed of hope in a sterile land. Here, Lewis says, we touch "upon one of Williams's fundamental principles . . . illustrated from the whole history of Judaism and Christianity. Israel is always failing, but there is always a 'remnant' left; out of that failure at its nadir, and that remnant at its smallest, salvation flows."[28] When we consider Logres in light of *this*, its peculiar role in *That Hideous Strength* begins making sense. It is not some little club or coterie, but a Williamsesque Logres, whose original pattern is seen in scripture. It is a faithful tribe in the midst of an idolatrous nation.

Lewis continues this idea of a remnant in another work. He says, "Arthurian Logres is for [Williams] the civilization to which the Grail was offered and which failed . . . to rise to the occasion, and so dwindled from being Logres into being merely Britain."[29] In addition to Logres as a remnant of Arthur's Kingdom, here we see Logres introduced in light of a tension which runs through *That Hideous Strength* from start to finish: Logres versus Britain. Margaret Hannay is right in calling Logres "the Arthurian ideal" which contrasts with Britain, "secular reality."[30] It is a division Lewis carried over from his friend. Yet, it is important to always remember that Logres and Britain "are not two worlds, but one."[31] Logres and Britain are not in opposition like alien versus native, but like yin versus yang. Logres does not hope to see Britain obliterated, but Britain restored to its true self.

This is where things take a surprising turn, especially for those readers living in countries other than Britain. Up to this point in *That Hideous Strength*, Arthurian Legend has been described in very British contexts. The first outline we get of it in the text is through Dr. Dimble, who discusses it in relation to Merlin, a figure who embodies the tension between Rome and Britain, between the Christian conquerors and the local Druids. Then, later in the text, we find Logres pitted against Britain. With this trajectory established, it seems that we should next anticipate a culmination in the restoration of a national identity; the book should get very "pro-Britain." But this never comes to pass. In fact, the reverse happens. Just when we expect Arthurian Legend to reach the height of its Britishness, it becomes universalized—one name for something we all experience.

We see this at the end of the novel, after everything is accomplished and

Belbury is destroyed. The company at St. Anne's is gathered round a fire after dinner, and Camilla asks Ransom, "Why Logres, Sir?" (*THS*, 365). Ransom defers to Dimble, who explains that their involvement with Logres stems from a discovery that Arthurian Legend is not just literary art, but a body of mostly true and historical accounts. "There was a moment in the Sixth Century," he describes, "when something that is always trying to break through into this country nearly succeeded. Logres was our name for it—it will do as well as another" (*THS*, 367). Dimble's answer here begins the most important shift in the book for our understanding of Logres and Arthurian Legend at large in the scope of the Trilogy. Not only does Lewis start hinting that Arthurian Legend is simply a way Britain participates in a larger and more universal story, he defictionalizes it as well; he indicates that Arthurian Legend is a collection of symbols—outward and visible signs of an inward, invisible grace.

Dimble goes on to say that something called Britain is always haunted by something called Logres. "This haunting," he says, "is no peculiarity of ours. Every people has its own haunter" (*THS*, 368). What we expected would end in "pro-British" admonitions, ends in pro-Spiritual, and therefore universal admonitions. When we thought we had reached the top of one country, we find ourselves at the top of the world. The names we often use to exclude and limit (*Arthurian* Legend, *Greek* Mythology, *Eastern* Meditation) are really the things which demonstrate membership in a universal story. They are part of the same signification system which all peoples use to point to the Spiritual pressing in on the physical (*THS*, 367).

This deepens the use of Arthurian Legend significantly. It makes it a part of something transtemporal and trans-spatial. Lewis is right, "Nations, cultures, arts, civilisations—these are mortal" and therefore passing.[32] To write about Britain alone would be to comment on a ship already disappearing in the horizon, for, as Lewis says, "All that is not eternal is eternally out of date."[33] *That Hideous Strength* is relevant to modern culture not primarily because it addresses so many modern issues, but because it addresses so many eternal issues, bearing, in our case, a rather technological face.

Avalon

Avalon is the fourth and final Arthurian element we will discuss in *That Hideous Strength*. Perhaps no other thread runs more fully through all of Lewis's creative works than Joy, than that "unsatisfied desire which is itself more desirable than any other satisfaction."[34] Lewis calls it *Sehnsucht*. This desire, "from a depth not of years but of centuries," akin to the "enormous bliss" of Eden which Milton speaks about, takes many forms in

Lewis's writing.[35] In the Ransom Trilogy, it is represented by Avalon and is specifically associated with, and eventually located on, Perelandra. This might be less obvious to readers because the name "Avalon," as we know it, is never actually mentioned in the Trilogy. In fact, Lewis seems to indicate his liberal appropriation of Avalon by presenting it, even linguistically, one step removed from the way it appears in Arthurian Legend proper—though, in the traditional Arthuriana, there are orthographic variations as well. The two times it is mentioned in *That Hideous Strength* (the only book in which Avalon is explicitly referenced), it is called "Abhalljin" and "Aphallin," which are, supposedly, old forms of "Avalon." Lewis's spelling, location, and peopling of Avalon might stray from traditional Arthuriana, but the heart and essence of Avalon is still intact.

Throughout the Trilogy, Avalon serves its traditional role as a place of healing and an object of longing. In early medieval narratives, the mortally wounded Arthur goes there to be cured. In later medieval narratives, Arthur is escorted to the mystical isle by magicians and enchantresses, supernatural forces reminiscent of the eldila. Ransom, who holds a title passed down from King Arthur, also intends to go there for healing by way of supernatural forces (*THS*, 366). The connection is clear.

But much more than a place of healing, Avalon, particularly in the Trilogy, is a place people long for. Avalon might only be mentioned in *That Hideous Strength*, but what it represents—painful, yet sweet, desire—courses through all three books. It courses through the Trilogy because it is the theme of its author's life. What holds the Trilogy together is Lewis himself, and what features so prominently in Lewis is desire, is Joy, is Avalon.

Sehnsucht might strike us as a vague or distant concept, but for Lewis, it was central. It denoted an acute longing—paradoxically both sweet and painful—which nothing in this world could fulfill, which is itself the closest thing we can get to its fulfillment. The longing has contours, borders, indications of shape and form. Lewis famously said that if we have longings that nothing in this world can satisfy, the most probable explanation is that we were made for another world.[36] The mystery and charm of "another world" might be, to some, mere child's play, figurative language, or, as the Fox says in *Till We Have Faces*, all "lies of poets."[37] Still, for others (especially American Evangelicals), this other "world" might be a way of saying "heaven"—the place where the Friend and Savior Jesus is, where there are pearly gates, streets of gold, crystal seas, and loved ones from all lands and eras. But for Lewis, this other world was at once more literal and more spiritual. If one were to have asked him what it looks like, he would have been able to paint pictures and "supposals." In fact, he did. One of them is Perelandra.

The significance of Avalon in *That Hideous Strength* is greatly deepened by the symbolic nature of Perelandra. Unlike the other Arthurian elements we discussed, this "cup-shaped land of Abhalljin, beyond the seas of Lur" is not so much something we learn about in *That Hideous Strength* as it is something we learned about in the previous novel that is given an Arthurian name in the present one (*THS*, 271). In the preface to *That Hideous Strength*, Lewis says that the novel can be read independently from the others (*THS*, 8). However, if one were to read *That Hideous Strength* without reading *Perelandra*, both the notion of Avalon and Ransom's inconsolable longing for it would remain mysteries.

Perhaps the clearest path for us in trying to understand Perelandra as a symbol of Joy—a symbol that is only later brought into an Arthurian landscape—is an analysis of Perelandra as a redeemed "system" of imagery.[38] Lewis was deeply affected by his moments of *Sehnsucht* from childhood onward and wrote about his longing in a number of ways. Joy was one central desire with a hundred faces. In his preface to the 1950 edition of *Dymer* (one of his first publications, released twenty-four years earlier while he was still a materialistic atheist), he says,

> Such longing is itself the very reverse of wishful thinking: it is more like thoughtful wishing. But it throws off what may be called systems of imagery. One among many such which it had thrown off for me was the Hesperian or Western Garden system, mainly derived from Euripides, Milton, Morris, and the early Yeats.[39]

Lewis goes on to explain that at the time *Dymer* was written, he understood Joy in "the Fool's Way" or "the Way of the Disillusioned 'Sensible Man,'" as he would later call them.[40] He experienced longing and hope for something that transcends earthly reality, but falsely put his hope in the things through which the longings came, not the things to which they pointed. He read about the Hesperian gardens in Greek mythology and believed that, if only he could reach such gardens, he would be satisfied. He did not recognize that the gardens themselves were a system of imagery which simply points to a place where true fulfillment lies. "These things," Lewis says, "—the beauty, the memory of our own past—are good images of what we really desire; but if they are mistaken for the thing itself, they turn into dumb idols, breaking the hearts of their worshippers."[41]

Lewis was in this brokenhearted state when he wrote "Dymer." He had idolized the Hesperian gardens, believing them to be the actual place where Joy exists, but they let him down. He says, "Instead of repenting of my idolatry I spat upon the images which only my own misunderstanding greed had ever made into idols."[42] Lewis thought the signposts were the destination and, because they were not, discarded them bitterly. He did not yet realize that, though they were not the destination, they could, nonetheless, be useful in pointing him to it. Only years later, after his conversion to Christianity, did he understand and harness their true use. Once Lewis understood the Hesperian gardens as a system of imagery, he could love them for what they are and not expect unreasonable fulfillment from them. He could, in other words, redeem the system of imagery which he cast aside. Instances of this redemption are everywhere in his writings: the myth of the Greek god, Hesperus, and his three daughters singing in a garden around a golden tree with fruit at the western edge of the world worked on Lewis's imagination in a deep way. Yet, in no other work does the Hesperian system of imagery, in its redeemed glory, feature more prominently and robustly than in *Perelandra*. Here, Lewis sets his love for the myth free, so much so, in fact, that Ransom wonders, "Were all the things which appeared as mythology on earth scattered through other worlds as realities?" (*PER*, 40). When Ransom wakes up on a floating island, we are told he "recognised the garden of Hesperides at once" (*PER*, 40). From the bubble trees to the docile dragon, the landscape and atmosphere of Perelandra bespeak Lewis's abiding love for the Hesperian setting. It is appropriate that Lewis sets the garden of Hesperides on Perelandra because the primary narratives he is working from in that novel are the creation narratives found in Genesis and in Milton's *Paradise Lost*. Both depict Eden and both resonate with the Hesperian imagery of the Greeks. Milton was well aware of this. In *Paradise Lost*, he envisions Eden, saying, "Groves whose rich trees wept odorous gums and balm, / Others whose fruit burnished with golden rind / Hung amiable, Hesperian fables true."[43] And in another work, *Comus*, (which Lewis thought was "one of the most perfect things in English poetry") Milton describes the Hesperian garden at some length.[44] He even places it outside of earth, a decision Lewis defended in a letter sent to the *Times Literary Supplement*, when *That Hideous Strength* was first being published.[45] Perhaps his defense was a preemptive move.

Lewis, therefore, incorporates Hesperian imagery into his science fiction through two routes: he draws from ancient sources he was familiar with and also from Milton, whom he loved. It is clear that the setting of Perelandra contains the Hesperian garden and that the Hesperian garden was a primary system of imagery Lewis used to express his longing or Joy. But how does a planet built on the Judeo-Christian creation narrative and certain settings from Greek mythology become Arthurian? What special role does Avalon play by being retroactively placed on Perelandra? One way of answering this is to pattern our conclusions after the ones we discussed in relation to the Pendragon and Fisher-King, enumerating the ways that Avalon functions as a nexus point of converging myths. However, this does not seem to capture the notion of hopefulness surrounding the mere mention of

Avalon nor the underlying orientation of longing, of *Sehnsucht*, itself. I believe the significance of the Arthurian Avalon in *That Hideous Strength*—something that brings to mind Perelandra and all its associations—is not found by examining it as a representation of immediate complexities, but of future simplicities. While the other Arthurian elements are part of a complex scheme of redemption in this life, Avalon functions as a symbol of simple glorification in another life. It symbolizes another kind of life, the life that exists in "the Third Heaven," "where an organism can last practically forever" (*THS*, 367; 366). Avalon is an Arthurian element that is derived from Celtic tradition—the Celts who "had ideas of the paradisal west going far beyond anything Greece could offer.'"[46] Lewis used the Arthurian idea of Avalon in *That Hideous Strength* rather than hearkening back to the Greek Hesperus not simply to superimpose another layer of mythology, but to pick up where Greece left off. The garden of Hesperides had run its farthest and Avalon picked up the next leg of the journey. By using Avalon as a symbol for Joy, Lewis was able to shift *That Hideous Strength* away from the pre-Christian notions of paradise and Eden and move it towards an ideal that is compatible with an era of history that contains the dystopian world of Belbury and the Christian remnant of St. Anne's. Arthurian Legend picks up where Greek mythology ends because, as established at the beginning of *That Hideous Strength*, Arthurian Legend is a hinge and turning point between the paganism of the Druids and the Christianity of the Romans. This falls in line with a running theme throughout *Perelandra*, that the Incarnation changed all of history, that Christ ushered in a new order: "Since our Beloved became a man," Tinidril says, everything is changed, "there is a time that turns a corner and everything this side of it is new" (*PER*, 54).

Arthurian Legend serves as a sort of stepping stone between Ransom's experience of pagan myth on Perelandra and his Christianity on Thulcandra. Avalon takes into consideration the Incarnation and brings together the Edenic atmosphere of Genesis, the Hesperian gardens of Lewis's youth, and the future life promised by Christianity. Joy proves itself once again to be one central longing with a hundred faces.

When considered together, the Arthurian elements in *That Hideous Strength* are deeply mythological, literary, and personal to Lewis. They are not simply an incorporation of outside sources, but are an expression of symbols and narratives that Lewis internalized. After all the wild adventures in Mars and Venus, these glimpses of Arthurian Legend are a reminder that the Silent Planet still has many stories to tell.

Endnotes

1 Margaret Drabble, ed. *The Oxford Companion to English Literature* (Oxford, UK: Oxford University Press, 1985), 43.
2 Walter Hooper, introduction to *The Weight of Glory: And Other Addresses*, by C. S. Lewis (New York: HarperCollins, 2009), 14.
3 Drabble, 43.
4 Geoffrey of Monmouth, *The History of the Kings of Britain*, trans. Sebastian Evans, rev. Charles W. Dunn (New York: E. P. Dutton & Co., 1958), 164.
5 Monmouth, 166.
6 Monmouth, 166.
7 C. S. Lewis, *Abolition of Man* (New York: HarperCollins, 2015), 55.
8 C. S. Lewis, "De Descriptione Temporum," in *Selected Literary Essays* by C. S. Lewis, ed. Walter Hooper (New York: Cambridge University Press, 1969), 7.
9 Drabble, 1019.
10 Monmouth, 5.
11 Walter Hooper, foreword to *C. S. Lewis's Lost Aeneid: Arms and the Exile*, ed. A. T. Reyes (New Haven, CT: Yale University Press, 2011), xii.
12 Margaret Hannay, "Arthurian and Cosmic Myth in *That Hideous Strength*," *Mythlore: A Journal of J. R. R. Tolkien, C. S. Lewis, Charles Williams, General Fantasy and Mythic Studies 2*, no. 2 (1970), 9.
13 Chrétien De Troyes, *Arthurian Romances*, trans. D. D. R. Owen (London, UK: Everyman Classic, 1993), 420–21.
14 Benjamin Shogren, "Those Kings of Lewis' Logres: Arthurian Figures as Lewisian Genders in *That Hideous Strength*," in *The Inklings and King Arthur: J. R. R. Tolkien, Charles Williams, C. S. Lewis, & Owen Barfield on the Matter of Britain*, ed. Sørina Higgins (Berkeley, CA: Apocryphile, 2017), 405.
15 Malory, *Works*, 2nd ed., ed. Eugène Vinaver (Oxford, UK: Oxford University Press, 1971), 714.
16 Shogren, 405.
17 Shogren, 405.
18 C. S. Lewis to Arthur Greeves, May 11, 1915, in *The Collected Letters of C. S. Lewis Volume 1: Family Letters (1905–1931)*, ed. Walter Hooper (New York: HarperCollins, 2000), 118.
19 Sørina Higgins, "The Matter of Logres: Arthuriana and the Inklings," in *The Inklings and King Arthur: J. R. R. Tolkien, Charles Williams, C. S. Lewis, & Owen Barfield on the Matter of Britain*, ed. Sørina Higgins (Berkeley, CA: Apocryphile, 2017), 49.
20 Shogren, 411.
21 Shogren, 387.
22 Higgins, 46.
23 Brenton D. G. Dickieson, "Mixed Metaphors and Hyperlinked Worlds: A Study of Intertextuality in C. S. Lewis' Ransom Cycle," in *The Inklings and King Arthur: J. R. R. Tolkien, Charles Williams, C. S. Lewis, & Owen Barfield on the Matter of Britain*, ed. Sørina Higgins (Berkeley, CA: Apocryphile, 2017), 106.
24 Charles A. Huttar, "Houses of Healing: The Idea of Avalon in Inklings Fiction and Poetry," in *The Inklings and King Arthur: J. R. R. Tolkien, Charles Williams, C. S. Lewis, & Owen Barfield on the Matter of Britain*, ed. Sørina Higgins (Berkeley, CA: Apocryphile, 2017), 116.
25 Higgins, 45.
26 Charles Williams and C. S. Lewis, *Arthurian Torso: Containing the Posthumous Fragments of The Figure of Arthur* (London, UK: Oxford University Press, 1969), 54.
27 Williams and Lewis, *Arthurian Torso*, 73.
28 Williams and Lewis, *Arthurian Torso*, 134.

29 C. S. Lewis, "Charles Williams, *Taliessin Through Logres* (London: Oxford University Press, 1945)," in *Image and Imagination*, by C. S. Lewis, ed. Walter Hooper (New York: Cambridge University Press, 2013), 138.

30 Hannay, 7.

31 Yannick Imbert, "From Myth to History and Back Again: Inklings Arthuriana in Historical Context," in *The Inklings and King Arthur: J. R. R. Tolkien, Charles Williams, C. S. Lewis, & Owen Barfield on the Matter of Britain*, ed. Sørina Higgins (Berkeley, CA: Apocryphile, 2017), 187.

32 C. S. Lewis, "The Weight of Glory," in *The Weight of Glory: And Other Addresses*, ed. Walter Hooper (New York: HarperCollins, 2009), 46.

33 C. S. Lewis, *The Four Loves* (New York: Mariner Books, 2012), 137.

34 Lewis, *Surprised by Joy* (New York: HarperCollins 2017), 19.

35 Lewis, *Surprised by Joy*, 17.

36 C. S. Lewis, *Mere Christianity: A revised and amplified edition, with a new introduction, of the three books, Broadcast Talks, Christian Behavior, and Beyond Personality* (New York: HarperCollins, 2015), 136–37.

37 C. S. Lewis, *Till We Have Faces: A Myth Retold* (New York: Mariner Books, 2012), 8.

38 Another term for this system of imagery is "myth" as it is described by Julianne Johnson in Chapter 1.

39 C. S. Lewis, "Preface by the Author to the 1950 Edition," in *Narrative Poems* by C. S. Lewis, ed. Walter Hooper (New York: Harcourt, 1969), 4.

40 Lewis, *Mere Christianity*, 136.

41 Lewis, "The Weight of Glory," 30–31.

42 Lewis, "Preface by the Author to the 1950 Edition," 5.

43 John Milton, *Paradise Lost*, ed. William Kerrigan, John Rumrich, and Stephen M. Fallon (New York: Random House, 2007), 132.

44 C. S. Lewis to Arthur Greeves, August 4, 1917, in *The Collected Letters of C. S. Lewis Volume I: Family Letters (1905–1931)*, ed. Walter Hooper (New York: HarperCollins, 2000), 332.

45 Huttar, 119.

46 Geoffrey Ashe, *Mythology of the British Isles* (North Pomfret, VT: Trafalgar, 1990), 262.

RANSOMING LOGRES

DANIEL Z. HSIEH

Arthurian Legend and Restoration

With the literary and historical details of the previous chapter in mind, let us continue our discussion by highlighting the distinct ways in which Arthurian Legend functions in *That Hideous Strength* to provide insights into the nature of human flourishing. This "'tall story' about devilry," becomes an even taller story, reaches even higher heights, when we consider how Lewis uses Arthurian Legend to paint a compelling picture of what spiritual restoration can look like on earth (*THS*, 7).

Perhaps, what emerges more prominently to readers of *That Hideous Strength* than restoration is a desperate *need* for restoration. Restoration comes, but only after a sort of hell-on-earth wreaks havoc. Why does Britain appear so desperately broken in Lewis's portrayal? To understand its restoration, it is helpful to understand its fallenness. To understand redemption, it is important to understand our sin.

According to Christopher Gaertner, the Inklings characterized modern civilization as a "demythologized era" in which "a new idolatry has been set up."[1] "This idolatry," Gaertner says, "is positivist materialism, mathematical and biological reductionism, and consequently, technocratic utilitarianism. Humanity experiences itself as subject, an inward-turned isolation from the objects in nature."[2] In essence, it is a corruption of how humankind relates to the most meaningful things in life and how it perceives itself. We are back at the Fall and the book of Genesis. The Catechism of the Catholic Church helpfully defines the Fall this way:

> Adam and Eve immediately lose the grace of original holiness. They become afraid of the God of whom they have conceived a distorted image.... The harmony in which they found themselves, thanks to original justice, is now destroyed: the control of the soul's spiritual faculties over the body is shattered; the union of man and woman becomes subject to tensions, their relations henceforth marked by lust and domination. Harmony with creation is broken: visible creation has become alien and hostile to man.[3]

In essence, as so many theologians have done, the Fall can be summarized as the severing of four relationships: 1) humans and God, 2) humans and humans, 3) humans and nature, and 4) humans and themselves. Christ has come and promised reconciliation, but until then, we live in between, in the "already but not yet." This is exactly where Lewis places Ransom and the company at St. Anne's. Ransom is holy, but still earthly. He uses crutches. He is aware that his interactions with *eldila* strain his human senses. He awaits his return to Perelandra with eager expectation. Likewise, St. Anne's is a beautiful place, holding to a different standard of values, but it still lies outside of town as a conscious minority.

Considering the eschatological placement of *That Hideous Strength*, we begin to see how Lewis uses Arthurian Legend to give us a picture of what redeemed, but unglorified, life can look like. I hope to show that, though Lewis may not have mapped out the correspondence between them, the four Arthurian elements we discussed in the previous chapter (Merlin, the Pendragon and Fisher-King, Logres, and Avalon) each depict a kind of earthly restoration of the relationships shattered at the Fall. In this way, the Trilogy not only warns us about the various evils to avoid in this world, but also warns us against living our lives *only* in avoidance of them. It tells us not only to hate what is evil, but also to cling to what is good.[4] It urges us to resist a certain existence in order to embrace a better one. And it gives us a picture of what this better existence can look like.

The Pendragon and Fisher-King: Restoration between Humans and God

When we finally encounter Ransom in *That Hideous Strength*, we discover that he is greatly changed. He is no longer simply Ransom the philologist, though his facility with languages and love for probing the depths of "essential speech" is still evident (*THS*, 319). Neither is he simply Ransom the space traveler, though his "disappearances" from earth form the structure of the story MacPhee tells Jane when describing him (*THS*, 188). There is a new quality about Ransom, a quality deeper and more transcendent than anything he has hitherto embodied. He is now the Pendragon and Fisher King—but even Arthurian Legend does not fully explain the supernatural quality of his character.

I believe this new dimension we see of Ransom in *That Hideous Strength*, is his resemblance to Christ Himself and to the perfect obedience Christ exhibited in every aspect of life. Ransom, through all his roles and Arthurian titles, becomes a model for us of what Christ-likeness—of what a restored relationship with God—can look like on Earth.

According to some theologians, one primary way that Christ fulfills the Old Testament and becomes the final mediator between God and humankind is by becoming the *Munus Triplex*, the "Triple Cure," the one who takes on the three roles of prophet, priest, and king. These three roles or offices, fulfilled by separate individuals throughout Israelite history, are brought together and perfected in the single person of Christ. It follows, then, that if we are to be conformed more and more to the likeness of Christ, we will inevitably begin reflecting, to some degree, these roles ourselves and begin helping others to have a restored relationship with God. This is exactly what we see when we look at Ransom, the Pendragon and Fisher-King.

As a king (one who is given authority "from above"), Ransom rules St. Anne's, protecting and providing for those under him, giving orders and relaying orders that he is given.[5] He literally holds the regal title by way of his Arthurian name, Fisher-King. When Jane first enters the Blue Room, the part of the house in which Ransom stays, she compares the whole experience to being in "a throne room" (*THS*, 140). When she lays eyes on him, "the bright solar blend of king and lover and magician" causes her to taste "the word *King*" for the first time (*THS*, 140). Ransom is often depicted with sunlight and gold, reminiscent of kings from almost every civilization. But, unlike the power-hungry monarchs that fill so many pages of our history books, Ransom is always acutely aware that his kingship is something he stewards, not something he merits. At one point, he tells MacPhee that his claim to authority rests neither on himself nor on consensus of those staying at St. Anne's (*THS*, 196). He sees his office of king as a role he plays, not his status or worth as a human being. And this recognition enables him to model what royal power, wielded humbly and tactfully, can look like.

Second, as a prophet (one who speaks "to the people on behalf of God"), Ransom stands between the Oyéresu and the company at St. Anne's, relaying to the company what his Masters foresee and command.[6] His intimacy with the Oyéresu and their *eldila* is constant throughout the novel. Ever since he has come back from space, he receives "continual visits" from them (*THS*, 188). Jane almost interacts with one when she first meets him. When Merlin refuses to believe that Ransom is the master at St. Anne's and tells him to call upon his master, Ransom replies, "'Do you really wish . . . that I call upon my Masters?'" (*THS*, 269). Ransom's relationship with the Oyéresu is analogous to the relationships that Moses and Isaiah had with the Lord. His intimacy with his Masters leads to prophetic insights that benefit, not just himself, but all those who come in contact with him. His attunement to heavenly powers shows us how regular communion with God can lead to prophetic roles which can aid in the spiritual and practical restoration of a community.

Third, as a priest (one who speaks "to God on behalf of the people"), Ransom intercedes with the Oyéresu on behalf of the company at St. Anne's and is associated with the sacraments.[7] Ransom represents both the Oyéresu to the company and the company to the Oyéresu. For example, after listening to Jane and her desire to join the company, Ransom tells her to talk to her husband while he consults his "authorities" (*THS*, 146). He consults his authorities on Jane's behalf because he knows Jane cannot be in the presence of the Oyéresu without experiencing trauma.

While instances of this intercession are present throughout the novel, it is Ransom's association with the Eucharist that, perhaps, indicates his priestly role more than anything. The only time we see Ransom at a meal is when he is on a sofa and is served red wine and bread—the elements of the Eucharist (*THS*, 146). When he is about to start eating, we are told, "With these words he broke the bread and poured himself out a glass of wine"—actions and descriptions similar to those of Christ at the Last Supper (*THS*, 146). These sacramental associations, together with the parallel between successive "Pendragons" and apostolic succession, lend themselves to viewing Ransom in a very spiritual and priestly light. In fact, Ransom's kingliness is reinforced by images of "battle, marriage, priesthood, mercy, and power"—priesthood being in the center of them (*THS*, 140).

Ransom's resemblance to Christ and his embodiment of prophet, priest, and king is quite deep. Yet, deeper still is the absolute obedience that he, in his various roles, shows his Masters. He does not obey his Masters like a servile employee submitting to his supervisors out of duty and necessity. He obeys them like musicians obeying a conductor or like Dante obeying Virgil in the *Divine Comedy*. Submission is simultaneously productive, proper, and delightful. Perhaps this is why Ransom compares obedience to a dance rather than a drill (*THS*, 147); or why the apostle Paul, in a single letter, can give long lists of instructions and yet continually say "rejoice in the Lord"; or why Christ tells us to obey His commands—that our "joy may be complete."[8]

Ransom recognizes that his true power as Pendragon and Fisher-King is not exercised by taking things into his own hands but by submitting them to his authorities, no matter how ridiculous their orders might seem. At one point, MacPhee comments on the absurdity of attempting to defeat the N.I.C.E. by staying within the walls of St. Anne's, pacing around, cultivating gardens, and training animals (*THS*, 189). He is, of course, looking only at outside appearances, regarding Ransom's patience as a lack of initiative rather than an act of obedience. It is no wonder that, in the end, he is forbidden to leave St. Anne's with the others to go search for Merlin. Unlike Ransom's patient obedience, MacPhee's fixation on empirical observation hinders his capacity for spiritual submission.

At the end of the novel, Ransom reveals the secret to St. Anne's success and a secret to spiritual success in general. He says that they had fulfilled what was asked of them, that they had "obeyed and waited" (*THS*, 368). It is a hard lesson, especially when one's enemies are a group like the N.I.C.E., which is constantly moving, taking over colleges, starting riots, and obtaining emergency powers from the government. Sitting patiently like a waiting Fisher-King in the rushing waters of modern society is no easy task. But, in some circumstances, that might just be exactly what is required.

Logres: Restoration of Human Relationships

After pages and pages of Mark's college drama, insecurities, and desperate attempts to penetrate the social rings of Belbury, Logres is a breath of fresh air. While the N.I.C.E. is a collection of busy-bodies with no strong center of gravity, the company at St. Anne's resembles a version—albeit, a very eclectic version—of King Arthur's court, where round tables establish true equality via mutual submission to a common authority. The difference between the N.I.C.E. and St. Anne's is as clear as night and day. In fact, one of the first times Jane visits St. Anne's, she literally sees it as a window of sunlight in a world of dark fog: she gets off the train and walks toward the manor, which, in contrast to the surrounded areas is "almost dazzling white" (*THS*, 134). It emerges as an island of sunshine, a city on a hill, a remnant of Israel in the midst of a plagued Egypt where there is "darkness that can be felt."[9]

Similar to the way the Pendragon and Fisher-King represent restoration between humans and God, the Arthurian element of Logres represents restoration between humans and humans. It is a community that is kept from degenerating into a collective. Like Lewis's description of true literary experiences, living in Logres "heals the wound, without undermining the privilege, of individuality."[10] How does it do this? What is the secret to this unique society?

I believe Logres garners its beauty and wonder in *That Hideous Strength* from being the exact opposite of the N.I.C.E., from being the complete anti-Belbury.

Of course, in reality, Logres's beauty and wonder is in no way dependent on Belbury, for Belbury is simply a corrupted Logres. Any vestige it has of being a productive society is derived from a goodness outside itself. In the words of Plato, "the wholly bad and perfectly unjust are also perfectly unable to accomplish anything."[11] The restorative nature of Logres, then, is this: unlike Belbury, which is built on vagueness, earning, and confusion of positions, Logres is built on hierarchy, grace, and clarity of roles.

Belbury as a place of deceit and oppression needs no detailing. Its atmosphere is established the moment it is introduced and sustained monotonously through the entire book. Granted, things are revealed, like "the Head" being the literal head of Alcasan. And personnel change, like Hingest being murdered upon leaving. But the predominant aura of the place stays the same. It is a static environment of fears and lies, held together by empty promises, the gibberish of which leads to its final destruction.

In almost every way, the workings of the N.I.C.E. are the fictionalized version of Lewis's famous address, "The Inner Ring." If *The Abolition of Man* is the serious, philosophical treatment of the larger themes in *That Hideous Strength*, then "The Inner Ring" is the serious, moral treatment of Belbury's toxic dynamics. Mark is the quintessential example of one seeking to be "in the *know*." He is constantly trying to figure out and advance in the ranks of "the second or unwritten systems" of Belbury.[12] Lewis compares these social maneuvers to peeling through the concentric rings of an onion—"if you succeed," Lewis says, "there will be nothing left."[13] Belbury is just "good" and "true" enough to be horrifically destructive, but just evil enough to be boring, hollow, and ultimately reduced to nothing but a bloody mush on the floor of a banquet hall.

Logres, on the other hand, shines as a beautiful bastion of hierarchy, grace, and clarity of roles. Ransom is the resplendent head of St. Anne's, and everyone submits readily to his good rule. Miss Ironwood curtsies politely before him, and the otherwise-obstinate Merlin bows to him when he learns that he is the Pendragon of Logres (*THS*, 139; 271). When Ransom is dressed in his blue robe and standing mysteriously at the top of the stairs, Jane's doubts verge on feelings of betrayal, which only prove her usual trust and loyalty towards him (*THS*, 275). Unlike the empty center of Belbury, Logres restores relationships between people by allowing them to share the common delight of submission to a good sovereign.

Furthermore, while Belbury is built on a system of striving, Logres is built on a foundation of grace. At Belbury, no one is even given the dignity of admission, only threats at the prospect of leaving. At Logres, however, admission is a great moment and privilege, and no one is under fear of expulsion. Mrs. Maggs is as much a member as Grace Ironwood, for they are all the "Director's charities" (*THS*, 165). In fact, Lewis's depiction of Logres is like his depiction of Heaven in

The Great Divorce. During one of the dialogues in that work, a ghost indignantly remarks, "'I'm not asking for anybody's bleeding charity,'" and a solid person replies, "'Ask for the Bleeding Charity. Everything is here for the asking and nothing can be bought.'"[14] Ransom might no longer be in Perelandra, but he certainly brings back to Earth the attitude inculcated in him during the coronation of Tor and Tinidril: "'All is gift'" (*PER*, 180). Logres is a symbol of restored relationships between humans, for it sets all its members on a foundation of grace. It brings all people to the level ground that is the foot of the cross.

Finally, although all the members of Logres are fundamentally united through their participation in grace, each member, nonetheless, is given a clear role to play. Some things seem to run very democratically, like shared kitchen duties between men and women, while other things are more individualized (*THS*, 164–65). MacPhee for example, often seems out of place in the trusting, reverential atmosphere of Logres, but he is no less significant in the role he plays. As Ransom says, he is the resident sceptic, "a very important office" (*THS*, 181). Everyone is a valuable part of the whole, which makes work—one's fulfilment of an ordained function—something dignified and even sacred. Relationships between humans are restored, not when "separate selves are pooled and . . . sink back into sub-individuality," but when separate selves are given worth through grace and, as an extension of that grace, are privileged with unique roles to play, interconnected but distinguishable.[15]

Logres, then, is a place of apparent paradoxes. On the one hand, there is a strong sense of hierarchy; on the other, there is a strong sense of shared worth. All are established on a foundation of grace, yet all must work, fulfilling a unique role for everyone else. Everyone belongs to each other, but no one loses his or her individual identity. If Belbury is an embodiment of "The Inner Ring," Logres is an embodiment of Lewis's address, "Membership," for in it he says that "worldlings are so monotonously alike compared with the almost fantastic variety of the saints. Obedience is the road to freedom, humility the road to pleasure, unity the road to personality."[16] Logres or St. Anne's—itself, according to Sanford Schwartz, bringing to mind Saint Anne, "the mother of the Virgin Mary"—is certainly one such collection of various saints.[17] Through hierarchy, grace, and clarity of roles, human relationships are restored at Logres and shown their particular excellence.

Merlin: Restoring the Relationship between Humans and Creation

As a wizard, Merlin is endowed with inherent, special powers. But, unlike modern portrayals of him, Lewis's depiction of this Arthurian figure highlights, not so much his power *over* nature, but the power *of* nature itself, which he harnesses.

We discussed in the previous chapter that, while Belbury is about the business of enslaving nature as a means of controlling other men, Merlin is concerned with having a relationship with nature, reverencing it from within, rather than manipulating it from without (*THS*, 283). For Belbury, the natural world is "something dead," but, for Merlin, "the spiritual qualities of Nature" make it an entity with life and character (*THS*, 283). Merlin represents what a restored relationship with nature can look like by consistently respecting the "personality" of nature. We see this particularly in the language he uses to describe his interactions with the woods and fields of Logres and the way he treats animals.

It is a grave fallacy to assume that the only alternative to pantheism is the ruthless exploitation of the natural world. Just because we do not regard nature as our god does not mean we can regard ourselves as *its* god. According to Christianity, humankind ought to relate with the natural world as fellow creation, almost as fellow creatures.[18] Humans and nature can exist in harmony because they share the same God, come from the same creative mind, are derived from the same Person. The language Merlin uses to describe his interactions with nature illustrates this point. When explaining to Ransom that he can cure pain, he expresses his desire to go about the woods of Logres and "renew old acquaintance" (*THS*, 184). Merlin always refers to nature like he would an old friend. He even tells Ransom that he and nature "have much to say to one another" and that Logres is in need of his "commerce with field and water" (*THS*, 284–85).

Of course, as a wizard, Merlin is especially attuned to the "inherent mythos" of the natural world.[19] A restored relationship with nature does not require us to speak to trees or renew old "acquaintance" with fields. Yet it should never exclude the possibility that things of this sort can be done. We might not communicate with the earth, but the problem does not lie in it being deaf or mute. According to the Scriptures, it is always declaring, proclaiming, and "pour[ing] forth speech."[20]

The second way Merlin shows us what a restored relationship with nature can look like is by relating to animals in a respectful manner. At Belbury, animals are simply things to be experimented on—creatures to be exterminated with the rest of organic life. They are given no dignity, and like many populations which are subjected to such treatment, are rarely interacted with in their native settings, or even the settings imposed on them. We are told that Mark "approved of vivisection," though he had never seen it firsthand (*THS*, 182). When the N.I.C.E. finds Mr. Bultitude outside of St. Anne's, the bear is only given attention when one of the workers says something about his monetary value (*THS*, 306). As Belbury is coming to an end, we find some animals badly maimed and needing to be put out of their misery (*THS*, 348). Humans are already shown little dignity there; it is no wonder that animals are abused without conscience.

In the presence of Merlin, however, animals are elevated to a status that, perhaps, they should always have. At St. Anne's, jackdaws, mice, and bears are all part of the company; beasts are "ennobled" rather than demeaned (*THS*, 305). Many characters, especially Ivy Maggs, are even depicted talking with animals. Merlin does not discount Mr. Bultitude from taking part in his conversations with Ransom (*THS*, 284). And during the banquet at Belbury, Merlin stirs up the animals to stampede over the N.I.C.E. personnel, "maddened with his voice and touch" (*THS*, 348). By contrasting the roles of animals at Logres and Belbury, Lewis paints a graphic picture of what respecting and disrespecting nature can lead to. The N.I.C.E. abused animals and are finally destroyed by them. Those at St. Anne's, especially Ransom and Merlin, ennoble animals and are served by them.

This is all consistent with Lewis himself, who loved animals and whose house was filled with them. Even his nickname, "Jack," is said to be associated with the name of a family dog. As a child, he had "a mouse, a canary, and a dog" as pets, and his early stories about Animal-Land reveal his fascination with big and small beasts alike.[21] This early love of animals remained with him throughout most of his adult life, famously indicated by the talking beasts of Narnia and in his letters to children. Thus, in addition to Merlin, Lewis's life demonstrates that an integral part of a restored relationship with nature is a recognition of nature's personality, including the personalities of animals. After all, as Lewis says in a poem, animals "all cry out to be used as symbols, / Masks for Man, cartoons, parodies by Nature."[22]

In consideration of these things, it is clear that Merlin functions in *That Hideous Strength* not only as an instrument for the destruction of Belbury, but also as a representation of how humanity can begin restoring its relationship with nature. In *Miracles,* Lewis describes nature "as one of the creatures, with her good points and her bad points and her own mistakable flavour running through them all."[23] Nature is not some huge mass of inchoate matter that we can abuse or exploit at will. We might succeed at doing so for a time, but our sins have consequences. In our praise of scientists, let us not forget the wizards. In our search for natural resources, let us not neglect the Source. Instead of enslaving nature, let us follow Lewis's advice to "Meet her and know her."[24]

Contrasting so starkly with the N.I.C.E., Merlin also warns us that mistreatment of nature goes hand-in-hand with a whole host of other evils, as Rachel M. Roller notes in Chapter 3. It is symptomatic of deeper issues. As Lewis says in "Vivisection," "In justifying cruelty to animals we put ourselves also on the animal level. We choose the jungle and must abide by our choice."[25] Belbury certainly had to abide by their choices. The final banquet was not a civilized dinner for humans, but a gruesome frenzy for animals. The leaders of the N.I.C.E. chose to ignore reason and ethics—those things which distinguish us from animals—and were treated like the weak animals they had become.

Avalon: Reintegrating the Self

Up until now, we have explored how Arthurian elements in *That Hideous Strength* help us to envision what life can be like in a redeemed, but unglorified, state. We have considered how Ransom points us to restoration with God, how Logres gives us a picture of true community, and how Merlin reacquaints us with the personality of nature. All three of these relationships reconnect us to things outside of ourselves. They help us rebuild vital bridges that we burned down at the Fall. But the restoration does not end there. The Arthurian elements in *That Hideous Strength* not only point to things outside ourselves that we can be reconciled to, but also point to something within us that will be reconciled by something outside us. By considering Avalon, especially Ransom's longing for it, we get a glimpse of what a reintegrated—that is, a reunified and whole—self looks like. We get a taste of what it might feel like when we are reconciled to our own souls and bodies.

Alienation from the self is a cause of perpetual grief and confusion. "Know Thyself" was inscribed by Plato above the doors of his academy. Philosophizing about the external world is perhaps an easy task compared to making sense of what goes on in one's own broken soul. In Romans, Paul bemoans, "I do not understand what I do. For what I want to do I do not do, but what I hate I do."[26] It is as if we are always at war within ourselves. Some part of us is always committing treason against the rest.

This frustrating reality of a fractured self is a key theme in *That Hideous Strength*. Jane is a character almost always divided upon herself. At one point, the narrator says there were "three, if not four, Janes" on the train leaving St. Anne's (*THS*, 147). Meeting Mr. Fisher-King left her acutely aware of her broken relationship with self. Yet, even Ransom, though supported by supernatural forces, is not a wholly integrated person, as he is continually battling physical pain and therefore feels a divide between his physical and spiritual selves. It is in light of the severed relationship between humans and themselves that Avalon stands as a beacon of hope. Avalon represents restoration by promising reconciliation between people and their bodies, fulfillment of humanity's deepest longings, and an end to death, decay, and time as we understand it.

Avalon as a place of reconciliation between humans and their bodies is very noticeable, for it is almost always mentioned in conjunction with Ransom's wound being healed. Toward the end of the novel, Ransom says his wound will be cured only "in the world where it was got" (*THS*, 366). He longs desperately for Perelandra, for his heel to stop bleeding, for his ageless body to be in an ageless world. However, when we pay closer attention to Ransom's language throughout the novel, we find that he does not portray reconciliation with his body as simply the absence of pain. He awaits something far more. When Merlin offers to wipe away his pain, Ransom says he could get drugs that can "cheat the pain" as well, if not better, than Merlin's "earth-magic" (*THS*, 285). But he never gets them. Why not?

When it comes to his heel, Ransom says it is his "business to bear it to the end" (*THS*, 285). When he nears his departure for Perelandra, he remarks that everything is beginning to feel like a happy dream—"even the pain"—and that he wants to stop talking so he can "taste every drop" (*THS*, 366). It becomes clear that Ransom's idea of reconciliation with his body is not simply a repairing of defects, but the *redemption* of all his pain and suffering. Avalon stands as a reminder not only that our pain will one day be wiped away, but also that our pain will one day be given a purpose and meaning that will transform our present understandings of it. The bridge we have burned down between ourselves and our bodies is restored not simply when the ashes are swept away, but when the Lord gives "a crown of beauty instead of ashes."[27]

The second way Avalon reintegrates the self is by promising fulfillment of humanity's deepest longings. As discussed in the previous chapter, Avalon is a symbol of Joy. It is bound up with that desire which nothing in this world can satisfy, that desire which is itself the closest thing we can experience of its satisfaction. Ransom is often overcome by this transcendent desire. When the Oyarsa of Perelandra descends on the Blue Room and Ransom smells sweet flowers and fragrances of her planet, he weeps (*THS*, 320). When the women at St. Anne's ready themselves for their final dinner, Mother Dimble notes that he has often "longed to go back to Perelandra" and that he is "sort of home-sick" (*THS*, 359). Ransom is never the same after his second voyage into space. Once he has tasted the object of his deepest desires, the object of his Joy, he lives with hopes set on another world.

Ransom, therefore, models for us how we can begin restoration and reintegration of the self while still living on earth. In regards to hope, he shows us how to reject the "The Fool's Way"—that is, setting our hope on earthly things themselves—by never mixing up signposts with the destination.[28] He also successfully resists "The Way of the Disillusioned 'Sensible Man'"—that is, resolving that there is no fulfillment to our deepest longings because nothing in this world seems to satisfy them.[29] This world is a waiting-period for Ransom. He does not have to take revenge on his Joy by "calling it names like Nostalgia and Romanticism and Adolescence."[30] He can relish his experiences of Joy and even nurture them, knowing that they have a proper object in another place.

And, contrary to what one might suspect, this does not make Ransom dreamy and hopelessly impractical. He is very concerned with the state of things on Earth, as we ought to be. Avalon does not cast the affairs of this world in a belittling light. A restored relationship with the self will, in one sense, attune us to things beyond Earth and yet, by correctly ordering our desires, prompt us to effect change *on* the earth. After all, as Lewis said, those "who did most for the present world were just those who thought most of the next."[31]

The final way Avalon represents reconciliation with the self is by promising an end to death, decay, and time as we know it. Those at the N.I.C.E. are always focused on time. Mark is either in a rush, wishing he had longer to finish writing his libelous articles, or wandering around idly, watching the minutes tick by. Time is a tease or a tyrant. The opposite is true of St. Anne's. They are conscious of time, but live by the rhythm and orders of those who exist outside of it. Ransom is always calm and deliberate. He is never worried about being early or late—only about being obedient.

It is important to understand these contrasting views of time because they cut to the heart of one's beliefs about life, death, and the meaning of existence. For those at Belbury, time and decay are inescapable and must therefore be fought against with everything science and technology can muster. For them, the meaning of life is simply "not death." Because transcendence of time is out of the question, prolonged existence within it becomes the goal. But for Ransom, time does not have the final say. He is well aware that "an organism can last practically forever" in many places throughout the universe (*THS*, 366). In fact, ever since his visit to Perelandra, he himself never grows older (*THS*, 192). He has "no natural death" awaiting him (*THS*, 366). Consequently, rather than living life in avoidance of death, he lives his life promoting things that transcend it—eternal things, like obedience, community, and hope. Ransom is a citizen of Avalon living on earth.

Is this not all eerily similar to how we ought to live as Christians? Isn't living in light of Avalon a lot like living in light of that "better country" described in the book of Hebrews?[32] Avalon represents the reintegration of the self because it helps to explain the discomfort we feel living within time, and it promises a day when this "inconsolable wound" will, at last, be cured (*THS*, 320). It shows us a way out of Belbury, a way out of the mindset that this world is all there is. In light of Avalon, we no longer have to live in fear of the past or the future. We are freed to live in the "eternal present," where "the tyranny, the unilinear poverty, of time" has no hold on us.[33]

Endnotes

1 Christopher Gaertner, "Shape and Direction: Human Consciousness in the Inklings' Mythological Geographies," in *The Inklings and King Arthur: J. R. R. Tolkien, Charles Williams, C. S. Lewis, & Owen Barfield on the Matter of Britain*, ed. Sørina Higgins (Berkeley, CA: Apocryphile, 2017), 152.
2 Gaertner, 152.
3 *Catechism of the Catholic Church* (Liguori, MO: Liguori Publications, 1994), 100.
4 Romans 12:9 (NIV).
5 John 19:11 (NIV).
6 R. C. Sproul, *Essential Truths of the Christian Faith* (Carol Stream, IL: Tyndale House, 1992), 105.
7 Sproul, 105.
8 John 15:11 (NIV).
9 Exodus 10:21 (NIV).
10 C. S. Lewis, *An Experiment in Criticism* (New York: Cambridge University Press, 2013), 140.
11 Plato, *The Republic of Plato*, 2nd ed., trans. with notes, interpretive essay, and a new introduction by Allan Bloom (Chicago: University of Chicago Press, 1991), 31.
12 C. S. Lewis, "The Inner Ring," in *The Weight of Glory: And Other Addresses* (New York: HarperCollins, 2009), 146.
13 Lewis, "Inner Ring," 154.
14 C. S. Lewis, *The Great Divorce* (New York: HarperCollins, 1973), 28.
15 Lewis, *Experiment in Criticism*, 140.
16 C. S. Lewis, "Membership," in *The Weight of Glory: And Other Addresses*, ed. Walter Hooper (New York: HarperCollins, 2009), 167.
17 Sanford Schwartz, *C. S. Lewis on the Final Frontier: Science and the Supernatural in the Space Trilogy* (New York: Oxford University Press, 2009), 94.
18 C. S. Lewis, *Miracles: A Preliminary Study* (New York: HarperCollins, 2015), 102.
19 Gaertner, 162.
20 Psalm 19:1–2 (NIV).
21 Walter Hooper, introduction to *Boxen: the Imaginary World of the Young C. S. Lewis*, by C. S. Lewis, ed. Walter Hooper (London, UK: Harcourt Brace, 1985), 12.
22 C. S. Lewis, "Impenitence," in *Poems*, by C. S. Lewis, ed. by Walter Hooper (San Diego: Harcourt Brace, 1992), 2.
23 Lewis, *Miracles*, 102.
24 Lewis, *Miracles*, 105.
25 C. S. Lewis, "Vivisection," in *God in the Dock: Essays on Theology and Ethics*, ed. Walter Hooper (Grand Rapids, MI: Eerdmans, 2014), 249.
26 Romans 7:15 (NIV).
27 Isaiah 61:3 (NIV).
28 Lewis, C. S. Lewis, *Mere Christianity: A revised and amplified edition, with a new introduction, of the three books, Broadcast Talks, Christian Behavior, and Beyond Personality* (New York: HarperCollins, 2015), 135–36.
29 Lewis, *Mere Christianity*, 136.
30 C. S. Lewis, "The Weight of Glory," in *The Weight of Glory: And Other Addresses*, ed. Walter Hooper (New York: HarperCollins, 2009), 30.
31 Lewis, *Mere Christianity*, 134.
32 Hebrews 11:16 (NIV).
33 C. S. Lewis, *Reflections on the Psalms: The Celebrated Musings on One of the Most Intriguing Books of the Bible* (New York: Houghton Mifflin Harcourt, 1986), 137–38.

THE COSMIC WAY

DANIEL J. FRIEND

C. S. Lewis spoils his last story in the Ransom Trilogy before it even begins. In the preface, he writes that the fairy-tale "is a 'tall story' about devilry, though it has behind it a serious 'point' which I have tried to make in my *Abolition of Man*" (*THS*, 7). To be fair, his spoiler had little to do with the plot of the story and everything to do with the theme. He was not breaking any conventions of storytelling but was returning to one of the oldest: stating the moral of the story at the beginning, a practice found in many ancient fairy tales and fables. Nonetheless, this "moral" is rather vague, leading us to ask, what exactly is the "serious 'point'" that Lewis has in mind? His point is the bedrock of all his warnings. Without it, everything else would crumble—from the belief that myth can be a vehicle of truth, to the notion that a medieval perspective can give us a clearer picture of reality, to the conviction that pride will drive us away from what is good. The serious point Lewis makes is that truth, reality, and goodness all exist. In a word, there is objectivity.

Both *That Hideous Strength* and *The Abolition of Man* address the philosophy of subjectivism directly. Subjectivism and objectivism disagree about our certainty in making judgments about truth and reality. Subjectivism is the belief that all such judgments are merely opinions. Objectivism, as used in this chapter, is the belief that absolute truths exist outside of individuals and are discernible by individuals. Within the academic community, Lewis observed a movement away from a belief in this objectivity and foresaw the tendency toward subjectivity spreading into places such as culture, politics, and even some Christian churches. To be clear, the predictions Lewis made about the spread of subjectivism were cautionary, not optimistic. He believed that the rejection of objective good and evil would, quite frankly, "damn our souls."[1] This is not to say that Lewis thought the world was hopeless, for, as we shall see later, he was hopeful about a gift to humanity that might point to salvation: natural law.

Subjectivism Defined

In his essay entitled "The Poison of Subjectivism," Lewis offers a framework to understand the idea of subjectivism. He argues that humanity's quest for knowledge has shifted from studying our environment to studying ourselves, writing, "[I]t is as if we took out our eyes to look at them."[2] In this process, reason—one's judgment of right and wrong—is placed under examination. However, because it can be examined only from an individual's biased perspective, it cannot be assumed to be objective. Although classical thinkers such as Plato and Aristotle would have had no doubt about the objectivity of their judgments, the modern view "does not believe that judgements are really judgements at all," but that they are simply socially conditioned sentiments or feelings.[3] In the modern, subjectivist view, there can be no objective basis for morality or beauty or anything "good." Ethics, aesthetics, and all other value judgments can simply be determined through the colloquial phrase, "You do you."

In *That Hideous Strength*, the N.I.C.E.'s "Objectivity Room" displays the goals of the modern view. Inductees to the inner circle of the organization would be brought into the room that was just a little "off." It was a cold, poorly lit room where everything was slightly disproportional, strangely painted dots were scattered against the ceiling and table, and artwork lined the room that was either plainly grotesque or simply odd (*THS*, 295). The purpose of the room was for a person to absorb all they initially thought was wrong until they no longer viewed it as wrong. The N.I.C.E. wanted its members to deconstruct their preexisting value judgments until they saw any emotional responses—even their own revulsion at grotesque images—as nothing more than feelings made relative to the subject by chemicals in the brain. Although the practice was overt indoctrination, it illustrates Lewis's concern that subjectivism would lead to "Men Without Chests."

Untrained Emotions

"Men Without Chests" is the title of the first chapter in *The Abolition of Man*, and Lewis uses the phrase to describe an inability to balance the three parts of a human that make one whole: the head (reason), the chest (emotion or sentiment), and the belly (appetites or wants).[4] As an example, Lewis contends that a human who is balanced in these three areas could objectively conclude that a magnificent waterfall is sublime. He argues that a person's ability to make such a judgment is an appropriate response to reality.[5] In this case, the trained emotion of humility allows one's reason (i.e. the ability to put oneself in perspective with the waterfall) to rule over one's belly (i.e. an alternative reaction, such as calling the waterfall "pretty"). When someone is shaped by virtue in this process of reason ruling the appetite through emotions, he or she becomes truly human.[6]

However, subjectivists would relegate such a judgment as an emotion relative to the individual. They would not say that the waterfall in and of itself is sublime but that the person viewing the waterfall was having sublime feelings toward it. This shift weakens its significance. If all emotions are relative and are not caused by an objective quality in something outside of an individual, what incentive does a person have to cultivate emotional responses? By eliminating all objective value, the modern view has broken down judgments of beauty, sublimity, and goodness, and has made them mere synonyms for experiences that hold no weight. Thus, subjectivism creates "Men Without Chests," people without emotions that are trained to respond appropriately to what they encounter.

When all value judgments are taken as subjective and there are no trained emotional responses, subjectivists can no longer base their actions on duty but must base them on desire.[7] The result is a habituated, irrational impulse to pursue pleasure or avoid pain.[8] As Lewis points out, with a subjective mindset, societies can choose their ideologies as arbitrarily as picking out an outfit to wear in the morning.[9] The N.I.C.E.'s historical counterpart as compared in Chapter 4 serves as a prime example. Looking at the Jews as something less than human, the Nazis saw no moral impediment to the Holocaust. The irrational impulse of society carried out the killing of millions. According to this view, the Nazis' actions cannot be objectively bad and there cannot be anything objectively better about the societal standards of today. A subjectivist cannot say that Nazism is bad; they can only say they have bad feelings about it. This introduces a conundrum for the modern view: how can society progress?

The Conditioners

In both "The Poison of Subjectivism" and *The Abolition of Man*, Lewis raises the problem of progress for a worldview without objectivity. I would not doubt that Lewis agreed with G. K. Chesterton's statement that "[t]he only intelligible sense that progress or advance can have among men, is that we have a definite vision, and that we wish to make the whole world like that vision."[10] The progress of moving toward some fixed end is impossible without objectivity, yet, as Lewis notes, there remains some subjectivist reformers seeking progress in society to make it "better."[11] These reformers become what Lewis calls the "Conditioners," who "know how to produce conscience and decide what kind of conscience they will produce."[12] They seek to overcome traditional moral judgments and create what they deem to be the right way of living.

The role of the N.I.C.E. in *That Hideous Strength* parallels Lewis's idea of Conditioners. Throughout the novel, the similarities abound. In the early chapters, we learn that the N.I.C.E. has already infiltrated the academy at Edgestow. Later on, we learn that they play a central role in propaganda, manipulating the public by writing articles in the newspaper that represent both sides of every argument; they take control of local communities with the use of their own police force; they experiment on man and animals alike, including the dissection of Alcasan's head; they manipulate their members through the use of the Objectivity Room, and so the list continues. In every way, the N.I.C.E. are the sort of Conditioners that Lewis cautions against. If the Conditioners could achieve their ultimate goal of conditioning the consciences of humankind, the results would look like something out of the pages of *Brave New World*, where all classes of people are under the subjection of an elite, educated few. Those at the bottom may experience some measure of contentment, but not without losing some central aspects of their humanity.

The dangers for those subjugated to the Conditioners are clear, but the Conditioners are ultimately under a sort of subjection themselves. As stated earlier, if humans cannot make objective value judgments or train their emotions, they must turn to something else to drive their actions. Lewis says that subjectivists will likely turn to their "Instincts," such as preserving humanity and pursuing their sexual desires.[13] Consequently, everyone—including the Conditioners—is ruled by irrational impulses. "Man's conquest of Nature turns out, in the moment of its consummation, to be Nature's conquest of Man," writes Lewis.[14] Although the Conditioners may wish to shape society in a way that they deem best through their scientism and technological advances, they are subject to their own "natural" impulses.[15] However, there is little guarantee that these instincts "which arise in minds thus emptied of all 'rational' or 'spiritual' motives" will be benevolent.[16] Take again the example of the Nazis: they sought to create the perfect race, but this plan was a product of their uncontrolled passions. In their rejection of what is objectively human, they were spiraling down a path to ultimately lose sight of their own humanity.

The subjection of the Conditioners to their own instinct inevitably leads to an implosion of the utopian society they sought to create. It is important to note that this danger does not apply solely to fascist Conditioners like the Nazis. In fact, Lewis argues that many democratic leaders are just as guilty as fascist leaders of trying to condition humanity through various means: "eugenics, psychological manipulation of infants, state education[,] and mass propaganda."[17] A subjectivist might suggest that though there are no objective values, a society can decide the most favorable values through a competition of ideas. However, even such a framework can lead to the erosion of trained emotions over time. As a society collectively moves little by little away from a belief in objectivity, "Nature's conquest of Man" through impulse will become obvious.

Within *That Hideous Strength*, the idea of "Nature's conquest of Man" is depicted most clearly by the destruction of the N.I.C.E. at the banquet scene near the end of the novel. Long before the banquet takes place, those at the N.I.C.E. willfully reject beauty and happiness. This rejection is not the result of a single Conditioner at the top of the organization but rather of a long series of choices. At the banquet, the consequences of this collective rejection of objectivity come to fruition. After everyone's speech is turned into babel, the unencumbered brutality of "Nature's conquest of Man" leaves each person to their conditioned impulses (*THS*, 342). The result is chaos and carnage. The N.I.C.E.'s desire to create a new and "better" world through the expulsion of objectivity brought ruin upon themselves.

The Problems of Subjectivism

The dangers of subjectivism aside, there are some serious flaws with the philosophy that make it so impractical that most people will always return to some sort of belief in objective morality.

In *Out of the Silent Planet*, Lewis clearly demonstrates the shortcomings of the modern view. Near the end of the novel, one of the main antagonists, Weston, defends his actions to the Oyarsa of Malacandra. He contends that preserving the life of humanity is more important than any sort of morality and that his mission is to extend human life through interplanetary colonization (*OSP*, 135). His sentiment echoes that of the Conditioners trying to subject future generations to what they deem best. The Oyarsa responds by saying that one traditional moral judgment is the "love of kindred" but that the fallen Oyarsa presiding over Earth has twisted morality so that only this principle remains and is warped to contradict all other principles (*OSP*, 137).

Lewis directly addresses the problem with Weston's subjectivist way of thinking in his essay "On Ethics." In it, he opposes the idea that humans have a "natural, unreflective, spontaneous impulse" to preserve all of humanity in the same way they have such an instinct to preserve their own offspring.[18] While he agrees that the preservation of humanity is a good thing, he denies that there is any connection to an instinct. For Lewis, this notion of an instinct was a frivolous excuse for what was a "purely moral maxim *That humanity ought to be preserved*."[19] He proceeds to argue that even if there was some legitimacy to the alleged instinct, it would still require moral precepts to "arrange our instincts in a hierarchy of comparative dignity," as different instincts frequently conflict.[20]

Weston's goal to preserve human life points to the reality of an objective right and wrong. If the desire to preserve the human race is a moral principle, what else could be its source other than an objective foundation? The principle is not something that Weston or thinkers like him could invent on their own. Rather, as Lewis argues, "They hold it by inheritance and training from the general (if not strictly universal) human tradition."[21] He goes on to say, "[I] t is no more possible to invent a new ethics than to place a new sun in the sky. Some precept from traditional morality always has to be assumed."[22] Despite what some may want to believe, they cannot create a "new morality" without drawing from the principles of objective morality. Weston's claim that preserving life is more important than morality falls apart when faced with the fact that seeking the preservation of human life is a distinctly moral claim. His inconsistency in clinging to some sort of ethics is a thread of hope that he still has, as Lewis writes in *Mere Christianity*, "that Moral Law which [God] has put into our minds."[23] This idea of a "Moral Law" or "natural law" was not Lewis's idea but a biblical concept. It can be seen vividly in the Epistle to the Romans, where Paul writes that the Gentiles "show that the requirements of the law are written on their hearts" when they follow God's law without being given it directly.[24]

Lewis on Law

Lewis vigorously fought for the ideas of natural law. If readers look closely at most of his works—or even just glance over the pages—they will be stumbling through a mountain of evidence that he believed in the existence of natural law. But what exactly is "natural law" as Lewis understood it? Like classical teachers such as Thomas Aquinas, Lewis understood natural law as a universal sense of a moral right and wrong. In *The Abolition of Man*, he provides a unique name for it, which sounds anything but Christian: the *Tao*. He writes:

> [The *Tao*] is the doctrine of objective value, the belief that certain attitudes are really true, and others really false, to the kind of thing the universe is and the kind of things we are. Those who know the *Tao* can hold that to call children delightful or old men venerable is not simply to record a psychological fact about our own parental or filial emotions at the moment, but to recognize a quality which *demands* a certain response from us whether we make it or not.[25]

Whereas the subjectivist makes each individual the sole arbiter of all meaning and value, the *Tao* holds that there is inherent meaning and value in actions or things. The word "Tao" literally refers to "the Way" or "the Right Way." The subjectivist says a person has sublime feelings toward a waterfall. The one who practices the *Tao* sees the sublimity inherent in the waterfall. Lewis's arguments in *The Abolition of Man* and elsewhere did not focus on asserting the extent to which this objectivity was discernible. He would leave that work for other philosophers and theologians. Instead of talking about how to know what is objectively right and wrong (i.e. a natural law "theorist"), Lewis first wanted his audience to see that there is an objective right and wrong (i.e. an "apologist").[26]

For Lewis, this concept of the *Tao* greatly informed his worldview and thereby his works of writing, as well. The most obvious connection, as previously mentioned, is in *That Hideous Strength*. Since the *The Abolition of Man* was published after *Perelandra*, it would not have had any direct influence on the first two novels of the Ransom Trilogy. However, the ideas that Lewis expressed in *The Abolition of Man* were clearly being developed in his mind much earlier, as he explicitly nods to natural law in *Out of the Silent Planet* and *Perelandra*. The manner in which Lewis expresses his ideas conveys an appreciation for the natural law, not because it places a limit on our freedom but because it guides us toward what is good for our souls. The progression of this thought will become clearer through an analysis of the three texts within the Trilogy.

The Bentness of Humanity

Through his work of science fiction, Lewis argues that turning away from the natural law is a spiritual sickness. He communicates this idea, especially in the first novel of the Trilogy, through use of the term "bentness." Ransom encounters the *hrossa* on Malacandra, a type of *hnau* or rational animal that rules over beasts and is ruled by *eldila* (*PER*, 41; *OSP*, 102). While the *hrossa* are rational like humans, there is one major difference between them and humanity: humanity is fallen and predisposed toward evil. When trying to explain to the natives of Malacandra that he is being pursued by evil kidnappers that want to harm him, he is lost at finding a word in their language to describe them. The closest term to "bad men" that Ransom can think of to use in the *hrossian* language is the term "bent men" (*OSP*, 68). This passage is the first time in the Trilogy that Lewis uses the term "bent" to describe sinfulness. Later in *Out of the Silent Planet*, he gives the reader a better idea of exactly what it means to be bent. In another conversation, Ransom asks if any *hrossa* has ever been bent. The *hross* he is speaking to responds by saying that he had heard about one who wanted to eat dirt—an impulse completely at odds with their nature (*OSP*, 75).

Lewis cleverly uses the concept of "bentness" to teach his audience about the nature of sin and the fallen state of humanity. The word describes something that is crooked and twisted away from its original design and purpose. Just as a yardstick that is bent would be incapable of serving its purpose of measuring to the fullest, the bentness of humanity reveals the shortcomings of the race. The desperate nature of humankind is seen in one of the tragic scenes of *Out of the Silent Planet*, where Hyoi, the close *hrossa* friend of Ransom, is shot and killed by Ransom's pursuers. As he tries to see if Hyoi is still alive, Ransom attempts to apologize to him on behalf of humanity but is at a loss as to how to translate words like "guilt" or "sorry" into the *hrossian* language. He falls short of communicating what he wants, only telling his friend that all of humanity is a bent race that has come to Malacandra to bring evil, concluding, "We are only half *hnau*" (*OSP*, 82).

Lewis continues the idea of bentness in *Perelandra*. Ransom is brought to the planet Perelandra, where the newly created *hnau* of the planet are tempted to break the one divine law established for them to follow, which is to never spend the night on the "Fixed Land." In being tempted to violate this law, they are being tempted to become bent. Lewis hearkens back to this idea in the description of the Great Dance at the end of the novel where he writes, "Where Maleldil is, there is the center. He is in every place.... There is no way out of the center save into the Bent Will which casts itself into the Nowhere" (*PER*, 185). For the unfallen Perelandra, the goodness of Maleldil radiates into all of life—the only thing that could escape the goodness would have been a bent, disobedient will. To bend away from God would be like a broken compass that no longer points toward true north.

The idea of "bentness" may not at first seem to connect with the idea of natural law, but the two ideas are actually inseparable. The natural law serves as a moral pattern to which actions ought to conform. Just as a human law concerning traffic serves to create order out of chaos, the natural law exists to guide humans toward an orderly way of living that is good for their souls. Introducing the terminology of "bentness" gives readers a way to visualize morality. The natural law is an indelible sense of right and wrong that can identify what is straight and what is crooked, guiding a person to know what actions need to be corrected.

Divine Law for Divine Good

Although he continues to use the idea of bentness throughout *Perelandra*, the more overt theme shifts from this to an explicit discussion of law. When Ransom first arrives on Perelandra, he discovers its unique landscape.

Interspersed amongst the vast oceans of the planet are two types of land: the "Fixed Lands" like those inhabited on Earth and the "floating islands" that roll with the waves of the ocean. It is while on the floating islands that Ransom first encounters the *hnau* of the planet, the Green Lady. As he interacts with her, he discovers the divine law that she has been given to obey. Similar to the command given to Adam and Eve in Genesis, the Green Lady explains that Maleldil does not want her and the king of Perelandra to sleep on the fixed land (*PER*, 64).

When first hearing about the law of the Fixed Land, Ransom seems confused. He instantly compares Perelandra with his world, asserting that such a law could never exist on Earth since there are no floating islands there (*PER*, 64). A reader might share in his confusion, as the certainty of resting on solid ground would seem preferable to resting on something so unstable. Moreover, the idea of being restricted from sleeping on the Fixed Land might seem like an arbitrary law to limit freedom. However, as we find out later in the novel, it is something that was put in place for the good of the planet's *hnau*.

After Ransom finds Weston tempting the Green Lady to think about living on the Fixed Island, the reader can begin to understand the goodness of the law. The Green Lady does not see what benefit breaking the law would bring, but Weston argues that it would make her wiser or, in her vocabulary, "older" (*PER*, 97). Ransom appeals to her trust in the one who gave the law, though, stating "[W]ill not Maleldil make you older in His own time and His own way, and will not that be far better?" (*PER*, 99). Weston counters this reasoning with another idea: Maleldil wants her to become older by her achieving independence, and he secretly wants her to break his law (*PER*, 100). The Green Lady sees through this temptation though, saying, "To walk out of His will is to walk into nowhere" (*PER*, 100). Although she does not understand the law's purpose, she understands that violating it would harm her fellowship with Maleldil.

The law on Perelandra may appear arbitrary, but it has an underlying purpose. The revelation of this purpose comes at the end of the book in a discussion between the Green Lady and Ransom as she tells him what she has learned:

> [Living on Fixed Land] was to reject the wave—to draw my hands out of Maleldil's, to say to Him, 'Not thus, but thus'—to put in our own power what times should roll towards us . . . as if you gathered fruits together today for tomorrow's eating instead of taking what came. That would have been cold love and feeble trust. And out of it how could we ever have climbed back into love and trust again? (*PER*, 179)

The law was not made arbitrarily by Maleldil but was put in place as a way to establish the Green Lady's trust in him. All of the circumstances in which she found herself were prepared by him to foster a dependence on him. Having to rest on a floating island that could move in any direction under the cover of a pitch-black night sky, all the while being able to see the Fixed Land during the daytime, required that the Green Lady relinquish control. There was no purpose to rest on the Fixed Land except to seek dependence on its stability, but doing so would display a lack of trust in Maleldil, who provided everything she needed for safety.

Ultimately, it became clear to the Green Lady that the purpose for the divine law was for her own good. Although she did not understand it at first, she did not resent it as a limit to her freedom. The law was not given to her for the purpose of constraining her; it was given for the purpose of driving her toward something good for her soul. The law was not a wall to restrict her freedom but a well to give her life. In the same way that this can be seen through the divine law in *Perelandra*, it can also be applied to the concept of natural law. Lewis saw that laws ordained by God, including the *Tao*, are not arbitrary laws created to restrict the freedom of humanity. Rather, they are established to drive people toward what is Good. In this manner, Lewis is echoing Paul when he writes, "I would not have known what sin was had it not been for the law."[27] The law is established to distinguish the bad from the good and to lead a person toward the latter.

Armor Against Evil

Having examined how the natural law can help diagnose what is wrong (i.e. bentness) and how it is an expression of God's goodness and a wellspring of blessing, *That Hideous Strength* provides two contrasting examples of how these aspects of natural law can drive individuals toward what is good for their souls. The first example is Mark, who sees wickedness in its face and is repelled by it. The second example is Jane, who sees goodness and is drawn in by it.

Throughout *That Hideous Strength*, Mark desperately wants to become a part of the "Inner Circle." Lewis first uses this term in the Trilogy when Mark is visiting the N.I.C.E. headquarters at Belbury, exploring a potential employment opportunity with them. When he begins to question his assignment to write propaganda for the newspapers, he considers returning to his position at Bracton College. He stops himself, though, because he is afraid that if he refuses to work for the N.I.C.E., then he will be pushed out of the "Inner Circle" of the elite "Progressive Element" at the school (*THS*, 99).

As Mark stays at Belbury and interacts with the leadership of the N.I.C.E., he is led further and further astray. His walking away from the *Tao* is encouraged by the employees of the N.I.C.E. In *The Abolition of Man*, Lewis makes it clear that this form of education is the most dangerous—"conditioning" men without any regard for morality. Mark was being educated to believe that everything is subjective and that there is no right and wrong.

The conditioning of Mark is most blatant when he is brought into the Objectivity Room for the second time. It is at this moment that the *Tao* ultimately pushes him to understand that something is wrong with the N.I.C.E. When he is brought into the room this time, there is a life-size crucifix lying on the table. Mark is surprised by it, largely because he had always treated Christianity as superstition (*THS*, 331). Frost commands Mark to deface the cross, but Mark refuses to do so, not out of a sense of obligation to God, but out of a sense of obligation to the "the Straight or Normal or Wholesome" (*THS*, 333). As Frost persists in his demands, Mark becomes increasingly adamant against giving into the absurd order. He does not yet believe in Christ, but deep down he knows that there is something intrinsically wrong in defacing a cross (*THS*, 334).

Mark's allegiance to the straight, normal, and wholesome demonstrates the *Tao* in action. Although he cannot explain where his sense of objectivity comes from, he acts upon it. Here, Lewis introduces a term synonymous to his use of "bentness" in *Out of the Silent Planet* and *Perelandra*: Mark begins to understand morality more clearly when faced with the "Crooked" demands of Frost (*THS*, 334). Following his obedience to the *Tao* and his rescue from the clutches of the N.I.C.E., his sense of objective value grows sharper. He realizes that in "his life-long eagerness to reach an inner circle he had chosen the *wrong* circle" (*THS*, 358). Where he really belonged was not with the elites at Bracton or the N.I.C.E.; he belonged with people like the Dimbles who possessed a certain joy in their lives (*THS*, 358). And by the end of the novel, Mark is walking steadfastly toward objective goodness, as he returns to Jane with an understanding of the true beauty and significance of their marriage (*THS*, 359).

Guide toward Good

Just as the *Tao* is seen in Mark's rejection of evil, it is also seen in Jane's acceptance of goodness. When Jane first visits the manor at St. Anne's, she is led through a large garden (*THS*, 60). Lewis spends a lengthy paragraph discussing Jane's reaction to the place. It is not the first time that a garden is brought up in the novel—when Jane visits the Dimbles in the first chapter, she notes the loveliness of their garden (*THS*, 27). The garden at St. Anne's is even more spectacular. To Jane, it represents a sort of feminine beauty, something appreciated by both men and women. She recalls a sentence describing this idea, noting how the goddess of Love came prior to the god of Love (*THS*, 60). The beauty that she is drawn toward by the garden shows that Jane is following in the tradition of the *Tao*. As Lewis references in *The Abolition of Man*, Plato in his *Republic* describes how well-nurtured youth are taught to have distaste for what is ugly and praise for what is beautiful.[28] Accordingly, Jane praises beauty.

As she interacts with Ransom and the others in the company at St. Anne's, Jane is continually drawn toward what is good and is challenged in her preconceived ideas about her own self-reliance. Unlike the N.I.C.E.'s "conditioning" of its members, the company at St. Anne's exemplifies what Lewis would consider to be proper, necessary education. In Lewis's view, education is essential in the persistence of the *Tao*. He compares this proper form of education to birds teaching younger birds how to fly, a process of initiation or "propagation" to pass down truths that have been learned.[29] Similarly, throughout the novel, Jane is taught by the men and women of St. Anne's through conversations with them and by witnessing their lives in action.

Jane's education builds up to a turning point in her life at the manor's garden, where she is arguably converted to Christianity. After a deep conversation with Ransom, she returns to this beautiful place where she had stood in awe when first arriving at the manor (*THS*, 314). Here, she spends time thinking about the conversation that she had with Ransom and how he had pointed out that the greatest stumbling block for Jane's faith was pride (*THS*, 312). While contemplating in the garden, Jane begins to think about how her own pride had made her reject both Mark's love and God's love. And then, Lewis says that in an instantaneous moment something happened, left to her only as a memory. He describes the bushes, path, and bricks of the garden as having changed, albeit not visibly (*THS*, 313). The change is in the way that Jane views the world. Just as she had begun contemplating the hugeness of humans from the perspective of mice earlier (*THS*, 147), now she was becoming aware of the hugeness of God. The pride that was standing in the way of surrendering her life to the God who made her was removed.[30]

While the connection is not absolute, Lewis probably connected the garden to Jane's conversion for a purpose. The same sense that allowed Jane to recognize the beauty in the garden allowed her to recognize her own relation to God. This sense is Lewis's *Tao*, the "doctrine of objective value." With her emotions trained to recognize the beauty and goodness of the garden, Jane can also see how she is not good, but bent. The humility this realization causes, combined with her understanding that something needs to change, drives her to consider more deeply her conversations with Ransom and the others at St. Anne's. This aspect of Lewis's narrative is consistent with a claim he makes in *Mere Christianity*: "It is after you have realized that there is a real Moral Law, and a Power behind the law, and that you have broken that law and put yourself wrong with that

Power—it is after all this, and not a moment sooner, that Christianity begins to talk."[31] As Jane sees the error in her pride, she begins to understand her position in relation to God. She realizes the Moral Law and the Power—that she is a sinner in need of a Savior—and then she begins to understand Christianity.[32]

Cosmic Counsel

As mentioned earlier, Lewis wrote that *That Hideous Strength* "is a 'tall story' about devilry, though it has behind it a serious 'point' which I have tried to make in my *Abolition of Man*" (*THS*, 7). The quotation marks around "tall story" and "point" are there for a reason. In the epigraph, we see that the title "*That Hideous Strength*" comes from a poem by Sir David Lyndsay, referring to the Tower of Babel (*THS*, 3). "Tall story" and "point," therefore, allude to the tower that was being built up to loom over the land like the N.I.C.E. over Britain.

Perhaps the reference to Genesis is the clearest image of the serious warning that Lewis is trying to make in *That Hideous Strength*. In Genesis 11, the whole earth came together full of pride in their ability to build a tower that would reach into heaven. But God, seeing their pride, scattered them by confusing their language.[33] Likewise, the N.I.C.E. sought to conquer nature and rule over the conscience of humanity. Yet, as Ransom says, "Their own strength has betrayed them .... [They have] pulled down Deep Heaven on their heads. Therefore, they will die" (*THS*, 291). And so they do—in a chaotic confusion of language. In both cases, there is grave judgment for those who wage war against our natural limits in order to become godlike.[34] Those at Babel sought to exalt themselves by conquering physical boundaries; those at the N.I.C.E. sought the same by conquering not only physical boundaries but also moral boundaries.

This, then, is the serious point behind Lewis's tall story: we ought to steer clear of the prideful dangers of subjectivism that make us the arbiters of right and wrong. We must return to the path of traditional morality—the cosmic *Tao*, acknowledging a universal and heavenly good. Like Jane, Mark, and even Weston, we all have this sense of objective value within us to some extent, even if it is bent to a great degree. No value judgment we make, however slight or unnoticeable, can be made without hearkening back to the *Tao*. It is a changeless guidepost in a changing world. Thus, we are left with a choice. We can either flee from the *Tao* and face the peril of subjectivism, or we can embrace the *Tao* and find rest in an increasingly clear sense of Truth. If we choose the latter, only then will we begin to see life as it really is, with all of its beauty and joy. And only then will we begin to see ourselves as we really are, in need of a ransom.

Endnotes

1 C. S. Lewis, "The Poison of Subjectivism," in *Christian Reflections*, ed. Walter Hooper (Grand Rapids, MI: Eerdmans, 2014), 89.
2 Lewis, "Poison of Subjectivism," 72.
3 Lewis, "Poison of Subjectivism," 73.
4 C. S. Lewis, *Abolition of Man* (New York: HarperCollins, 2015), 16.
5 Lewis, *Abolition of Man*, 20.
6 Scott Key, "Metaphors of Meaning: The Dance of Truth and Imagination in *That Hideous Strength*," in *Contemporary Perspectives on C. S. Lewis' The Abolition of Man*, eds. Timothy Mosteller and Gayne Anacker (London, UK: Bloomsbury Publishing, 2017), 160.
7 Lewis, *Abolition of Man*, 65.
8 Of course, as Lewis notes in *The Abolition of Man* (36), desires or "instincts" are often in conflict with one another. A subjectivist must therefore make value judgments in deciding which desire is more important. Over time, this conditions impulses similarly to the way emotions are trained. However, the impulses are conditioned without any regard to reason (32).
9 Lewis, "Poison of Subjectivism," 73.
10 G. K. Chesterton, *Orthodoxy* (San Francisco: Ignatius, 1995), 112.
11 Lewis, "Poison of Subjectivism," 74.
12 Lewis, *Abolition of Man*, 61.
13 Lewis, *Abolition of Man*, 33.
14 Lewis, *Abolition of Man*, 68.
15 Lewis also explains this idea in a second way, arguing that when humans reduce even humanity to nature, humanity becomes subject to nature. For more details on this explanation, see Rachel M. Roller's discussion of the subject in Chapter 3.
16 Lewis, *Abolition of Man*, 66.
17 Lewis, "Poison of Subjectivism," 81.
18 C. S. Lewis, "On Ethics," in *Christian Reflections*, ed. Walter Hooper (Grand Rapids, MI: Eerdmans, 2014), 61.
19 Lewis, "On Ethics," 62.
20 Lewis, "On Ethics," 62.
21 Lewis, "On Ethics," 64.
22 Lewis, "On Ethics," 66.
23 C. S. Lewis, *Mere Christianity: A revised and amplified edition, with a new introduction, of the three books, Broadcast Talks, Christian Behavior, and Beyond Personality* (New York: HarperCollins, 2015), 29.
24 Romans 2:14–15 (NIV).
25 Lewis, *Abolition of Man*, 18.
26 Micah Watson, "Natural Moral Law in *The Abolition of Man*," in *Contemporary Perspectives on C. S. Lewis' The Abolition of Man*, eds. Timothy Mosteller and Gayne Anacker (London, UK: Bloomsbury Publishing, 2017), 32.
27 Romans 7:7 (NIV).
28 Lewis, *Abolition of Man*, 17.
29 Lewis, *Abolition of Man*, 23.
30 Gavin Ortlund, "Conversion in C. S. Lewis's *That Hideous Strength*," *Themelios* 41, no. 1 (2016): 13.

31 Lewis, *Mere Christianity*, 31.

32 Micah Watson, "C. S. Lewis as Natural Law Evangelist: Evangelical Political Thought and the People in the Pew," in *Natural Law and Evangelical Political Thought*, eds. Jesse Covington, Bryan McGraw, and Micah Watson (Lanham, MD: Lexington Books, 2013), 203. It should be noted that in addition to preparing a person to understand their need for salvation, Lewis believed that natural law provides a way for people to recognize common human nature. Although there is not room in this chapter to explore the relation between the Trilogy and the idea that natural law can serve as a source of unity in depth, it is worth consideration.

33 Genesis 11:1–9 (NIV).

34 See Nolan Andrew's contribution in Chapter 6 for a more in-depth look at this perilous problem of pride.

VOICES IN HIS HEAD

EVANGELINE M. PRIOR

Each of the chapters so far has demonstrated that C. S. Lewis's science fiction trilogy is rich with metaphor, social commentary, and public exhortation which invites a thoughtful reading and demands a responsible life. The diverse thematic complexity of this work all stems from Lewis's own eclectically furnished mind. While the previous chapters detail these significant aspects of Lewis's own life and their influence on the science fiction trilogy, this final chapter focuses on the application of those influences: how Lewis's experience speaks through the voices of Ransom, Mark, and Jane.

As discussed in Chapter 5, the medieval, geocentric conception of the universe is one which underlies the Trilogy as a whole and eventually reshapes and redeems the perspectives of the three protagonists. The planets—or wandering stars—were seen as inherently spiritual, not at all like the sterile, scientific view taught in modern education. Michael Ward explains, "In the pre-Copernican model of the cosmos the planets were silent and sounding at the same time: their music was not heard on earth because it was always heard. And it is this sort of silence, a pregnant silence, resonant with significance" that becomes a focal point of the Trilogy. Each wandering star sings its own song of universal import and beauty, each silence a mere rest in the divine music. With this glorious view of the heavens, Lewis's terming of Earth as Thulcandra—meaning 'Silent Planet'—becomes a rather morbid assertion. Earth is not singing its cosmic song, perhaps because it is dead, perhaps asleep. Amid this silence in the Ransom Trilogy, a great cosmic battle is waged.

In order to navigate the pitfalls and hazards of this silent planet, Lewis encourages his readers to become like Ransom, Mark, and Jane: to plot course and chase after the good, right, and true. Through Ransom, Lewis demonstrates the importance of identity. An astute philologist, Ransom becomes the translator for Old Solar, bridging the gap between the world and the universe and shifting the paradigm from a cold and void outer space to a warm and living heaven. Through Mark, Lewis shows the importance of taking action. Mark's perspective shifts from passive to active good when confronted with the reality of evil. And through Jane, Lewis encourages humility. A hypocritical academic, Jane is not content with her life until she recognizes the natural law created by Divine order and submits to it. Lewis's medieval understanding of the cosmos along with his portrayal of good and evil underscore the tone of the voices of these three characters. These are the voices which speak the clearest in the Ransom Trilogy, and these are the voices that, in the end, sing the song of the Silent Planet.

Literary Criticism

Certainly, the Ransom Trilogy serves as a pleasurable science fiction read for the casual reader. But those who look deeper are rewarded with a richer meaning. In one of Lewis's forays into literary theory, a book entitled, *An Experiment in Criticism*, he contends that "good readers" entrust their intellect, emotion, and morality into a work of literature in order to understand "the facts as they are."[1] As literary critic, Wayne Shumaker says, "To serious students of fiction [the books of the Trilogy] can suggest that the formal complexity so prized nowadays by a perceptive minority need not always entail the sacrifice of meaning for the less perceptive majority."[2] Enjoyment and enrichment are not mutually exclusive qualities in insightful books like those of the Trilogy. However, in these books, neither enjoyment nor enrichment is as easily attained as a reader might hope. In fact, the first efforts to delve into Ransom's account result in a near cacophony as the voices of medieval philosophy, Christian theology, human psychology, and other imageries sing Ransom's epic. True to his classical education, significant insight can be gained into Lewis's Trilogy through the lens of moral criticism—a theory that began with Plato and Aristotle—that seeks out the moral lessons the author intended to convey.

As mentioned previously, Lewis's well-established theology of good and evil along with his fearless social critique work together to create what we have termed a "compass" for navigating universal truths and cosmic dangers. At the end of *Out of the Silent Planet*, the author explains that the names and places have been changed so as "to publish in the form of *fiction* what would certainly not be listened to as fact," further insisting that "there would be indications enough in the narrative for the few readers—the very few—who at *present* were prepared to go further into the matter" (*OSP*, 152). We take joy in going further into the matter, discerning the truth behind the myths, the reality underlying the fiction, the instructions amid the tale. For Lewis, these veiled truths are the foundation of the moral compass which he encourages his readers to seek out.

In expounding the morals written into the Trilogy, it is helpful to recognize the varied literary style from book to book. Though the Trilogy is classified under the genre of science fiction, each of the three books contains a subgenre that shapes the characters, settings, and exhortations. *Out of the Silent Planet* is a true science fiction text that "is used to reveal a medieval cosmology," setting the stage with precarious cosmic tension and creating costly stakes for each choice and action.[3] *Perelandra* is a biblical retelling, like Milton's *Paradise Lost*, that clarifies the definitions of good and evil, fallen and redeemed, truth and falsehood. Finally, *That Hideous Strength* is built upon the philosophic and theological principles of the first two books, using gothic novel themes—Arthurian legend, character tropes, and spiritual enlightenment—to stress the interdependence of the cosmic and the individual.[4] Throughout these books, the three main characters each have their own biases of education and character, their own pitfalls their own coming of age, and eventually their own cosmic redemption.

Meet the Voices

Decoding Lewis's moral discourse through the words of his characters requires a detailed understanding of these narrators themselves. The first narrative perspective of the Trilogy is that of Dr. Elwin Ransom, a "philologist, and a fellow of a Cambridge college" (*OSP*, 10). Ransom is steeped in the study of linguistics and the origin of words, and his worldview is shaped by academia and language. One ramification of this framework is the "prodigious emotional consequences" that occur when Ransom first hears the Old Solar tongue on Malacandra (*OSP*, 56). The native *hross* who first addresses Ransom upon his landing on Malacandra awakens his linguistic spirit to the song of the cosmos and expands his perspective of the universe to reflect Lewis's medieval one. Another aspect of Ransom's linguistic identity is the importance of his own words, both in describing himself and later in translating truth about the cosmos from Old Solar to English and vice versa.

Part of Ransom's description of himself at the outset of *Out of the Silent Planet* includes the underestimation of his own courage. The stark contrast of his childish bravery and his gruesome experience in war incited in Ransom a "view of his own unheroic qualities" (*OSP*, 38). Perhaps recalling his own experience in war, Lewis parallels Ransom's role in the war on Earth and his role in the war being waged in the heavens. As a literary trope, his combatant humility marks Ransom as the ideal hero simply awaiting transformation in the subsequent events.

After taking center stage in the stories of *Out of the Silent Planet* and *Perelandra*, Ransom fades into a supporting-character position as Mark and Jane Studdock become the focal point in *That Hideous Strength*. Mark Studdock is a sociologist by vocation and, like Ransom, has been awarded a fellowship at university. Compared with Ransom's academic self-assurance, Mark's vocational identity is young, insecure, and people-pleasing. Mark desires nothing more than to be in the inner circle or in whatever "gang" he perceives to be in the know (*THS*, 15). Early in *That Hideous Strength*, Mark's employer at Bracton College, Sub-Warden Curry, discusses the agenda of "the Progressive Element," referring to Mark, himself, and other notable Bracton scholars as "we" (*THS*, 15). This inclusive language spurs in Mark an "intense pleasure" (*THS*, 15). Though privately he hopes to win favor and enter into the special few, Mark is not proactive in achieving this hope. From his wife Jane's perspective, "he was always either sleepy or intellectually preoccupied" (*THS*, 12). Due to his consistent sleepiness or busyness, Mark is regularly distracted from the work of communication, both in his work and in his marriage.

The metaphor of sleep and waking is used repeatedly to portray ignorance and enlightenment in the Trilogy. Shumaker explains that Mark's "world view rests on a conviction that behind the apparently mechanical processes of the universe are both Divine awareness and Divine purpose," processes which are represented in sleep and waking, in silence and singing respectively.[5] Lewis does not only use this metaphor in his presentation of Mark. The *eldila*, who represent an angel-like intelligence full of pure wisdom, possess "unsleeping minds," which contrast with Mark's passivity. (*THS*, 199). So thorough is Mark's metaphorical sleepiness that Jane observes, "only one thing ever seemed able to keep him awake after he had gone to bed, and even that did not keep him awake for long," an observation that hints at Mark's redemption later in the novel (*THS*, 12).

Jane parallels her new husband's narrative, shifting perspectives within each chapter, creating a "monotonous rhythm" on which the story progresses.[6] *That Hideous Strength* opens with Jane recalling the words of her marriage ceremony just six months prior. Though she and Mark have agreed not to have children so that Jane can continue her academic career and further develop her thesis, Jane makes little to no progress on this thesis, pulling out her notes and texts each day, but remaining wholly unfruitful. Lewis's use of irony here is acute, for the very thesis that causes Jane to reject her own body's healthy sexuality and desire for procreation is a commentary on John Donne and the "triumphant vindication of the body" (*THS*, 12).

While her research details the value of subduing one's body with the superior mind, her bodily life suffers, constrained by her own cold and distant academic air. Rather than marry her mind and body in the hierarchy outlined by her thesis, Jane prefers to separate her own body and mind. Thus, the unproductivity in her thesis is reflective of her unproductive marriage. What Jane professes to know in theory, she rejects in reality. Because of this hypocrisy, Jane finds that the comradeship she imagined would come with her marriage instead seems more like prison or isolation (*THS*, 12). Jane grows increasingly irritable and bitter with her husband.

Though Jane is an academic, she is a fairly ordinary thinker—as depicted by her somewhat unoriginal and overworked thesis proposal—but her dreams or visions, which describe the future, are extraordinary. In the first few pages, Jane recalls her dream of a French prisoner whose head was detached from its body, carried away, and artificially resurrected. That morning, the headlines of Jane's newspaper detail a French prisoner sent to the guillotine for poisoning his wife. Literary scholar Sanford Schwartz considers this opening chapter of the novel and sees in Jane several tropes traditional of Gothic heroines. From the marital stagnancy, to the ability to see beyond in her dreams, to the shocks and paradigm shifts that come later in the novel, Jane's "Gothic credentials" are prevalent throughout.[7] Viewed within the Gothic novel paradigm, Jane's narrative in *That Hideous Strength* gains further significance in her spiritual coming-of-age.

While They Were Sleeping

Each of the three speakers experiences an "awakening" from their individual sleep. For Ransom, sleep came in the form of a drug-induced blackout. Travelling along the road in fog at the beginning of *Out of the Silent Planet*, Ransom runs into a woman who is distraught because her son has not been sent home from his hired labor at a professor's house. Ransom offers to call on this professor and ask for the boy to be sent home, secretly hoping to seek lodging with like-minded academics. Far from being similar men, Ransom finds the cruel Weston and his greedy compatriot, Richard Devine—the academics—trying to overpower the boy. Ransom asks that the boy be sent to his mother, and Weston begrudgingly consents when it is revealed that Ransom and Devine attended school together.

After a few minutes of food and drink, the reader next finds Ransom waking up in a spaceship bound for Mars, and Ransom realizes that Weston and Devine have drugged him—as they intended to do to the hired boy before Ransom entered. While asleep both physically and spiritually, Ransom is carried toward

Malacandra where he will soon hear the Old Solar tongue for the first time and meet the Oyarsa of that planet. Upon his arrival, Ransom's "first impression [of the planet] was of a bright, pale world—a watercolour world out of a child's paint-box" (*OSP*, 43). The first moments on Malacandra are blurry and bright, like the first glimpses of sunrise viewed through waking eyes. This moment serves its literary purpose by using the imagery of waking up to describe Ransom's enlightenment and introduction to the heavens.

Mark is more obviously portrayed as a sleepy intellectual. As *That Hideous Strength* unfolds, Mark enters into problematic situations with his docile silence. By the time of *That Hideous Strength*, Devine has championed the late Weston's cause of controlling nature, the heavens, and life itself through science. Giving himself the new name Lord Feverstone, Devine tells Mark that Weston was murdered for "being on our side" (*THS*, 39). Again seduced by that inclusive pronoun "our," Mark becomes more interested in the N.I.C.E., declaring his alignment with Weston's side (*THS*, 40). When invited to work with the organization, Mark goes to their base at Belbury to spend a few days. However, this puts his fellowship at Bracton College into question, and both Bracton and Belbury interpret Mark's unassertive participation in the inner circle to mean that Mark has joined Belbury and declined his fellowship. Mark hopes he can continue to affiliate with both institutions, keeping himself in the particular companies of the leaders of each, but realizes that he must choose.

In an attempt to clarify his duties with the Deputy Director John Wither if he commits to the N.I.C.E., Mark receives only vague answers assuring him that he is most valuable to the Institute, that he is among friends, and that his questions will be satisfied. After this, Mark does not confront the leaders of the N.I.C.E. regarding his duties. In part, this passivity is driven by the impression that the leaders expected Mark already to know his responsibilities and the fear that he, in fact, did not know them. Mark's resistance to confrontation is further enhanced by "the warm and almost drugged atmosphere" of the N.I.C.E. (*THS*, 52). Here, Lewis's acronym gains another layer of significance: the N.I.C.E. and its members certainly seem nice, insofar as they are inoffensive. However, this very inoffensiveness is the hallmark of their falsehood. Though Mark does not yet realize it, the work of Weston and Devine has put life and natural order into jeopardy. When such war is afoot, it is often necessary to take the offensive. Mark's rather noncommittal participation inadvertently resigns him to association with the evil desires and missions of the N.I.C.E., a sleepy prison in which Mark will eventually awake.

As for Jane's sleep, it is both literal and metaphorical. While she literally sleeps, terrifying dreams come to her that are made all the more disconcerting by their real-life parallels. Frightened by her dream of the French prisoner

Alcasan, she seeks consolation in purchasing a new hat and, along the way, meets her old tutor's wife, Mother Dimble. Mother Dimble invites Jane for tea, and the two women chat until Mrs. Dimble asks a question about marriage and Jane melts into tears, overwhelmed with worry at her dreams. Much later that night, still deeply anxious of the vivid occurrences in her sleep, her usual uptight irritability momentarily deserts Jane as she sobbingly embraces her husband upon his return home (*THS*, 42). Following the Dimbles' recommendation that Jane visit their friend, Grace Ironwood, in order to understand the nature of these visions, Jane almost accidentally stumbles into the manor at St. Anne's, not realizing where she was walking until she had arrived (*THS*, 134). Without plan or preparation, Jane arrives at St. Anne's unready for the impending plot.

Upon speaking with the aloof Miss Ironwood, Jane learns that her visions—or "dreaming realities"—are inherited from her Tudor ancestry, a surname she tries not to take pride in but one that later connects her to Arthurian rulership (*THS*, 65). Still amid her own cosmic sleepiness, Jane joins the community at St. Anne's where Ransom has become Director, and it is upon meeting him that Jane is awakened to the cosmos. After a few days of Mark spending time in the N.I.C.E. and Jane investing in relationships at St. Anne's, the couple spends a night together at home. Their interaction is all pretense and poise, much like the plumage of mating birds. These two "were young, and if neither loved very much, each was still anxious to be admired" (*THS*, 87). At this point in Mark and Jane's relationship, they are both still sleepy, or—as the Green Lady on Perelandra would say—young.

Coming of Age

Each character, having experienced his or her own personal enlightenment, then undergoes a coming-of-age. For Ransom, this is a process that begins most vibrantly on Malacandra, but continues on Perelandra. After humbling himself to the *hrossa*'s teachings on the three species of Malacandra and the nature of the universe overseen by Maleldil, the *hrossa* invite Ransom to join their hunt of the sea creature, the *hnakra*. In the middle of this hunt, an *eldil* messenger summons Ransom to the Oyarsa of Malacandra. Overwhelmed with the prospect of beholding a planetary deity, Ransom's courage quavers and he insists on finishing the hunt first "to hold on to his new-found manhood; now or never—with such companions or with none" (*OSP*, 81). In a flurry of rising waves and hurled spears, Ransom and Hyoi kill the *hnakra*. Alluding to Ransom's experience in the First World War and foreshadowing the battles to come, the account depicts Ransom's pride of completion, "They were all *hnau*. They had stood shoulder to shoulder in the face of the enemy, and the shapes of their heads no longer mattered. And he, even Ransom, had come through it and not been disgraced. He had grown up" (*OSP*, 82).

Though Ransom is certainly not a traditional *bildungsroman* character—he is a grown man already quite certain of his personal identity—Lewis's repetition of a coming-of-age theme stresses the necessity of a steadfast spiritual growth for the characters involved in the cosmic battle. Schwartz asserts that "Lewis addresses the collective trauma of his own generation and attempts to instill . . . the *good* element in the martial spirit, the discipline and freedom from anxiety," virtues that are confirmed later as Ransom finally meets Malacandra.[8]

Marking the death of his ignorance, Ransom travels to Perelandra, not in a science-propelled spaceship but in a coffin moved by Maleldil. In a parallel of hunting the *hnakra*, Ransom faces a necessary battle on Perelandra when he is confronted with the Un-man. The Un-man and Ransom both talk to the Green Lady, trying to make her "older," but the ideological warfare soon dissolves into hand-to-hand combat where Ransom strangles the Un-man, bashes in his head, and hurls him into the lake of fire. In hunting the *hnakra* and murdering embodied evil, Ransom has slain his dragons so that in the third and final narrative he can receive honor.

Mark's moment of enlightenment and the beginning of his spiritual maturation occur in a single horrific moment. The Head of the prisoner—which Jane saw in her first vision—was taken by the N.I.C.E., artificially resurrected with an evil concoction of science and dark magic, and enthroned as the N.I.C.E.'s little Oyarsa. As Jane determines from her vision of Mark's encounter with the speaking Head, Mark faints (*THS*, 180). Disgusted with the hideous strength that vandalized natural law, Mark suddenly takes an active initiative to leave the N.I.C.E. Leaving, however, is not so simple. The N.I.C.E. police chief Miss Hardcastle captures Mark and accuses him of the murder of another member who attempted to escape from the institution, but then offers to suppress her supposed "facts" if he continues to work for the N.I.C.E. and brings his visionary wife into their team as well (*THS*, 207). When Mark refuses to bring his wife into their cruel company, he is taken prisoner and sentenced to death. For Mark, this moment is death to passivity and ignorance. Mark realizes that what appears *nice* is, in fact, truly evil (*THS*, 296). In beholding the Head, Mark stares evil in the face, defeats his own passivity, and comes of age.

As for Jane, her encounter with Ransom, who is now the Fisher-King, reorients her worldview. Just by standing in his presence, "her world was unmade . . . Anything might happen now" (*THS*, 140). As described in Chapter 7, the Fisher-King of Arthurian legend was a wounded king who led young souls, like Parzival, toward the Holy Grail. Similarly, Ransom was wounded, will eventually become a king, and continues to lead the souls at St. Anne's toward cosmic enlightenment. Calling upon Gothic tropes, Schwartz explains that this moment "sublimates the classic Gothic encounter with a mysterious male authority into an unforeseen spiritual transformation, and translates the reader from the stifling air of Gothic oppression to the 'marvelous' realm of traditional romance" reminding the reader of Psyche and Cupid and of Parzival and the original Mr. Fisher-King.[9] Opening herself to this mystical romance eventually leads to Jane's personal redemption, but that is prefaced by a long trial that ages Jane emotionally and spiritually. Like her husband, Jane is arrested by the N.I.C.E. interrogated, and tortured by Miss Hardcastle. As the policewoman pesters Jane to ascertain information about their rival, St. Anne's, the Gothic "ogress" burns Jane with a lit cigar in a symbolic trial by fire.[10] But Jane has become older, and she refuses to answer her interrogator. She recognizes that the N.I.C.E. is an enemy of the human race, even though terror causes such a scene to become unreal. As if "between sleeping and waking," Jane resists the pressure of this Institution representative, demonstrating the effects of her cosmic awakening at St. Anne's (*THS*, 152).

Redeeming the Voices

As each of these narrators comes into their own and begins to understand the cosmic battle between the Oyéresu of other planets and the Bent One of Thulcandra, these three voices also adopt the voices of other planets, becoming their representatives on the silent Earth. Having navigated the order of heavens physically and metaphorically, Ransom, Mark, and Jane begin to live out a changed morality which is reflective of the great cosmic order, thus finalizing their redemption. During a conversation with Jane about her visions, Ransom asks, "Did you know that all the planets are represented in each?" (*THS*, 313). Ransom explains that each Oyarsa in Heaven appoints an Earthly representative. The first representative of Heaven comes to maturation in Ransom. His initial taste of this responsibility comes on Perelandra when he is chosen as the heavenly Oyéresu's representative to combat the "representative of Hell," the Un-man (*PER*, 120). Lewis highlights this connection by the use of messianic language. For example, the Un-man wounds Ransom's ankle, and Ransom bashes in the head of the Un-man. From Lewis's Christian worldview, this is reminiscent of the curse of Satan in Genesis, where God tells Satan that the Messiah would crush his head, but he would strike the heel of the Messiah.[11] Lewis also uses Ransom's exclamatory language—"By Jove" and "Good God,"—to connect him with Glund-Oyarsa, the ruler of Jupiter and high king over the other Oyéresu (*PER*, 19). Later at the manor at St. Anne's, the Oyéresu come to hold council with Ransom, Merlin, and company as they strategize the defeat of the N.I.C.E. Before this council, Ransom explains to Merlin that he has become a bridge between the earth and the heavens (*THS*, 288). On Thulcandra, the spirits of the planets work via incarnation. When the Oyéresu come, Ransom, who is already called to be the Pendragon, now receives the power of the "King of Kings" (*THS*, 324).

As suggested by the meaning of his name, Mark—consecrated to Mars—is redeemed and called into representing Malacandra on Earth. The connection that Lewis draws between these two is not a trite transformation of Mark becoming more combative, but rather as deep, assured, and wise as the inhabitants of Malacandra themselves. According to Schwartz, Lewis "portrays the Malacandrans not as untried innocents but as courageous and disciplined rational beings."[12] It is these very qualities of courage, discipline, and reason that Mark gains as a result of his terrifying encounter with the Head. Juxtaposed with his passive insecurity at the outset of the narrative, Mark becomes demonstratively masculine in his marriage. By the end of *That Hideous Strength*, Mark learns to view his marriage not as an asset to bolster his image among the elite, but rather as something more poetic. He realizes the error of believing that marriage was merely a status symbol. Rather, he comes to understand that "one might as well have thought one could buy a sunset by buying the field from which one had seen it" (*THS*, 359). Ward further expounds the medieval Martian imagery, "The complexity Lewis finds in such imagery is perhaps best expressed if we refer to *Till We Have Faces* and say that Malacandra is a 'weaponed' world, where 'weaponed' means a man who is not a eunuch."[13] This aspect of cosmic masculinity makes Mark and Jane's marital consummation at the end of *That Hideous Strength* significant, for it is in this moment that Mark becomes fully representative of Malacandra on Thulcandra.

Jane—meaning "God is gracious"—becomes a planetary representative for Perelandra, standing as Lewis's depiction of Venus in all her poise, fertility, and pure love. While working alongside Mrs. Dimble and Jane's former housekeeper, Ivy Maggs, to prepare a bedroom for Ivy and her husband, Jane is overwhelmed with "age-old superstitions, jokes, and sentimentalities about bridal beds and marriage bowers" (*THS*, 298). This work reminds her of her own falsely accused and imprisoned husband and incites another vision full of bright colors that seem similar to the colorful warmth with which Ransom describes Perelandra (*THS*, 302). Lewis uses this similarity of color to parallel Ransom's and Jane's awakening and redemption. Earlier in the novel, Jane strolls the gardens of St. Anne's considering the imagery of gardens. She recalls Freud's assertion that people find beauty in gardens because they symbolize the beauty of the female body. Though Freud intended something less wholesome by his connection, the observation holds true: Jane's mind is as fertile as a garden, producing dreams pregnant with reality.

Here, the hypocrisy of Jane's thesis on the wondrous body and her own rejection of that body are held accountable. The nature of the garden teaches Jane natural law, thus initiating her redemption. Later, preparing for the council of the planets at St. Anne's, Mother Dimble, Ivy, Camilla, and Jane find a wardrobe of women's gowns, and each tries on a robe or mantle. As they dress, each woman seems to become an archetype of some kind; Ivy becomes a "fairy," Camilla a "Valkyrie," and Mother Dimble "an old tribal matriarch" (*THS*, 360). At first Jane thinks her gown too "fussy" and has no ancient words of compliment for herself, but later, when Perelandra rests on St. Anne's, it becomes clearer that she has become Perelandra herself on Earth (*THS*, 361). Schwartz highlights in Jane's redemption "the shift from Being to Becoming... and the psychological, spiritual, and cosmological implications" that ensue.[14] Jane is ransomed in her Perelandrian contentment with her community and her marriage—a profound transformation from the opening chapter—and her Venereal fertility, consummated with Mark in the last chapter. Jane's voice has become that of Perelandra.

Awake and Sing

The voices of these three speakers change as they are woken from their spiritual sleep, matured through trials, and eventually redeemed by encounters with Maleldil, becoming earthly representatives of the planets themselves. Using the imagery of sleeping and waking, silence and song, Lewis portrays these three protagonists as "self-divided, self-exiled, diseased Tellurians," and thus, "dramatizes the meaning of alienation from the Divine Will."[15] In so doing, Lewis brings the arc of his exhortation to a conclusion. Schwartz says, "If 'bad things are good things perverted,' as Lewis faithfully maintained, then the ultimate act of transfiguration is the regeneration and 'raising up' of an anguished creation into new life, or as [Lewis] put it elsewhere, 'the process of turning finite creatures (with free wills) into—well, into Gods.'"[16] His underlying theological ideals, expressed so carefully in the narrative of the Ransom Trilogy, are brought to completion as the cosmic work, which began in the Heavens, is brought to Earth in the persons of Ransom, Mark, and Jane, "For it is not on Mars or Venus, but on Earth, that the real test... must come."[17] Amid the cosmic song of the planets, the Silent Planet must begin its song—a song that will either align with the rhythm of Maleldil or the Bent One. In the redemption of Ransom, Mark, and Jane, they wake to the voice of Maleldil and assume the voices of Glundandra, Malacandra, and Perelandra upon Earth, beginning the song of the Silent Planet.

In the portrayal of these three protagonist voices, Lewis's exhortation to the reader echoes that in the epistle to the Ephesians, "Wake up, sleeper, rise from the dead."[18] A great cosmic battle is being waged, and sleepy silence will not do. Many voices will filter what is heard: the smooth science, the modern education, the preservation of self. Take care to discern the redeemed voices from the bent ones. Those under the influence of the Bent One, like Weston, will try to further sleep by administering the drug of some sweet-sounding ideology. Do not give in. Wake up to the Solar tongue and know thyself like Ransom. Though silence may open the door to the prestigious inner circle, it will also open the very gates of Hell. Wake up to the voice of Maleldil, be aware and be called to action like Mark. Keep sleeping, and reality will become merely glimpses in a dream, causing unproductive dissatisfaction. Be transformed by and contented in His presence like Jane. Awake and speak and sing with the planets the cosmic song "Blessed be He," for "Only the least part has served, or ever shall, a beast, a man, or a god. But always . . . it is what it is and utters the heart of the Holy One with its own voice" (*PER*, 185). Like Ransom, Mark, and Jane, assume the voice of Maleldil, and wake the Silent Planet.

Endnotes

1 C. S. Lewis, *An Experiment in Criticism* (Cambridge, UK: Cambridge University Press, 2013), 138.
2 Wayne Shumaker, "The Cosmic Trilogy," in *The Longing for a Form: Essays on the Fiction of C. S. Lewis*, ed. Peter J. Schakel (Kent, OH: Kent State University Press, 1977), 63.
3 David C. Downing, *Planets in Peril: A Critical Study of C. S. Lewis's Ransom Trilogy* (Amherst, MA: University of Massachusetts Press, 1995), 139.
4 Downing, *Planets in Peril*, 139.
5 Shumaker, 55.
6 Sanford Schwartz, *C. S. Lewis on the Final Frontier: Science and the Supernatural in the Space Trilogy* (New York: Oxford University Press, 2009), 91.
7 Schwartz, 96.
8 Schwartz, 33.
9 Schwartz, 107.
10 Schwartz, 110.
11 Genesis 3:14–15 (NIV).
12 Schwartz, 13.
13 Michael Ward, *Planet Narnia: The Seven Heavens in the Imagination of C. S. Lewis* (New York: Oxford University Press, 2008), 81.
14 Schwartz, 15.
15 Schumaker, 53.
16 Schwartz, 149.
17 Schumaker, 63.
18 Ephesians 5:14 (NIV).

ACKNOWLEDGMENTS

We would like to thank the following mentors, scholars, friends, and family:

DANIEL F.: Dr. Scott Key, for providing insight into the philosophy of Lewis; Dr. Micah Watson, for his scholarly work on Lewis's political philosophy and understanding of natural law; and Dr. David Weeks, for his exemplary leadership in the Honors College and dedication to the moral and intellectual development of his students.

DANIEL H.: Sørina Higgins, for her careful and unprecedented work in the growing field of Inklings and Arthurian Legend studies; and Brenton Dickieson, for his work on Lewis's early poems and his popular, yet well-informed, blog: A Pilgrim in Narnia.

EVANGELINE: Dr. Richard Lawes, for embodying the classic Oxford Don; Glen Prior, for introducing me to science fiction; and Reilly, for providing words when I only have thoughts.

JACOB: Mike Glyer, for being the guiding voice of contemporary science fiction during my writing process; Prof. Michael Lee, for being another musician fascinated with the world of the classics and science fiction; and my father Tom Meyer for inspiring and fostering interest in science fiction from a very early age.

J.D.: Tim DeMarse, for his insight on the historical period of WWII; Josh Randall, for sharing his historical knowledge, reviewing our work, and providing illustrations; and special thanks to Barbara Hayes for her help in editing these pages with such care and attention.

JULIANNE: The Johnson family, for their endless support and love; Dr. Charlie W. Starr, for his enlightening work in Lewis scholarship and for taking the time to be a mentor to me; and Dr. Roger White for pointing me in the right direction in my research.

MAYA: Dr. Adams, for her insight into the universes of the ancients and medievals; Dr. White, for his guidance in researching the work of C. S. Lewis; Michael Ward, for his incredible works; Chris Armstrong, for sharing practical wisdom; my family and friends, for being my support through this writing process; and my parents, for always being in my corner.

NOLAN: Dr. Adam Green, for providing authoritative critique; John and Janet Croce, for unconditionally loving me and supporting my academic endeavors; Will Vaus, for creating *Mere Theology*, a comprehensive guide to Lewis's theology that informed the beginnings of my research and let me know I was headed in the right direction; and Pershing Lum, for listening to me go on and on about the Trilogy.

RACHEL: Dr. Bob Roller, for reading stories; Wanda Roller, for listening to endless rants and critiquing countless drafts; and Dr. Joshua Morris, for opening the closed box of ontological naturalism.

SARAH: Walter Hooper, for the work he has done to shed light on C. S. Lewis; Ron Jensen, for introducing me to the Trilogy; and Dr. Roger White for helping me to explore the far reaches of Lewissian thought.

GLOSSARY

Alcasan, Francois. A radiologist beheaded for poisoning his wife. His disembodied head is kept artificially alive by the N.I.C.E.

Arthurian legend. A term that describes the body of literature (primarily English, French, and German) pertaining to King Arthur and the adventures of his court. These legends are expressed in many different literary genres, from historical accounts to cycles of romances, and they thrived during the Middle Ages.

Arbol, Field of. The realm of the heavens that encompasses the modern Solar System.

Avalon. According to some accounts, Avalon is an island King Arthur goes to for final rest and healing.

Barfield, Owen. A member of the Inklings and one of Lewis's closest friends. Much of Barfield's writing deals with the philosophy of language.

Belbury. The town where the headquarters of the N.I.C.E. is located.

Bent One. A Malacandrian name for the fallen Oyarsa of Thulcandra, the Satan or Devil of Christian theology.

bentness. The closest term for "evil" in the language of the unfallen Malacandrians.

Bracton College. The small, graduate-only college in Edgestow where Mark Studdock is employed before he joins the N.I.C.E.

Bragdon Wood. An ancient, walled forest on the grounds of Bracton College, containing a site known as Merlin's Well.

Mr. Bultitude. A bear who lives at St. Anne's. He is the last of the seven bears of Logres.

cosmology. A doctrine that describes the purpose, origin, nature, and order of the universe.

chronological snobbery. Overconfidence in present ideas coupled with a disdain for the past; the assumption that new ideas are always better than old ones.

deep heaven. Old-Solar term for outer space. The dwelling place of the *eldila.*

Denniston, Arthur. An old friend of Mark who lives at St. Anne's. Married to Camilla Denniston.

Denniston, Camilla. Wife of Arthur Denniston. She encourages Jane to join the company at St. Anne's.

Devine, Richard. One of the two men who kidnap Ransom at the beginning of *Out of the Silent Planet.* Charming and manipulative, he is later known as Lord Feverstone.

Dimble, Dr. Cecil. An academic and friend of Mark who lives at St. Anne's.

Dimble, "Mother" Margaret. Wife of Cecil Dimble. She has no children, yet she is very motherly toward Jane. Lives at St. Anne's.

Dyson, Hugo. A member of the Inklings, known for his role in Lewis's conversion to Christianity and for his vocal dislike of Tolkien's *Lord of the Rings.*

Edgestow. The small country town at the center of the action in *That Hideous Strength,* home to the University that includes Bracton College.

eldil. The angel-like servants of Maleldil. Plural *eldila* or *eldils.*

evolutionism. Belief in the myth of inevitable progress, championed by science fiction author H. G. Wells.

Filostrato. A scientist in the N.I.C.E. who works with the Head and believes in the complete conquest of nature and eradication of organic life.

Fisher-King. A character in the Grail Quest (a subgenre of Arthurian Legend). Sometimes he is portrayed as a badly-wounded king who passes time by fishing. In *That Hideous Strength,* it is the surname of Ransom's sister, which Ransom adopts.

Fixed Land. The portion of land on Perelandra that was not floating on the surface of the water. Tor and Tinidril were forbidden to sleep upon it.

Frost, Augustus. A member of the inner circle of the N.I.C.E. along with Wither. He focuses on teaching Mark "objectivity."

Glundandra. In Old Solar, the name of the planet Jupiter.

Glund-Oyarsa. The Oyarsa (or ruler) of Glundandra, a planetary spirit of majestic pomp and jollity.

Greeves, Arthur. A close friend of Lewis, the pair exchanged letters throughout their lives.

Haldane, J. B. S. British biochemist, advocate of eugenics, author of "The Last Judgment" and "Auld Hornie, F. R. S."

handramit. Old Solar word for "low earth." The warm valleys of Malacandra where the *hrossa* live.

harandra. Old Solar word for "high earth." The cold mountains of Malacandra where the *séroni* live.

Miss Hardcastle. Also called "The Fairy," she is the head of the N.I.C.E. Institutional Police and known for her cruelty.

the Head. The disembodied head of a criminal named Francois Alcasan. The N.I.C.E. keeps it alive by using a complicated (and unexplained) technology.

Hingest, William. A physical chemist at the N.I.C.E., Hingest is killed while attempting to leave the organization.

hnakra. A vicious aquatic creature native to Malacandra. Plural *hnéraki.*

hnau. A term used to identify any rational being made in the image of Maleldil.

hross. One of the three species of *hnau* on Malacandra. Tribal, seal-like poets who live in the *handramits.* Plural *hrossa,* feminine plural *hressni.*

Huxley, Aldous. British writer and philosopher known for writing *Brave New World.*

Hyoi. The first *hross* Ransom encounters on Malacandra. They become close friends.

Inklings. A writers' group that included C. S. Lewis, Warren Hamilton Lewis, J.R.R. Tolkien, Christopher Tolkien, Owen Barfield, and Charles Williams.

Ironwood, Grace. A psychologist who lives at St. Anne's and helps Jane interpret her dreams.

Joy. In the Lewissian sense of *Surprised by Joy,* a deep longing for the transcendent.

Jules, Horace. The figurehead director of the N.I.C.E.

King of Perelandra. The Adam-figure of *Perelandra.* Also called Tor.

Lewis, Warren. Brother of C. S. Lewis and a member of the Inklings. Served as an officer in the British Army. Published on French history.

Lindsay, David. Scottish science fiction writer. Author of *A Voyage to Arcturus.*

Logres. The Kingdom of Arthur, interpreted by Charles Williams as a true remnant, a faithful minority akin to the biblical accounts of a tribe of godly Jews in idolatrous Israel.

Lord Feverstone. A title given to Richard Devine.

Lurga. Old Solar name for Saturn. Also the Oyarsa (or ruler) of Lurga, planetary spirit of old age, sorrow, and death.

MacDonald, George. Scottish writer and theologian whose works greatly inspired Lewis.

MacPhee, Andrew. A scientist and skeptic who lives at St. Anne's.

Maggs, Ivy. A woman who once worked for Jane as a maid and now lives at St. Anne's.

Malacandra. Old Solar name for Mars. Also the Oyarsa (or ruler) of Malacandra, planetary spirit of fearless military vigilance and masculinity.

Maleldil. Old Solar name for God.

Meldilorn. The paradisiacal island where the Oyarsa of Malacandra held council.

Merlin. A magician from Arthurian Legend who appears in *That Hideous Strength* as a key ally for the Company at St. Anne's.

myth. A term Lewis often uses to describe a story that offers a taste of divine reality and truth.

N.I.C.E. The National Institute of Co-ordinated Experiments. The villains of *That Hideous Strength.*

objectivity. Belief in objective or absolute value.

"objectivity." Perverted sense of objectivity. The belief that science is the only source of objective fact. Similar to Logical Positivism.

Old Solar. In Lewis's mythology, Old Solar is the language spoken universally before the Tower of Babel. Also called *Hressa-Hlab,* it is still spoken by the *hrossa* of Malacandra.

Oyarsa. Ruler of a planet, usually an *eldil,* but also given to Tor and Tinidril as rulers of Perelandra. Plural Oyéresu.

Parzival. A character from Arthurian legend known for seeking the Holy Grail. The Parzival archetype is a pure-hearted "chosen one" who is sent on a quest.

Pendragon. The King of Logres in the line of Aeneas of Rome and King Arthur. The true spiritual leader of Britain.

Perelandra. Old Solar name for Venus. Also the Oyarsa of Perelandra, planetary spirit of charity, Joy, and femininity.

pfifltrigg. One of the three species of *hnau* on Malacandra. Busy, frog-like, skilled artisans who live in the dry sea beds. Plural *pfifltitriggi.*

Queen of Perelandra. The Eve of *Perelandra.* Also called Tinidril.

Ransom, Elwin. Protagonist of the Ransom Trilogy. Initially described as a middle-aged philologist and a veteran of the first World War with a penchant for walking tours, he becomes the 79th Pendragon after his journeys to Malacandra and Perelandra.

scientism. The belief that mere human survival is of greater moral import than human pity, happiness, or freedom. Also the belief that science is the only reliable source of knowledge.

Silent Planet. Another term used by those in deep heaven to describe Earth.

sorn. One of the three species of *hnau* on Malacandra. Wise, tall, feathery intellectuals who live on the *harandra.* Plural séroni or sorns.

St. Anne's. Also referred to as the Company at St. Anne's. The community in *That Hideous Strength* that opposes the N.I.C.E. and the dark eldila. Led by Ransom.

Stapledon, Olaf. British science fiction author. Wrote novels such as *Odd John, Star Maker,* and *Last and First Men.*

Straik. A reverend who uses the Bible to justify the actions of the N.I.C.E. He is a candidate for induction into the inner circle along with Mark.

Studdock, Jane Tudor. Protagonist of *That Hideous Strength.* Married to Mark Studdock. A seer, gifted with second sight or the ability to see present and future realities in dreams.

Studdock, Mark Gainsby. Protagonist of *That Hideous Strength.* Married to Jane. An insecure young academic at Bracton College who becomes entangled in the plots of the N.I.C.E.

subjectivism. The belief that there is no external or objective truth.

Tao. Chinese for the "Way." The doctrine of objective value.

Tellus. Old Solar name for Earth before it became the silent planet.

Thulcandra. Earth. Old Solar name meaning "the silent planet."

Tinidril. Queen of Perelandra and the Eve-figure of *Perelandra,* wife of Tor. Also called the "Green Lady."

Tolkien, J.R.R. British writer, philologist, and a member of the Inklings. Best known for writing *The Hobbit* and *The Lord of the Rings.*

Tor. King of Perelandra and the Adam-figure of *Perelandra,* husband of Tinidril.

Treaty of Versailles. Treaty that ended the war between the Allies and the Central Powers in World War I. Its punishing terms are considered to be a contributing cause to the collapse of the German economy in the interim between the wars.

Un-man. Weston, after he has been overtaken by a dark spirit in *Perelandra.*

Viritrilbia. Old Solar name for Mercury. Also the Oyarsa of Viritrilbia, planetary spirit of language and meaning.

Wells, H. G. British author often considered the father of science fiction. Wrote *The Time Machine* and *The First Men in the Moon.*

Weston, Edward Rolles. A physicist who builds a spaceship to travel to Malacandra in *Out of the Silent Planet* and later becomes the Un-man in *Perelandra.*

Williams, Charles. A British poet, novelist, literary critic, and member of the Inklings, whose poetic work Lewis highly praised.

Wither, John. Deputy Director of the N.I.C.E. and member of the inner ring. He speaks a lot but says nothing.

RECOMMENDED READING

Alighieri, Dante. *The Divine Comedy,* translated by John Ciardi, 2003. An enduring classic, essential for understanding the medieval mindset and its influence on Lewis.

Armstrong, Chris R. *Medieval Wisdom for Modern Christians: Finding Authentic Faith in a Forgotten Age with C. S. Lewis,* 2016. An accessible source for understanding and applying the medieval wisdom that Lewis embraced.

Downing, David C. *Planets in Peril,* 1995. An approachable, scholarly examination of the Ransom Trilogy.

Glyer, Diana Pavlac. *Bandersnatch: C. S. Lewis, J. R. R. Tolkien, and the Creative Collaboration of the Inklings*, 2015. An inspiring account of the Inklings' creative process.

Higgins, Sørina. *The Inklings and King Arthur*, 2017. The most comprehensive study to date of the Inklings' interaction with Arthuriana.

Lewis, C.S. "A Reply to Professor Haldane," 2017. A concise explanation and biting critique of scientism.

———. *The Abolition of Man,* 2015. One of Lewis's most prophetic works, and the non-fiction presentation of themes explored fictionally in *That Hideous Strength.*

———. "The Poison of Subjectivism," 1995. One of Lewis's essays that compliments the *Abolition* in explaining his views on the philosophy of subjectivism.

———. *The Screwtape Letters*, 2015. Lewis's convicting and satirical look at temptation from the perspective of a demon, and a helpful resource for understanding *Perelandra*.

Lewis, Warren H. and Walter Hooper, eds. *Letters of C. S. Lewis,* 2017. The best way to understand Lewis is to read his own words about his works.

Milton, John. *Paradise Lost,* 2007. Milton's classic epic retelling of the Genesis Fall narrative, which influenced Lewis's *Perelandra.*

Sayer, George. *Jack: A Life of C. S. Lewis,* 1988. A faithful account of Lewis's life.

Schakel, Peter J. *The Longing for a Form,* 1977. A collection of scholarly essays on several of Lewis's fiction works, serving as an introductory literary criticism.

Starr, Charlie W. *The Faun's Bookshelf,* 2018. An excellent examination of myth in Lewis's life and works.

Wells, H. G. *The First Men in the Moon,* 1969. Wells' early science fiction novel that detailed two men journeying to the Moon and strongly influenced *Out of the Silent Planet.*

———. *The Time Machine*, 2000. Wells' first novel, which introduced the theme of evolutionism that Lewis opposed.

BIBLIOGRAPHY

Aldiss, Brian W., Kingsley Amis, and C. S. Lewis. "Unreal Estates." In *Of Other Worlds: Essays and Stories*, edited by Walter Hooper, 135–51. New York: HarperCollins, 2017.

Alighieri, Dante. *The Divine Comedy.* Translated by John Ciardi. New York: New American Library, 2003.

Aquinas, Thomas. *Summa of the Summa.* Translated by the Fathers of the English Dominican Province. Edited by Peter Kreeft. San Francisco: Ignatius, 2012.

Armstrong, Chris R. *Medieval Wisdom for Modern Christians.* Grand Rapids, MI: Brazos, 2016.

Ashe, Geoffrey. *Mythology of the British Isles.* North Pomfret, VT: Trafalgar, 1990.

Baxendale, John, review of *Half the Battle: Civilian Morale in Britain During the Second World War,* by Robert Mackay. *Reviews in History* (June 2003). https://www.history.ac.uk/reviews/review/332#author-response.

Boenig, Robert. "The Face of the Materialist Magician: Lewis, Tolkien, and the Art of Crossing Perilous Streets." *Mythlore 35*, no. 1 (2016): 5–22.

Brazier, Paul H. *C. S. Lewis—On the Christ of a Religious Economy.* Eugene, OR: Pickwick, 2013.

Buber, Martin. *I and Thou.* Translated by Ronald Gregor Smith. New York: Scribner Classics, 1986.

Card, Orson Scott. Introduction to H. G. Wells, *The War of the Worlds*. New York: Scholastic Incorporated, 2005.

Carpenter, Humphrey. *The Inklings: C. S. Lewis, J. R. R. Tolkien, Charles Williams, and Their Friends*. New York: HarperCollins, 1997.

Castillo, Daniel. "German Economy in the 1920s." December 2003. http://www.history.ucsb.edu/faculty/marcuse/classes/33d/projects/1920s/Econ20s.

Catechism of the Catholic Church. Liguori, MO: Liguori Publications, 1994.

Chesterton, G. K. *The Everlasting Man*. New York: Dodd, Mead, & Company, 1925.

———. *Orthodoxy*. San Francisco: Ignatius, 1995.

Clark, David G. *C. S. Lewis: A Guide to his Theology*. Malden, MA: Blackwell, 2007.

De Troyes, Chrétien. *Arthurian Romances*. Translated and notes by D. D. R. Owen. London, UK: Everyman Classic, 1993.

Deasy, Philip. "God, Science, and C. S. Lewis." *Commonweal* 68 (1958): 421–23.

Dickieson, Brenton D. G. "Mixed Metaphors and Hyperlinked Worlds: A Study of Intertextuality in C. S. Lewis' Ransom Cycle." In *The Inklings and King Arthur: J. R. R. Tolkien, Charles Williams, C. S. Lewis, & Owen Barfield on the Matter of Britain*, edited by Sørina Higgins, 81–113. Berkeley, CA: Apocryphile, 2017.

Downing, David. C. *Into the Region of Awe: Mysticism in C. S. Lewis*. Downers Grove, IL: InterVarsity, 2005.

———. *The Most Reluctant Convert: C. S. Lewis's Journey to Faith*. Downers Grove, IL: InterVarsity, 2002.

———. *Planets in Peril: A Critical Study of C. S. Lewis's Ransom Trilogy*. Amherst, MA: University of Massachusetts Press, 1995.

Drabble, Margaret, ed. *The Oxford Companion to English Literature*. Oxford, UK: Oxford University Press, 1985.

Duriez, Colin. *Bedeviled: Lewis, Tolkien, and the Shadow of Evil*. Downers Grove, IL: InterVarsity, 2015.

Gaertner, Christopher. "Shape and Direction: Human Consciousness in the Inklings' Mythological Geographies." In *The Inklings and King Arthur: J. R. R. Tolkien, Charles Williams, C. S. Lewis, & Owen Barfield on the Matter of Britain*, edited by Sørina Higgins, 149–172. Berkeley, CA: Apocryphile, 2017.

Garth, John. "When J. R. R Tolkien Bet C. S. Lewis: The Wager that Gave Birth to *The Lord of the Rings*." *The Telegraph*. December 8, 2016. https://www.telegraph.co.uk/books/what-to-read/jrr-tolkien-bet-cs-lewis-wager-gave-birth-lord-rings.

Glyer, Diana Pavlac. *The Company They Keep: C. S. Lewis and J. R. R. Tolkien as Writers in Community*. Kent, OH: Kent State University Press, 2007.

Haggard, H. Rider. *King Solomon's Mines*. New York: Oxford University Press, 2008

———. *She*. New York: Oxford University Press, 2008.

Haldane, J. B. S. "Auld Hornie, F.R.S." In *Everything Has a History*. London, UK: Allen & Unwin, 1951. http://lewisiana.nl/haldane/.

———. "The Last Judgment." In *Possible Worlds and Other Essays*. London, UK: Chatto and Windus, 1927.

———. "Science and Politics." In *Possible Worlds and Other Essays*. London, UK: Chatto and Windus, 1927.

Hannay, Margaret. "Arthurian and Cosmic Myth in *That Hideous Strength*." *Mythlore: A Journal of J. R. R. Tolkien, C. S. Lewis, Charles Williams, General Fantasy and Mythic Studies 2*, no. 2 (1970): 7–9.

Higgins, Sørina. "The Matter of Logres: Arthuriana and the Inklings." In *The Inklings and King Arthur: J. R. R. Tolkien, Charles Williams, C. S. Lewis, & Owen Barfield on the Matter of Britain*, edited by Sørina Higgins, 25–59. Berkeley, CA: Apocryphile, 2017.

Hooper, Walter. *C. S. Lewis: A Companion and Guide*. New York: HarperCollins, 1996.

———. Foreword to *C. S. Lewis's Lost Aeneid: Arms and the Exile*, edited by A. T. Reyes, xi-xv. New Haven, CT: Yale University Press, 2011.

———. Introduction to *Boxen: The Imaginary World of the Young C. S. Lewis*, by C. S. Lewis, edited by Walter Hooper. London, UK: Harcourt Brace, 1985.

———. Introduction to *The Weight of Glory: And Other Addresses*, by C. S. Lewis. New York: HarperCollins, 2009.

———. Preface to *On Stories: And Other Essays on Literature*, by C. S. Lewis, edited by Walter Hooper, ix-xxi. New York: Harcourt Brace, 1982.

Huttar, Charles A. "Houses of Healing: The Idea of Avalon in Inklings Fiction and Poetry." In *The Inklings and King Arthur: J. R. R. Tolkien, Charles Williams, C. S. Lewis, & Owen Barfield on the Matter of Britain*, edited by Sørina Higgins, 115–147. Berkeley, CA: Apocryphile, 2017.

Huxley, Aldous. *Brave New World*. New York: HarperCollins, 1998.

Hynes, Samuel. "Guardian of the Old Ways." Review of *C. S. Lewis at the Breakfast Table: And Other Reminiscences*, edited by James T. Como, *New York Times*. July 8, 1979. https://www.nytimes.com/1979/07/08/archives/guardian-of-the-old-ways-guardian.html.

Imbert, Yannick. "From Myth to History and Back Again: Inklings Arthuriana in Historical Context." In *The Inklings and King Arthur: J. R. R. Tolkien, Charles Williams, C. S. Lewis, & Owen Barfield on the Matter of Britain*, edited by Sørina Higgins, 175–204. Berkeley, CA: Apocryphile, 2017.

Key, Scott. "Metaphors of Meaning: The Dance of Truth and Imagination in *That Hideous Strength*." In *Contemporary Perspectives on C. S. Lewis' The Abolition of Man*, edited by Timothy Mosteller and Gayne Anacker, 155–73. London, UK: Bloomsbury, 2017.

Lambert, Carole J. *Against Indifference*. New York: Peter Lang Publishing, 2015.

Lazo, Andrew. "Did C. S. Lewis Get it Wrong?" AndrewLazo.com. February 19, 2013. http://www.andrewlazo.com/2013/02/did-c-s-lewis-get-it-wrong/.

Lewis, C.S. *The Abolition of Man*. New York: HarperCollins, 2015.

———. "Answers to Questions on Christianity." In *God in the Dock: Essays on Theology and Ethics*. Grand Rapids, MI: Eerdmans, 2014.

———. "Charles Williams, *Taliessin Through Logres* (London: Oxford University Press, 1945)." Review of *Taliessin Through Logres,* by Charles Williams. In *Image and Imagination*, by C. S. Lewis, edited by Walter Hooper, 137–146. New York: Cambridge University Press, 2013.

———. "Christian Apologetics." In *God in the Dock: Essays on Theology and Ethics*. Grand Rapids, MI: Eerdmans, 2014.

———. *The Collected Letters of C. S. Lewis, Volume 1: Family Letters (1905–1931)*. Edited by Walter Hooper. New York: HarperCollins, 2000.

———. *The Collected Letters of C. S. Lewis, Volume 2: Books, Broadcasts and War (1931–1949)*. Edited by Walter Hooper. New York: HarperCollins, 2004.

———. *The Collected Letters of C. S. Lewis, Volume 3: Narnia, Cambridge and Joy (1950–1963)*. Edited by Walter Hooper. New York: HarperCollins, 2009.

———. "Cross-Examination." In *God in the Dock: Essays on Theology and Ethics*. Grand Rapids, MI: Eerdmans, 2014.

———. "De Descriptione Temporum." In *Selected Literary Essays* by C. S. Lewis, edited by Walter Hooper, 1–14. New York: Cambridge University Press, 1969.

———. *The Discarded Image*. Cambridge, UK: Cambridge University Press, 1964.

———. "Dymer." In *Narrative Poems* by C. S. Lewis, edited by Walter Hooper, 1–91. New York: Harcourt, 1969.

———. *An Experiment in Criticism*. New York: Cambridge University Press, 2013.

———. "Forms of Things Unknown." In *Of Other Worlds: Essays and Stories*, edited by Walter Hooper. New York: HarperCollins, 2017.

———. *The Four Loves*. New York: Mariner Books, 2012.

———. "The Funeral of a Great Myth." In *Christian Reflections*, edited by Walter Hooper. Grand Rapids, MI: Eerdmans, 2014.

———. Preface to *George MacDonald: An Anthology.* Edited by C. S. Lewis. New York: HarperCollins, 2009.

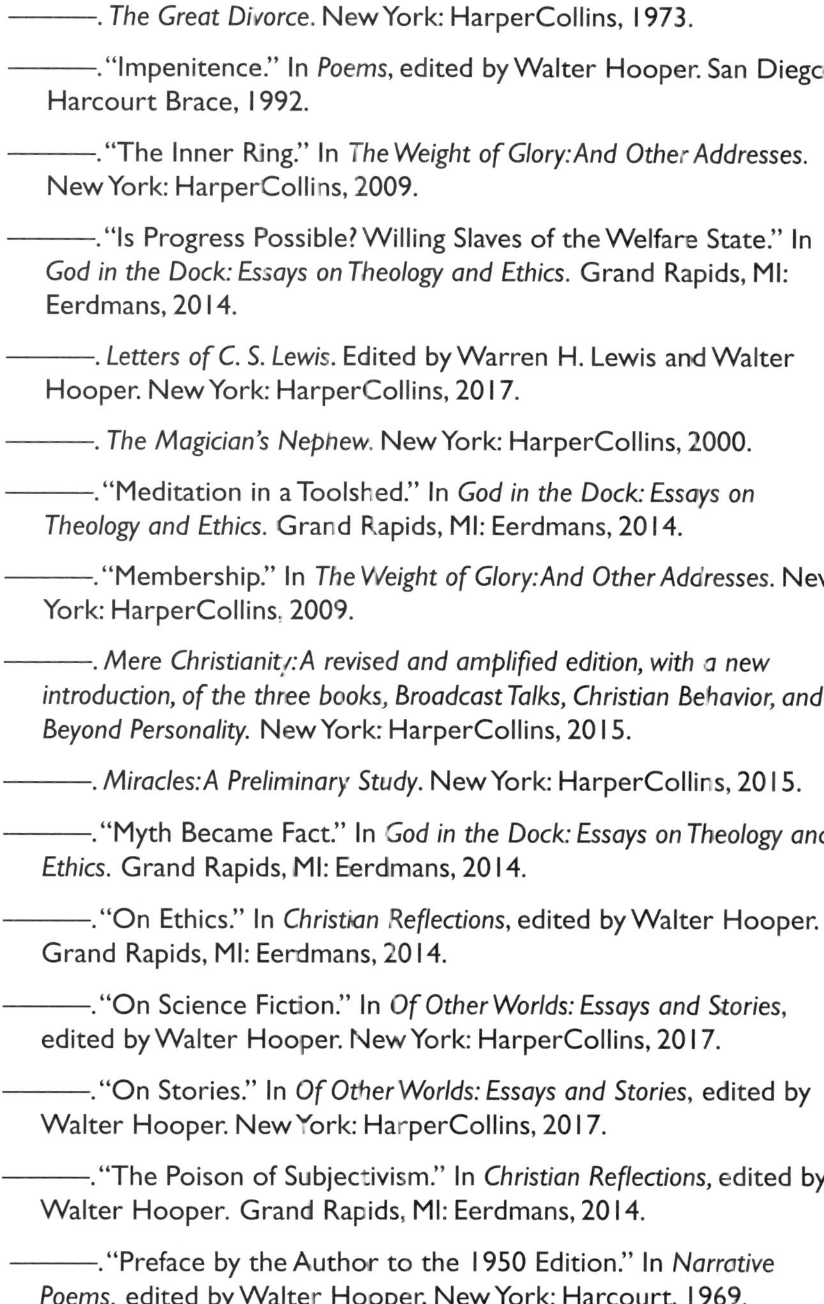

———. *The Great Divorce*. New York: HarperCollins, 1973.

———. "Impenitence." In *Poems*, edited by Walter Hooper. San Diego: Harcourt Brace, 1992.

———. "The Inner Ring." In *The Weight of Glory: And Other Addresses*. New York: HarperCollins, 2009.

———. "Is Progress Possible? Willing Slaves of the Welfare State." In *God in the Dock: Essays on Theology and Ethics*. Grand Rapids, MI: Eerdmans, 2014.

———. *Letters of C. S. Lewis*. Edited by Warren H. Lewis and Walter Hooper. New York: HarperCollins, 2017.

———. *The Magician's Nephew*. New York: HarperCollins, 2000.

———. "Meditation in a Toolshed." In *God in the Dock: Essays on Theology and Ethics*. Grand Rapids, MI: Eerdmans, 2014.

———. "Membership." In *The Weight of Glory: And Other Addresses*. New York: HarperCollins, 2009.

———. *Mere Christianity: A revised and amplified edition, with a new introduction, of the three books, Broadcast Talks, Christian Behavior, and Beyond Personality*. New York: HarperCollins, 2015.

———. *Miracles: A Preliminary Study*. New York: HarperCollins, 2015.

———. "Myth Became Fact." In *God in the Dock: Essays on Theology and Ethics*. Grand Rapids, MI: Eerdmans, 2014.

———. "On Ethics." In *Christian Reflections*, edited by Walter Hooper. Grand Rapids, MI: Eerdmans, 2014.

———. "On Science Fiction." In *Of Other Worlds: Essays and Stories*, edited by Walter Hooper. New York: HarperCollins, 2017.

———. "On Stories." In *Of Other Worlds: Essays and Stories*, edited by Walter Hooper. New York: HarperCollins, 2017.

———. "The Poison of Subjectivism." In *Christian Reflections*, edited by Walter Hooper. Grand Rapids, MI: Eerdmans, 2014.

———. "Preface by the Author to the 1950 Edition." In *Narrative Poems*, edited by Walter Hooper, New York: Harcourt, 1969.

———. *A Preface to Paradise Lost*. London, UK: Oxford University Press, 1969.

———. *Reflections on the Psalms: The Celebrated Musings on One of the Most Intriguing Books of the Bible*. New York: Houghton Mifflin Harcourt, 1986.

———. "Religion Without Dogma?" In *God in the Dock: Essays on Theology and Ethics*. Grand Rapids, MI: Eerdmans, 2014.

———. "A Reply to Professor Haldane." In *Of Other Worlds: Essays and Stories*, edited by Walter Hooper. New York: HarperCollins, 2017.

———. *The Screwtape Letters*. New York: HarperCollins, 2015.

———. "Sometimes Fairy Stories May Say Best What's to Be Said." In *Of Other Worlds: Essays and Stories*, edited by Walter Hooper. New York: HarperCollins, 2017.

———. *The Space Trilogy*. Reissue edition. New York: Simon & Schuster, 2011.

———. *Surprised by Joy*. New York: HarperCollins, 2017.

———. *Till We Have Faces: A Myth Retold*. New York: Mariner Books, 2012.

———. "Two Ways with the Self." In *The Weight of Glory: And Other Addresses*. New York: HarperCollins, 2009.

———. "Vivisection" In *God in the Dock: Essays on Theology and Ethics*. Grand Rapids, MI: Eerdmans, 2014.

———. *The Voyage of the Dawn Treader*. New York: HarperCollins, 2000.

———. "The Weight of Glory." In *The Weight of Glory: And Other Addresses*. New York: HarperCollins, 2009.

———. *Yours, Jack: Spiritual Direction from C. S. Lewis*. Edited by Paul F. Ford. New York: HarperCollins, 2008.

Lindsay, David. *A Voyage to Arcturus*. Auckland, NZ: Floating Press, 2011.

MacDonald, George. *Phantastes*. Grand Rapids, MI: Eerdmans, 1981.

Malory. *Works*. 2nd ed. Edited by Eugène Vinaver. Oxford, UK: Oxford University Press, 1971.

McGrath, Alister. *C. S. Lewis - A Life: Eccentric Genius, Reluctant Prophet.* Carol Stream, IL: Tyndale House, 2013.

McLeish, Tom. *Faith and Wisdom in Science*. Oxford, UK: Oxford University Press, 2014.

Milton, John. *Paradise Lost*. Edited by William Kerrigan, John Rumrich, and Stephen M. Fallon. New York: Random House, 2007.

Monmouth, Geoffrey. *The History of the Kings of Britain*. Translated by Sebastian Evans. Revisions by Charles W. Dunn. New York: E. P. Dutton & Co., 1958.

Moorman, Charles. "Space Ship and Grail: The Myths of C. S. Lewis." *College English 18*, no. 8 (1957): 401–05.

Mounts, Karen. "C. S. Lewis's Space Trilogy: A Study in Allegory." Honors thesis, Ball State University, 1997.

Mueller, Steven Paul. "Christology in the Writings of C. S. Lewis: A Lutheran's Evaluation." PhD thesis, University of Durham, 1997.

Ortlund, Gavin. "Conversion in C. S. Lewis's *That Hideous Strength*," *Themelios 41*, no. 1 (2016), 8–19.

Pasquini, Robert. "Evacuated Ecologies: H.G. Wells and the Evolutionary Aesthetics of Extinction." *Interdisciplinary Humanities 32*, no. 2 (2015): 48–62.

Plantinga, Alvin. *Where the Conflict Really Lies*. New York: Oxford University Press, 2011.

Plato. *The Republic of Plato*. 2nd edition. Translated with notes, an interpretive essay, and a new introduction by Allan Bloom. Chicago: University of Chicago Press, 1991.

Sayer, George. *Jack: A Life of C. S. Lewis*. Wheaton, IL: Crossway, 1988.

Schaefer, Henry F. III. "C. S. Lewis: Science and Scientism." In *Science and Christianity: Conflict or Coherence?,* 121–36. Athens, GA: The Apollos Trust, 2003.

Schultz, Jeffery D. and John G. West Jr. *The C. S. Lewis Readers' Encyclopedia*. Grand Rapids, MI: Zondervan, 1998.

Schwartz, Sanford. *C. S. Lewis on the Final Frontier: Science and the Supernatural in the Space Trilogy.* New York: Oxford University Press, 2009.

Shogren, Benjamin. "Those Kings of Lewis' Logres: Arthurian Figures as Lewisian Genders in *That Hideous Strength*." In *The Inklings and King Arthur: J. R. R. Tolkien, Charles Williams, C. S. Lewis, & Owen Barfield on the Matter of Britain*, edited by Sørina Higgins, 387–412. Berkeley, CA: Apocryphile, 2017.

Shumaker, Wayne. "The Cosmic Trilogy." In *The Longing for a Form,* edited by Peter J. Schakel. Kent, OH: Kent State University Press, 1977.

Simpson, Margo Lee. "The Anti-Modern Imagination: C. S. Lewis and 'The Cosmic Trilogy.'" Thesis, University of Ottawa, 1999.

Sproul, R. C. *Essential Truths of the Christian Faith*. Carol Stream, IL: Tyndale House, 1992.

Starr, Charlie W. *The Faun's Bookshelf: C. S. Lewis on Why Myth Matters*. Kent, OH: Kent State University Press, 2018.

Tolkien, J. R. R. *The Letters of J. R. R. Tolkien.* Edited by Humphrey Carpenter. New York: Houghton Mifflin, 2000.

———. *The Lord of the Rings*. Boston, MA: Houghton Mifflin Harcourt, 2012.

———. *The Lost Road and Other Writings (The History of Middle-Earth, Vol. 5)*. New York: Del Rey, 1996.

Tozer, A. W. *The Pursuit of God.* In *Three Spiritual Classics in One Volume*. Chicago: Moody Publishers, 2018.

Vaus, Will. *Mere Theology: A Guide to the Thought of C. S. Lewis*. Downers Grove, IL: InterVarsity, 2004.

Wagner, Richard. *Siegfried & the Twilight of the Gods*. Translated by Margaret Armour. Warwickshire, UK: Pook Press, 2011.

Walker, Leslie. *The Catholic Encyclopedia*. Vol. 12. New York: Robert Appleton Company, 1911. http://www.newadvent.org/cathen/12510a.htm.

Walsh, Chad. *The Literary Legacy of C. S. Lewis.* New York: Harcourt Brace Jovanovich, 1979.

Ward, Michael. *The Narnia Code: C. S. Lewis and the Secret of the Seven Heavens.* Carol Stream, IL: Tyndale House, 2010.

———. *Planet Narnia: The Seven Heavens in the Imagination of C. S. Lewis* New York: Oxford University Press, 2008.

———. "Science and Religion in the Writings of C. S. Lewis." *Science & Christian Belief* 25, no. 1 (April 2013): 3–16.

Watson, Micah. "C. S. Lewis as Natural Law Evangelist: Evangelical Political Thought and the People in the Pew." In *Natural Law and Evangelical Political Thought*, edited by Jesse Covington, Bryan McGraw, and Micah Watson, 195–224. Lanham, MD: Lexington Books, 2013.

———. "Natural Moral Law in *The Abolition of Man*." In *Contemporary Perspectives on C. S. Lewis' The Abolition of Man*, edited by Timothy Mosteller and Gayne Anacker, 25–46. London, UK: Bloomsbury, 2017.

Wells, H. G. *The First Men in the Moon*. New York: Lancer Books, 1969.

———. *The Time Machine*. Rockville, MD: Phoenix Pick, 2009.

———. *The War of the Worlds*. New York: Scholastic Incorporated, 2005.

Williams, Charles, and C. S. Lewis. *Arthurian Torso: Containing the Posthumous Fragments of The Figure of Arthur*. London, UK: Oxford University Press, 1969.

CONTRIBUTORS

Diana Pavlac Glyer is an award-winning writer who has spent more than 40 years combing through archives and studying old manuscripts. She is a leading expert on C. S. Lewis and J. R. R. Tolkien; her book *The Company They Keep* changed the way we talk about these writers. Dr. Glyer teaches fulltime in the Honors College at Azusa Pacific University.

S. L. Jensen has been a Lewis fan for much of her life. She grew up reading the Chronicles of Narnia and listening to the series as audiobooks. She feels blessed for the opportunity to study more of Lewis's fiction and nonfiction works during her time as an undergraduate student at Azusa Pacific University, where she graduated with a double major in political science and humanities. Currently, she works as an enrollment counselor at Colorado Christian University.

Julianne Johnson studied English, humanities, and graphic design at Azusa Pacific University and has since worked in book publishing and ministry near Los Angeles. She is the kids pastor at the West Covina campus of ONE&ALL Church. Her writing has appeared in several books, including *Read Me, Los Angeles: Exploring L.A.'s Book Culture.*

Jacob E. Meyer studied audio engineering and music at Azusa Pacific University. His interest in science fiction started from a young age with the works of Jules Verne and H. G. Wells and later fell in love with authors such as Ray Bradbury and Isaac Asimov. He spends the majority of his time behind an audio console or camera as a freelance audio engineer in Los Angeles or out in the field as an amateur night-sky photographer.

Rachel M. Roller studied chemistry and humanities at Azusa Pacific University. She has loved reading C. S. Lewis for as long as she can remember, so she was thrilled to spend a summer studying his works at Oxford, where she received a de Jager award for her research on C. S. Lewis and Science and Religion. She is currently pursuing a doctorate in analytical chemistry at the University of Notre Dame.

J. D. Wunderly studied business management at Azusa Pacific University. He is currently the office manager at a California branch of a tutoring company. He has a love of fantasy and reading as well as a firm belief in the importance of history and its impact on our present and future.

Maya Maley loves asking challenging questions and working through complex problems. She graduated from Azusa Pacific University with a degree in political science and now works on the development team at HOPE International, a Christ-centered microenterprise development organization.

Nolan Andrew was first introduced to Lewis through the Chronicles of Narnia film franchise and has been haunted by the image of the lamppost ever since. Faith, fiction, and film have always been at the center of his attention. Originally from southern New Jersey, Nolan now works for the pharmaceutical industry in Orlando, Florida with his spouse and robot vacuum named Alcasan (relation to the Lewis character is unconfirmed).

Daniel Z. Hsieh is a native of Southern California and an incurable reader of literature, particularly of classics and Lewis. He has studied Lewis at the undergraduate and graduate levels and is especially interested in exploring Lewis's reading habits.

Daniel J. Friend is fascinated with political philosophy, rhetoric, and the relation between the two with Christianity. He lives in Austin, Texas and works as a reporter on state politics for *The Texan*. In his free time, he has created his own novel inspired by Lewis's *Abolition of Man* and *That Hideous Strength*.

Evangeline M. Prior is a spare-time science fiction aficionado. Currently working as a music teacher in Orange County, CA, Evangeline considers herself a life-long learner. In everything she does, Evangeline seeks out and enjoys the beauty of the world, whether in music, literature, or friendship. Though trained in music at Azusa Pacific University, she spent a term in Oxford researching C. S. Lewis where she won a de Jager award for a version of the research presented in this book.

MORE ABOUT **C.S. LEWIS** AND **SPACESHIPS** FROM SQUARE HALO BOOKS

C.S. LEWIS AND THE ARTS: CREATIVITY IN THE SHADOWLANDS

"Even fifty years after his death, C. S. Lewis remains one the most popular and influential Christian writers and thinkers of the twentieth century. So much has been written about him, one wonders what else can possibly be said. But this book is a fascinating exploration of Lewis's thinking about the arts, making it a must read book for anyone who loves Lewis and loves the arts."
—Mary McCleary, Regents Professor Emeritus at Stephen F. Austin State University

DEEPER MAGIC: THE THEOLOGY BEHIND THE WRITINGS OF C.S. LEWIS

"Lewis opens more than wardrobe doors, but for most, the door has been locked. Williams has picked the lock and allows readers to see how Lewis—the great Oxford and Cambridge scholar—made his faith the means to an integrated scholarship. It is a model for all who want to see an embodiment of what it is to actually think Christianly about any given topic. I highly recommend this book!"
—Jerry Root, C.S. Lewis Scholar and Professor, Wheaton College

BIGGER ON THE INSIDE: CHRISTIANITY AND DOCTOR WHO

Like the TARDIS itself, the fanatically popular series *Doctor Who* is bigger on the inside, full of profound ideas about time and history, the nature of humanity, and the mysteries of the universe. The stories are full of wonder and hope. Perhaps these sci-fi parables can even illuminate the mysteries of faith. *Bigger On The Inside* is determined to find out, exploring key episodes of the series to discover what light they shed on the contours of Christian thought.

SQUAREHALOBOOKS.COM